THE ASSASSINATION
OF THEO VAN GOGH

THE ASSASSINATION
OF THEO VAN GOGH

From Social Drama to Cultural Trauma

Ron Eyerman

Duke University Press

Durham and London

2008

© 2008 Duke University Press
All rights reserved
Printed in the United States of America
on acid-free paper ∞
Designed by Amy Ruth Buchanan
Typeset in Quadraat by Keystone
Typesetting, Inc.
Library of Congress Cataloging-in-
Publication Data appear on the last
printed page of this book.

To Johanna

CONTENTS

ACKNOWLEDGMENTS

Thanks to Yale University's generous sabbatical program, I was able to spend the spring of 2006 in Amsterdam at the Institute for Social Research (ASSR). I thank Jeff Alexander, Wendell Bell, Nicolas Demertzis, John Dickson, Joke Esseveld, Al Hadi Khalaf, Lisa McCormick, Dick Pels (who also opened his vast network of contacts), Justus Uitermark, and Frederic Vandenberghe for their thoughtful comments on earlier drafts of this book. No one could ask for better criticism than that provided by Marc de Leeuw and Sonja van Wechelen, to whom enormous gratitude is due. Thanks go to the participants of the Workshop at Yale University's Center for Cultural Sociology and the other Yale colleagues, including those at the "Senior's Seminar," who listened to my presentations and offered their comments. I am grateful to Nadine Casey, whose creative secretarial assistance included wonderful advice on my artwork. I appreciate the ASSR's hospitality during my sabbatical, its wonderful secretarial staff and to the participants at the staff seminar for their comments and criticisms of my work. I am especially thankful to Dutch friends and colleagues Hans Sonneveld, Dick Pels and Baukje Prins, Mohammed Baba, Nico and Mahmod, and Marja and Hans Schoonhoven. Nadine Mignoni and Hans Hoogendoorn helped arrange interviews I never thought possible. Thanks also to Irene Stengs, who allowed me to read her manuscript on the art of mourning. Finally, I want to acknowledge the support of my family spread over the Netherlands, Sweden, England, and the United States.

CHAPTER 1

ASSASSINATION AS PUBLIC

PERFORMANCE: THE MURDER

OF THEO VAN GOGH

Every work of art is an uncommitted crime.—**Theodor Adorno**

Three positive things one can say about Amsterdam: you can buy anything you want; you are free; you are safe.—**René Descartes**

On November 2, 2004, the Dutch filmmaker Theo van Gogh was killed while cycling to work in the morning rush hour on a busy street in the heart of Amsterdam. The murderer, who also arrived on bicycle, first shot his victim, then slit his throat, and finally, with a separate knife, pinned a five-page note to his body. Written in Dutch verse, the note contained an indictment of Western society and was addressed not to van Gogh but to Ayaan Hirsi Ali, a Somali refugee and member of the Dutch parliament, and other well-known politicians. In addition to being an outspoken proponent of Muslim women's rights, Hirsi Ali had written the screenplay for a short film, *Submission Part One*, directed by van Gogh.

A work of fiction, the film had been recently shown on Dutch public television and depicted the bruised bodies of young women with text from the Koran written on their semi-naked bodies. The film aroused great public debate and the already controversial Hirsi Ali was forced into hiding and twenty-four hour police protection. Despite receiving the same threats, Van Gogh continued his very public life and became the victim of this well-publicized crime. The murder set off a series of reactions, including arson against Muslim schools and mosques.[1] The murderer was almost immediately identified as Mohammed Bouyeri, a citizen of the Netherlands, but with roots (and citizenship) in Morocco. Bouyeri was tried, convicted and sentenced to life imprisonment under the new antiterrorism law.[2] A second trial, which concerned the alleged involvement of co-conspirators, members of a so-called "Hofstad group" (Court or Capital City group), was carried out, resulting in the "group" being officially labeled a terrorist organization; some of its alleged members were later sentenced to prison. Strong doubts remain, however, about both the status of the group and any conspiracy in the murder of van Gogh. Named as one of its leaders, Mohammed B. spoke for over an hour during the second trial, using the occasion to discourse on his personal mission and the role of jihad or sacred struggle in Islam. This was in sharp contrast to his behavior at the first trial, when, except for saying a few words, he chose to remain silent.

The media coverage of the murder and its follow-up has been worldwide and extensive. Following approximately two and a half years after the murder of Pim Fortuyn (May 2002), a leading politician with outspoken ideas on immigration policies, many local commentators saw the murder of Theo van Gogh as part of a clash of civilizations and forecast a turning point of historical proportion in Dutch society. The international media also followed the story closely. In the United States for example, Ayaan Hirsi Ali was the subject of extensive coverage, including an article in the *New York Times Magazine* that featured a full-page color photo and the headline "Daughter of the Enlightenment." Interviewed on the CBS television news magazine *60 Minutes* soon after the murder (where the program host introduced her as a "star"), Hirsi Ali insisted she had no regrets and claimed to be making a sequel to the film, something she repeated in a follow-up broadcast on July 10, 2005. Hirsi Ali has since moved to the United States and become an international celebrity. Also interviewed on *60 Minutes* was Theodor Holman, identified as a columnist and radio commentator and "one of van Gogh's closest friends." Explaining why the Netherlands was shocked by van Gogh's death, even if he was a controversial figure, Holman said, "The country did love him. . . . He had his own television show, he had a radio show, he made movies. So he embodied what you can do in this country and what you can say" (*60 Minutes* transcript, p. 3).[3] In addition to van Gogh and Hirsi Ali, Mohammed Bouyeri, his life, and his possible motivations have also been the subject of great media scrutiny. President George W. Bush referred to Bouyeri in a speech given just after the latter's trial: "In a courtroom in the Netherlands, the killer of Theo van Gogh turned to the victim's grieving mother and said, 'I do not feel your pain—because I believe you are an infidel.' "[4] Clearly the death of a Dutch filmmaker is of more than just local interest.

An analysis of the murder of Theo van Gogh has several perspectives and frameworks to draw upon. The selection of one analytic frame or another is neither innocent nor obvious. In fact, the framework through which one chooses to respond to the question "what really happened here?" goes some way to providing its own answer. One can fruitfully look at this occurrence as a "hate crime," which as defined by Kelly and Maghan (1998:222), would mean viewing it as a criminal act that also possesses "dynamic racial, political, ideological and cultural dimensions that magnify their impact on victims and on the communities in which they occur." From this perspective one could study aspects of this "dynamic," such as the role of "media performance" (Cottle 2004), which would highlight processes of media construction. However, calling the murder of van Gogh a "hate crime" (was the murder of a native Dutchman "racist"?) is already to categorize and thus to prescribe interpretation. Another alternative is to analyze the murder and the associated reportage as a "moral panic," which would call attention to another aspect of the media's role in dramatizing the occurrence and in prescribing its effects. The German translation of the Dutch historian Geert Mak's (2005c) account of the murder carries the subtitle "history of a moral panic" (though the author himself claims no responsibility for that choice).[5] Framing the murder as a moral panic means highlighting a form of public hysteria induced through media orchestration. In his rich account, Mak focuses on the lack of what he considers a proper response from Dutch leaders and opinion makers and what this might mean for Dutch society. His own position comes out clearly: we have been through this before. If Protestants, Catholics, and Jews have been incorporated into Dutch society, why can't Muslims be as well? From another point of view, one could call the murder an "assassination," which would imply a political motivation. This might also be fruitful, but it would push the investigation primarily to the assassin, to the person and the structural conditions that might drive or motivate him or her (see Wilkenson's [1976] analysis of assassinations according to a theory of status inconsistency). Finally, one might apply the notion of "artistic transgression" as Julius (2002) does; this turns the question into a moral and legal dispute suggesting historical and cultural comparisons, where the notions of blasphemy and artistic license come under scrutiny.

In my own approach to the murder of Theo van Gogh I will make use of aspects from these various perspectives. Over the following chapters I will apply three types of analysis, geared to three levels of approach. I begin with a performative approach that focuses on the prediscursive performance of action (Alexander et al. 2006). Issues of concern here are who was killed and why, how it was carried out, and what it meant to actors and audience. Second, use is made of discourse theory in analyzing how these actions were transformed into an event as they were represented and reconstructed through mass media reports and other accounts. Here the concern is also who was killed and why, but with a focus on media representation and framing. Third, the theories of social drama and cultural trauma are applied as means to understanding the social processes triggered by the murder and as means toward assessing its long-term effects. Issues here concern the meaning and changing nature of social inclusion, the boundaries of "Dutchness," of Dutch "multiculturalism" and the very nature of Dutch collective identity.

THE EPISODE

The stage for the murder of Theo van Gogh had already been set by preceding events. Let me mention some of the most significant: the arrival of waves of immigrants from former Dutch colonies from the 1950s onward, the emergence of Amsterdam as a magnet for a "counterculture" in the 1960s, and the importation of "guest workers," largely from Turkey and Morocco, in the 1970s. In October 2003, the Central Bureau of Statistics (CBS) would report that there were "nearly as many Muslims as Calvinists in the Netherlands" (web magazine *www.cbs.nl*) and that the number of Muslims in the country was increasing dramatically, to nearly 6 percent of the total population.[6] According to a member of the Dutch parliament at the time (someone of Moroccan heritage), "Muslims are expected to outnumber non-Muslims in Europe by 2050," and in some European cities, "Muslim school children will be in the majority within the next decade" (Cherribi 2003:195). There were also media-circulated reports that Mohammed had become the most popular name for newborn boys. More directly connected to our purpose was the publication in a leading newspaper of an essay titled "Het multiculturele drama" (The multicultural drama) by the sociologist and political commentator Paul Scheffer. This article, which appeared in January 2000, castigated the lack of public discussion of immigration policy and, more significantly, the apparent lack of any such policy at all. This set in motion widespread debate about the alleged "failure of Dutch immigration," especially as it concerned the assimilation of Muslims. Aspects of this discussion were transformed into a political platform by Pim Fortuyn, a sociology professor turned social critic and populist politician, whose enormous success effectively ended with his assassination just prior to what was expected to be a triumphal national election in 2002. In between came the September 11 terrorist attacks on targets in the United States, which helped catapult Fortuyn to prominence. When the murder of Fortuyn first occurred it was widely assumed that the assassin was an Islamic militant, a fear shared by Hirsi Ali (2007) that turned out to be false. The killer was announced as Volkert van der Graaf, an animal rights activist, who, at his trial, would claim to have acted on behalf of Muslim immigrants. It was in this tense context that Theo van Gogh used his public presence to make vulgar remarks about Muslims and Jews, that Hirsi Ali drove her campaign for the rights of Muslim women as a member of parliament and media figure, and that their film *Submission* was broadcast.

The actual murder has been well documented and my recounting builds on Benschop (2005) and Chorous and Olgun (2005) (see also Buruma 2006b). Both assassin and victim were cycling when Mohammed B. began shooting. The latter fired several times, severely wounding his victim. The final shots were fired as van Gogh was being chased (twice) around a parked car, while shouting, "We can still talk about this, don't do it," something that Hirsi Ali (2007) calls typically Dutch. After van Gogh was dead, the assailant cut his throat with a small machete (attempting, perhaps, to decapitate his victim). This was something the assailant had apparently rehearsed on sheep in the hallway to his apartment. The killer then stuck a filet knife into his victim's body so deeply that it touched the spine. Attached through the knife (which perhaps was meant as a dagger) was a note that contained threatening references not to van Gogh but to Ayaan Hirsi Ali. In his pocket Mohammed B. had another, more personal, note written to friends and colleagues, in which he declared his martyrdom. After kicking his victim to ensure he was dead, the assailant reloaded his weapon (a 15-shot semi-automatic pistol manufactured in Croatia) and walked calmly across the crowded street toward a nearby park. There were fifty-three eyewitnesses, including one who supplied the media photos that were taken through his cell phone camera. One of the onlookers is reported to have said to Mohammed B. "You can't do that," to which the latter replied, "Oh yes, I can, he asked for it, and now you know what to expect." When the police arrived, the assailant fired off twelve more shots in their direction, wounding a motorcycle policeman. Wounded in the leg by a police bullet, Mohammed B. was finally arrested. In the ambulance, an accompanying police officer told him that he was lucky not to have been killed, to which Mohammed B. replied, "That was precisely my intention." At his trial he would repeat these sentiments, telling the wounded policeman to his face that he had intended to shoot to kill and to be killed himself.

Hirsi Ali and not Theo van Gogh may well have been the prime target for assassination, something we will directly address. The note pinned to van Gogh's body (available on http://en.wikipedia.org/wiki/Image: Afscheidsbrief.jpg), was addressed to "Mrs. Hirshi Ali" (the name was misspelled throughout), calling her an "infidel fundamentalist" who "terrorizes Islam" and "marches with the soldiers of evil." It labeled Hirsi Ali an "unbelieving fundamentalist" and a heretic in the service of lying "Jewish masters," "products of the Talmud" who "dominate Dutch politics" (according to the translation by Ian Buruma [2005]). The note also contained the phrase "I know for sure that you, O America, are going to meet with disaster. I know for sure that you, O Holland, are going to meet with disaster" and is signed Saifu Deen al-Muwahhied. According to official accounts this letter was most likely written by someone other than Mohammed B., though this is a name he allegedly used on the Internet. The style of address appears to reflect its author's desire to link urban street rhetoric with poetic prophecy from an imagined past and could very well have been written by Mohammed B.

On Mohammed B.'s person, the police recovered the following suicide note:

BAPTIZED IN BLOOD
So these are my last words . . .
Riddled with bullets . . .
Baptized in blood . . .
As I had hoped.

I am leaving a message . . .
For you . . . the fighter . . .
The Tawheed tree is waiting . . .

Yearning for your blood . . .
Enter the bargain . . .
And Allah opens the way . . .
He gives you a garden . . .
Instead of the Earthy rubble.

To the enemy I say . . .
You will surely die . . .
Wherever in the world you go . . .
Death is waiting for you . . .
Chased by the knights of DEATH . . .
Who paint the streets with Red.

For the hypocrites I have one final word . . .
Wish for DEATH or hold your tongue . . . and sit.

Dear Brothers and Sisters, my end is nigh . . .
But this does not end the story.

The killing appears staged as ritual assassination, though I would rather see it as a social performance.[7] The killer prepared himself for assassination and martyrdom, yet the fact that he felt it necessary to carry textual messages reveals that he felt the acts did not speak for themselves. Although he was born and raised in Amsterdam, Mohammed B. chose to die as a martyr to Islam and, to judge by the written texts and the mode of killing, to link himself and his act to a tradition where murder was a sacred duty and where even a kitchen knife could pass for a dagger, the only permissible weapon of ritual assassination (Buruma and Margalit 2004:69). The shots may have been necessary on city streets, but the real killing was done in a prescribed way.

The Principals
A twenty-six-year-old Dutchman of Moroccan descent, Mohammed Bouyeri (referred to by the Dutch as Mohammed B., as I have been doing), until recently had been a model of integration, a success story for the Dutch multicultural society. Buruma (2005) calls his background "typical for a second-generation Moroccan immigrant": a father disabled by years of menial labor, speaking only halting Dutch, and a mother who arrived in the Netherlands through an arranged marriage and a change in Dutch immigration policy. Mohammed B. was active in community affairs and

had six years of higher education, leaving college just prior to finishing his degree. While events in his personal life may have "triggered" his move toward political extremism, the picture is more complex, as will be shown in the chapters that follow.[8] In the space of a few months in 2004, Bouyeri changed his manner of dress, his rhetoric, and his place of worship, moving from the conservative, local mosque of his father to one led by a more radical Syrian cleric. He began writing fantasy articles and "open letters," on the Internet, using different names, "Abu Zubair" (the powerful) and "Saifu Deen al-Muwahhied ("Saifu Deen" literally means "the Sword of Faith"), the name on the letter pinned to van Gogh's body. His letters contained a list of groups and people to "hit," including Hirsi Ali and other prominent Dutch politicians.

Three intended victims were identified in Mohammed B.'s letters on the Internet: Ayaan Hirsi Ali; Ahmed Aboutaleb, an Amsterdam politician born in Morocco, with an opposite view on Muslim assimilation; and Geert Wilders, a Dutch politician following in the footsteps of Pim Fortuyn. The most internationally prominent was Ayaan Hirsi Ali, who was born in Somalia but had been a Dutch citizen since 1997. She was elected to parliament on a list for the Volkspartij voor Vrijheid en Democratie (People's Party for Liberty and Democracy, vvd). In both public and private life, she has lobbied forcefully against female circumcision and spoken out on issues concerning immigrants to Europe.

Theo van Gogh, a Dutch filmmaker and enfant terrible, was forty-six years old at the time of his death and the great-grandson of another Theo van Gogh, brother of the painter Vincent van Gogh. A law school dropout, van Gogh worked as a stage manager and as a film and television actor. He wrote regularly for the Dutch Metro, a free newspaper, and was the author of several books; his last book, written in 2003 and called *Allah weet het beter* (Allah knows best), was mockingly critical of Islam. Van Gogh was a member of the Dutch republican society (Republikeins Genootschap), against the monarchy, and a friend and supporter of Pim Fortuyn. He was well known for his derogatory statements about Muslims and Jews, including some directed against Job Cohen, the mayor of Amsterdam, whom he called a "collaborator," evoking images of the Second World War. In addition to *Submission*, van Gogh had just completed a film about the murder of Pim Fortuyn. One of his television films, a remake of *Romeo and Juliet*, in which one of the lead characters is a Moroccan immigrant, continues to be used in Dutch classrooms to stimulate positive views of integration. Clearly an ambiguous figure, van Gogh often characterized himself as an "intellectual terrorist."

The Film

Submission is an eleven-minute fictional account of four young Muslim women, including one who is forced into an arranged marriage with a man who physically abuses her, who is raped by her uncle, and who is later punished for falling in love with another man. In the film, the women wear transparent gowns that reveal bruises as well as nakedness. Scriptures from the Koran appear painted on naked backs and the voice-over (in English) strongly suggests that the Koran justifies violence against women. With regard to its aesthetic framework, the film makes reference to previous motion pictures such as Peter Greenaway's *The Pillow Book* (1996), and one can also find links to the work of the Iranian photographer Shirin Neshat (one look at Hirsi Ali's web homepage confirms this), where body and text are conjoined in communicating a message. It was first broadcast over Dutch public television (VPRO) on August 29, 2004 (following the murder of van Gogh, it was broadcast on Danish television on November 11, 2004, and in Italy on May 12, 2005).

The voices of critics are essential to the interpretation and evaluation of a performative event. Providing answers to "What it all means" is the role of the critic, and in this case they ranged from local commentators and newspaper and magazine writers to representatives of the international media, bloggers, the police, and government analysts. For Albert Benschop (2005), the meaning is both deeply rooted and ominous: "The murder of Theo van Gogh wasn't a tragic incident or anomaly, but an almost logical result of a fight getting out of hand between autochthonous 'kaaskoppen' (cheese heads) who felt increasingly overrun by a horde of maladjusted and asocial, violent and criminal foreigners and the allochthonous foreigners who emigrated or fled to Holland. This conflict, which had been smouldering for years, was explosively brought to the surface by the murder of van Gogh."[9] Other voices were present, but a consensus would soon emerge around the alleged success or failure of immigration policy.

Then we have to consider the multilayered audience. There is the local, Amsterdam-based artistic and intellectual subculture with its own traditions and norms of propriety; the wider national public, with access filtered through Dutch language media with its regional, political, and confessional differences; the local and international Muslim community; the radical Islamic movement; and, finally, the international audience, filtered through various mass media, including the Internet. The function and use of the Internet will be of prime importance in this study, not only as a means of communication, but also as a means of organization and interpretation in its own right. The Internet has facilitated new organizational forms, such as the "all-channel network" and led some theorists and strategists to speak of "netwar," as a form of conflict that might increasingly replace more traditional forms of warfare. According to Arquilla and Ronfeldt (1999:194) netwar "refers to an emerging mode of conflict (and crime) at societal levels, involving measures short of traditional war, in which the protagonists use network forms of organization and related doctrines, strategies, and technologies attuned to the information age. These protagonists are likely to consist of disparate small groups who communicate, coordinate, and conduct their campaigns in an inter-netted manner, without a precise command center."

LAYERS OF MEANING

What an action means cannot simply be deduced from the intentions of the actor or the context within which it occurs. The meaning of an action depends as much on who is viewing as on who is doing. In the interpretation of meaning, one must take into account the mediated process of framing and narrating of actions and events, including those that guide actors and audiences, as these are part of the conditions structuring actions. This includes not only mass-mediated accounts, but also historically rooted traditions. One way of interpreting the making of the film *Submission* is as an expression of artistic license and freedom of speech. The murder of van Gogh has been framed in some mass-mediated accounts as a matter of free speech, and the filmmaker as a martyr for that societal value. In describing himself as a "radical libertarian" and a "provocateur," van Gogh claimed the right of art and the artist to expose and test societal norms and values by exposing taboos. This position can also be situated in the traditions of the Amsterdam art world and various intellectual traditions of the country. This largely urban culture created a distinctive social space that permitted, even encouraged, outrageous behavior. In her own accounts, the scriptwriter Hirsi Ali (2007 for the latest) claims that the film was intended as an intervention into the debate on violence against women, particularly Muslim women. In media accounts, she has been portrayed as the "Daughter of the Enlightenment," as was mentioned above, and also as a potential martyr for the cause of free speech. How the intentions of the filmmaker and the scriptwriter were actually realized in the film, who their intended audience was, and how they could expect to reach this audience are matters thoroughly discussed by de Leeuw and van Wichelen (2005) and will be further analyzed in subsequent chapters.[10]

Much like Salman Rushdie's *Satanic Verses* (1988) and more recently the so-called Mohammed Cartoons published in a Danish newspaper (2006), both subjects discussed in a later chapter, *Submission* was apparently interpreted by many Muslims as blasphemous, as an attack on religious beliefs. For them and for others, non-Muslims included, this might explain, if not legitimate, the murder of its creators. During the afternoon of the day of the murder of van Gogh, several organizations associated with the municipal government of Amsterdam organized meetings with Muslim organizations around the city to help quiet the disturbing and uncertain atmosphere. They also organized a televised press conference with Muslim political representatives and some sympathetic associates of Theo van Gogh that same evening. According to the Dutch historian Geert Mak (2005b:22), of those "Muslim" immigrants to the Netherlands who might constitute an audience, less than 20 percent report that they attend a mosque regularly. By his calculation the size of the potential audience for a "radical" Islamic message is about .04 percent (the number for Europe as a whole has been put at 400,000, per Tausch et al. 2006). A study carried out in Amsterdam by Slootman and Tillie (2006) revealed that 2 percent of the city's Muslim population had a "potential" for radicalization.[11] However, it is not so much numbers but perceptions that count here, especially the perceptions guided and amplified by mass-media projections and representations. As has been seen in the more recent controversy following the Mohammed Cartoon affair, many interpretations, and uses, can be made of controversies of this sort.

At least at first, for the police authorities the event was a murder carried out by one person. This has now been extended to include several co-conspirators. For some (Dutch and American) authorities and commentators, it was much more than a murder or even an assassination, it was a terrorist plot, with possible links to Al Qaeda and Takfir Wal Hijra, the latter an Egyptian-based group responsible among other things for the assassination of Anwar Sadat in 1981.

For at least a number of Dutch citizens the murder is an example of tolerant immigration gone too far. (A poll taken after the event suggested that 40 percent of Dutch citizens hope that Muslim immigrants "no longer feel at home in the Netherlands" and that more than 80 percent want tougher restrictions against immigrants.) In 2005, a Pew Survey reported that 51 percent of native Dutch "admitted to unfavourable views of Muslims" (Haan 2007:2).

For those concerned with law and tolerance, the event was a questionable artistic transgression, testing the line between freedom of expression and discriminatory, even criminal, remarks about another's religious beliefs.[12]

ASSASSINATION AS PERFORMANCE

Interestingly enough for the present case, the term *assassination* itself derives from the Arabic and the words *assassiyun* (fundamentalist) and *hashishiyyin* (consumers of hashish) (Laucella 1998:xi). It was first applied to a Muslim sect active in Syria and Persia between 1090 and 1272. The sects' chief objective was the murder of those it considered its doctrinal enemies, the elimination of which it took to be "a sacred religious duty" (Wilkinson 1976:3). A workable, formal definition of assassination could be "assassination refers to those killings or murders, usually directed against individuals in public life, motivated by political rather than by personal relationships. . . . Assassination is the deliberate, extralegal killing of an individual for political purposes" (Murray Havens cited in Wilkinson 1976:3). Wilkinson's book carries the subtitle "the sociology of political murder," and the essays collected in it reveal both the atmosphere in which it was compiled (the common feeling that the United States was a "violent and sick" society) and the desire to find a plausible sociological, rather than psychological, explanation for the rash of violence and killing that occurred in the 1960s and early 1970s. The underlying theoretical framework is provided by variations of collective behavior, with emphasis on "structural strain" and "status inconsistency" as developed most systematically by Neil Smelser (1962). Smelser's six "determinants" for explaining the emergence of relatively spontaneous collective behavior, such as riotous crowds, strikes and social movements, provide the authors with tools to identify and understand the often less than collective act of political assassination.[13] This model is useful for our purposes, especially in accounting for the behavior of Mohammed Bouyeri; another concept useful in this endeavor is that of martyr. Bouyeri's letter makes clear that he planned to die along with his victim in the assassination. That he did not must surely have been a disappointment and to have created a problem in terms of how to behave in the aftermath, especially during the trial. In fact, he chose a well-scripted path, one used by politically motivated actors and common criminals alike: mainly silence, with a minimum of well-chosen words.[14]

In addition to the social-structural moorings, which Wilkenson and her coauthors identify, there is a history and a conventional repertoire in religious and political assassination. The fanatic breaks through the throng to point a pistol at the admired or despised leader in full public view or the hidden gunman, working alone or in conspiracy with others, to fire the shot that he or she hopes will change the course of history. There are performative aspects to be identified and studied in the very act of assassination. Further, many political assassinations are followed by attempts at a return to normalcy, accompanied by rituals of closure, elaborate state funerals, and periods of mourning, which are also rituals of reconciliation, where opposing sides may publicly present themselves as co-participant. The still unresolved murder of Swedish prime minister Olaf Palme in 1986 and the continuing controversy surrounding that of John F. Kennedy in 1963 are examples of such a process, where political opponents unite in mourning a fallen leader to signify the unity and resolve of a nation in crisis. This is highly significant public performance.

The assassination of Theo van Gogh was a performative event in several senses, most important perhaps in that it seemed to create a new reality. The political and cultural climate in the Netherlands changed with and through this event, even if one can identify other significant occurrences that preceded it and that added to its effect, like the assassination of Pim Fortuyn in May 2002, the first political assassination in the Netherlands in more than three centuries. The assassination of van Gogh was a highly symbolic and stylized performance, a carefully staged occurrence, while the murder of Fortuyn appears to be more the relatively spontaneous act of an enraged individual.[15] One murder occurred in a dimly lit parking lot, the other in full public view on a busy street. The multitude of possible intentions and coded meanings that were embedded in these acts where differently drawn upon, represented, and orchestrated in various media. Van Gogh's film and violent death provoked in a very conscious way many of the reactions that followed, such as the call for a defense of artistic freedom by his friends and colleagues. Mohammed Bouyeri's actions were highly scripted; he knew what he was doing and what interpretations his actions would encourage, though probably not many would have predicted the violent outrage, including the burning of schools and mosques. His act, however, set off a barrage of public and private speculation as to its meaning, triggering a struggle over meaning that included many layers of interpretation and many interpreters.

What transformed this political/religious action into a performative event was in part the way it was carried out and why. As important, however, was the potentially explosive context in which it occurred and the potential meanings that this imposed on it. Highly significant here was the note, which contained the message that the person killed was not the real target and, of course, that the murder of Fortuyn had so recently occurred. A cultural sociology should investigate and analyze the scripts, the mise-en-scène and the performance, and the struggle to fix meaning.

ASSASSINATION AS SOCIAL DRAMA

According to Turner's model, a social drama opens with "a breach of a norm, the infraction of a rule of morality, law, custom, or etiquette, in some public arena" (Turner 1980:150).[16] This can be deliberate or spontaneous, but usually involves a highly visible or valued person in a social group or society. In our case, there are several to be identified, though *Submission* is not one of them. The film did not break the established norms of Dutch society, at least as they are understood formally by the law and informally by the rules and norms concerning artistic expression and the behavior of the Amsterdam artistic subculture. It may, however, have had a different effect in the Muslim immigrant community, making it possible to speak of a layered breach or even of two. The breach, in other words, may be a complex multifactor process involving a cumulative series of "traumas," as will be discussed in later chapters. Following Turner (1974:35), one could say that while the breach of a norm may abruptly occur, as a phase of social drama, it opens a liminal space that "bring(s) fundamental aspects of society, normally overlaid by customs and habits of daily intercourse, into frightening prominence" (Wagner-

Pacifici 1986 and Jacobs 2000:9 make similar points). A breach requires a striking occurrence, one "rich in symbolic presentation," but this only serves to expose and agitate deeper divisions, which can then be articulated in the ensuing struggle to interpret and to attribute and fix meaning. In this process as well, aesthetic or dramatic performances are connected to political outcomes. The struggle over meaning clarifies perpetrators and victim, a process that is inherently political and that is a step toward crisis. The role of the mass media in this process is central, as the media help "signalize," as Turner calls it, a specific occurrence as a "breach," "prompting a wider public crisis" (Cottle 2004:72).

Setting is important: "The setting can provide or deprive the protagonists of a necessary symbolic arsenal" (ibid.:69). The open street and time of day were important aspects in the murder of van Gogh; to be attacked on an open public thoroughfare in the early morning rush hour carries great symbolic weight. It exposes the vulnerability of a citizen in the practice of basic taken-for-granted rights, free passage and public safety. The bicycle as means of transport and the knife as means of murder were also highly symbolic. The former was such not only because it expresses Dutchness (Buruma 2006b) but also because it makes its user both vulnerable and free at the same time. Like the bicycle, the use of a knife as murder weapon requires direct personal contact between perpetrator and victim.

A breach implies a major and very public occurrence, which, as Turner notes, cannot be denied once it has happened. Such an occurrence, which creates opposition, forces taking of sides, the formation of factions with reference to its meaning and significance. A breach creates controversy, conflict, and, if not healed quickly and formally, crisis. This crisis may expose long-hidden or simmering fissures in a collective; it also may create the opportunity for new groupings to form. In our case, the various reactions, from inter-ethnic conflict to public debate did both. Those already critical of immigration policies found new fodder for their beliefs and force for their arguments; in the same process, others regrouped, and some new alliances were formed and older ones refitted. The mass media played a crucial role in this process, both as a medium of exchange and as resource in the struggle.

In this stage of the social drama, specific legal measures and ritual practices are employed in order to quell the crisis and restore order. Naming those responsible and a trial of those considered guilty of transgression are classic examples of redress. Here authority can be performed and routines reestablished. It is important that such processes be public, as well as orderly and just. Mohammed Bouyeri's trial was closely followed and made available to a large audience. As noted, the trial was televised and commented on daily in the mass media. In addition to the media performance, (Cottle 2004) which includes print and other media such as the talk shows, other arenas of redress can be identified: the public meetings between various factions formed during the crisis stage, where in highly controlled and stylized settings differences could be aired in the attempt to promote understanding and, one could hope, reconciliation. Important also were public displays of protest against violence and solidarity with its victims. A spontaneous memorial of flowers and notes grew immediately at the scene of the murder and after the ritualized press conference, where public officials could perform their authority; a demonstration was organized in Amsterdam's central square. Van Gogh's funeral was a major public event, where both the Dutch royal family and his own family were at center stage.

What the outcome of the social drama surrounding the van Gogh murder will be remains to be seen. One central process of redress and reintegration is the return to order through the reestablishment of authority and normalization of daily life. The trials of those deemed responsible have ended, and the guilty parties are in prison. A government has fallen as an indirect outcome of the murder, and a new one has been put in place. New laws have been enacted in the attempt to deal with such acts of violence, both in the real world and the virtual world of the Internet. At least on the surface, daily routines have been reinstated. However, the debate concerning the assimilation of immigrants generally and Muslims in particular is still ongoing, and a general unease can be sensed not only in the Netherlands but also in Europe generally. The tear in the social fabric has been patched. How long and in what form this will remain in place is still an open question.

FROM OCCURRENCE TO EVENT: THE RHETORICALLY RECONSTRUCTED INTERPRETATIONS

Events take shape through a dialectic of action and interpretation (Mast 2006). Actions occur in delimited time and space, while events unfold in more ambiguous and unpredictable sequences. Events crystallize in the interplay between protagonists, interpreters, and audience, as sense and meaning is attributed and various interpretations compete with each other. As this meaning struggle proceeds, various accounts stabilize, with perhaps one achieving some sort of hegemony, but counterinterpretations or stories may continue to exist alongside, as several variations may become rooted in the collective memory of different agents or groups. Language and the formation of social texts are vital objects of analysis in social drama. A basic proposition in what Robin Wagner-Pacifici (1986:18) calls the "dramaturgical method" is that "language is symbolic action and that, as such, it leads both inwards to the world of individual meanings and outward to social action." Protagonists in a social drama construct their own stories and the researcher must reconstruct them. Equally important are those accounts represented through mass media. In our contemporary world, mass media is central in the making of events and in fixing meaning. Mass media help occurrences to crystallize as events before the eyes of the public (Molotch and Lester 1974). "Media events are social performances whose contents are dictated by writers and photographers and whose distribution is decided by corporate or state organization" (Alexander 2006:67). Like the public however, mass media are multilayered and various, implying that an "event" might crystallize at different moments and in different ways depending on the mediated forms of representation and the audience (Jacobs 2000). The analysis of mass-mediated social drama should be sensitive to this and seek to identify those moments of crystallization.

There is plenty of evidence of a dramatic self-consciousness in this murder. The carefully planned street scene, the knives, notes, and the style of dress point to a keen awareness of a sense of drama and audience. In analyzing this awareness, the distinction between tragedy and melodrama might be useful here. While the latter is an "intense emotional and ethical drama based on the manichaeistic struggle of good and evil" (Wagner-Pacifici 1986:279, quoting Peter Brooks), where the characters are one-dimensional bearers of one side or the other, the characters in a tragedy are much more complex and the outcomes more ambiguous. Tragedy can even lead to a positive outcome, where the audience recognizes an important issue and can adjust its behavior; as Wagner-Pacifici (1986:279) puts it, "This audience would recognize itself as the ultimate source of the conflict and of the possibility of overcoming it." This could very well be one outcome in the Dutch case. How will the audience react? How is the drama represented in the media, as tragedy or as melodrama?

Besides drama, there are also the reactions of the various, multilayered audiences: who was being addressed and how were the messages received? One of the immediate triggers to the murder was the film *Submission*, and the question of its audience and reception should be addressed. The first audience to view the film was the more liberal, sophisticated members of the Dutch public sphere, a relatively closed and select group with its own norms of propriety and address. This audience was widened by the film's being aired on public television, at the same time as it was discussed and interpreted by critics in various mass media. While still relatively small and known, this new audience potentially included "outsiders," those who might not share the norms of the primary audience. It was the broadcasting of the film and the wide public debate afterward that opened the possibility of a counterperformance, at the extreme the threats to those deemed responsible, and the murder itself. We will have a chance to discuss this in more detail later on; here we can offer a few speculations and hunches. The ritualistic acts, the symbolic dress, and the note are highly pregnant clues with which to begin making an interpretation. The choice of place, on the other hand, may well have been only pragmatic and opportunistic, chosen for access, though clearly not for escape. Even if this were the case, it would be no less symbolic for that; the open street and free public access are central to Western democracies and thus available to perpetrator and victim. It appears from all the evidence that the mise-en-scène, the setting, the mode of killing, and the costuming of the perpetrator were chosen for their symbolic reference and are thus telling in terms of intended audience. These symbols mean something significant to the Dutch and international public. A highly stylized act of violence carried out in full public view makes explicit reference to embodied values and traditions, sending a message, however coded, to an audience, however multiple, that decodes it. For one audience, the message of the murder seemed clear: your way of life is threatened from within; it is insulting, and there are those who are willing to die to reveal and revenge that. The message to another audience, the Dutch Muslim "community," which was again made aware of its otherness through this action and the events that followed, was also clear, at least from the side of the perpetrator: I am acting in your name. The reception from that audience was much more ambiguous, however.

For the Dutch audience generally, including the Muslim community, another intended message by the assassin might well be to symbolize the "failure" of integration, a message that was apparently read by many. Here what the actors represented would be crucial. As a "model of successful integration," Mohammed Bouyeri seems perfectly cast to symbolize failed integration through his murderous actions. This possibly intended and received message would also make it clear that van Gogh was not the prime target, though he might well have served as a representative figure of all that was wrong with Western civilization in the eyes of his killer. Hirsi Ali, on the other hand, might well have symbolized successful integration, having moved with stunning speed from political refugee to member of parliament. In this case, she would have been someone to target, especially if there were to be only two paths available: joining the decadent and polluted West or the pure East. In this sense, the murder could be viewed as ritualized political assassination, with the aim of eliminating any of the middle ground, a very common tactic. What makes for powerful drama in that case is that the perpetrator was himself once a touted example of exactly that middle ground.[17] The murder would thus symbolize at one and the same time the failure of multiculturalism and the foolishness of any other alternative.

Dress or costume was significant in the murder of van Gogh in the sense of symbolizing good and evil (Wagner-Pacifici 1986:282). The clothing chosen by the perpetrator was the equivalent of the white hat worn by the Hollywood hero, and the work clothes of the bohemian van Gogh stood in for the black hat of the evil and decadent West. Was it merely coincidence that the latter was wearing red, white, and blue suspenders when he died? In this sense, van Gogh *was* important and not merely a substitute for Hirsi Ali: he embodied the contaminated culture in appearance as well as in practice. Even the name he bore, with its obvious linkage to one of the icons of Western art, increased his symbolic value as the target. Further, the suicide note recovered from the perpetrator proclaimed the desire for martyrdom. This too was meant to be read and interpreted as a symbolic message to multiple audiences: to one it repeated what Mohammed B. said at the scene, "Now you know what to expect," to the other it conveyed, "I am one of you." The symbolic acts of such a performance are also intended to be interpreted by a global audience as another expression of Islamic militancy, part of a worldwide movement against Western hegemony. Political analysts in the United States and elsewhere were quick to see an Al Qaeda connection and to propose another battleground in the "war on terror" and the "clash of civilizations." The pronounced ethnicity of the perpetrator, his clothing, the fiery rhetoric of the notes, and the manner of killing all lend themselves to this particular reading. All of this is to say that the killing of van Gogh was a performance and not merely, as some have viewed it, a ritual murder or the act of a "loser." Performers have a clear sense of audience, though there is never a guarantee of a successful fusion between the two (Alexander 2006). Rituals, however, focus more on the agent than the audience, and even the desired martyrdom of the perpetrator was a type that required being seen.

Analyzing media representation will be the subject of the next chapter, but a few remarks can be made here with respect to shaping not only audience response but also future actions and performances. While the assassination of Pim Fortuyn might have more easily been made to fit into the traditional political cleavages of left and right, as the victim himself founded a political party within that spectrum, the murder of van Gogh is not so easily contained. It does not "make sense" within these familiar categories. How then was it framed? Hajer and Maussen (2004) have identified three frames representative of the Dutch media: an attack on free expression; part of the clash of civilizations, the war on terror, and the holy war; and an example of failed integration. For many members of the artistic and intellectual community, for many journalists and for Amsterdam's mayor, the murder was interpreted as an attack on the right to free expression. At issue here is one of the most coveted of rights of democratic society, one affecting every citizen, but most especially writers, intellectuals, and artists. Since this right is protected by law as well as by group norms, how far this freedom extends is a matter for the courts to decide; but it is considered as almost a duty of modern artists to continually test these borders (Heinich 2000). The second frame, clash of civilizations or war frame, implies that social polarization was the issue and that religious extremism was the problem. Hajer and Maussen cite the headline that the left-liberal newspaper De Volkskrant ran on the morning after the killing: "Moord begin heilige oorlog in Nederland" (Murder starts a holy war in the Netherlands). As the debate developed, perpetrators (radical Muslim extremists) and victims (Dutch civil society) were identified. Failed integration is the third frame that Hajer and Maussen posit. Here the polarities are the "success" and "failure" of Dutch immigration policies regarding the integration of immigrants, most particularly those identified as Muslim (about 6 percent of the Dutch population as a whole and 13 percent of the population of Amsterdam). Some politicians were cast as being "soft and naïve" regarding the possibility of accommodating the Islamic faith into a modern, liberal society (which recalls American debates in the 1950s in which liberal politicians were accused of being "soft on Communism"). This frame locates the discussion on a left-right continuum. Here the identity and background of the assassin, Mohammed Bouyeri, carries heavy symbolic weight. As a model of success turned murderer, he seems to embody policy failure. The perpetrators in this account are liberal politicians, and the victims are again the Dutch public, who were misled.

The mass media of modern society are more than a lens or filter through which occurrences are reported; they are also protagonists in that they provide a stage on which actors may perform and represent their own stories. This was clear in the case of the murder of van Gogh: all those concerned were keenly aware of the presence and power of mass media and took this into account in their actions. The mass media are protagonists in a social drama in that they represent occurrences as dramatic stories, creating a spectacle for audiences already predisposed to receive them. To an increasing extent, modern audiences have come to expect to see news as entertainment, to be presented in dramatic format; at the same time, they are keen to be on hand as a story unfolds. News should be exciting, as well as informative. The question of how stories are told, in other words, is a matter of form and content, making it important to analyze the ways in which the Dutch media told this story. How far along the road to news as entertainment the Dutch media has come will be discussed in the following chapters. The extent to which mass media present occurrences as spectacles also has implications for audiences. The more audiences are predisposed to want to witness spectacle, the more passive they are, in the sense that they come to see and to be entertained, not to be engaged in discussion. The social drama is thus once again a matter of interaction between audience and performer, the latter in this case being the mass media.

FROM SOCIAL DRAMA TO CULTURAL TRAUMA

As discussed above, the model of social drama conceptualizes occurrences in terms of sequences of performance and counterperformance, as a process that begins unexpectedly with some transgression of taken-for-granted norms and routines. To quote again Turner (1974:38), "Such a breach is signalized by the public, overt breach or deliberate nonfulfillment of some crucial norm regulating the intercourse of the parties. To flout such a norm is one obvious symbol of dissonance. In a social drama it is not a crime, though it may formally resemble one; it is, in reality a symbolic trigger of confrontation or encounter." In our case, the action triggering a breach *was* a crime, though we will not focus on that aspect, but rather on the dynamic process the actions of the perpetrator set in motion and their actual and potential effects. In extraordinary cases, a social drama can expose and threaten the social contract and the stable collective identity of a society. Should this occur, one could speak of the possibility of social drama developing into cultural trauma. As developed by Alexander et al. (2004), the theory of cultural trauma refers to a fundamental tear in the social fabric of society, which requires both interpretation and repair. It represents a fundamental threat to established individual and collective identity.

In the dynamic process of social drama, what Turner and Wagner-Pacifici call the "root paradigms" of a society can be exposed and become objects of public debate and reflection. Root paradigms are those largely taken-for-granted frameworks of meaning that guide everyday social actions and aid actors in making sense of themselves and their world. Root paradigms, which include at their most fundamental level the founding myths of a collective, also demarcate the boundaries between those who are part of "us" and those who are excluded. As I will elaborate in a later chapter, one central root paradigm exposed in the social drama set off by the murder of Theo van Gogh concerns the very meaning of "Dutchness," that is, who is included in the collective and who is not and what those who might want to join must do to be included. It should be obvious that this is not a matter of formal citizenship. A key element in this root paradigm makes reference to the Second World War. This reference not only helps identify who is Dutch and who is not, but also provides a moral measure of proper and improper behavior, which carries great emotional import. Guilt and shame, as well as pride and valor, are part of this collective narrative as it was reconstructed in the postwar era, when the "good" Dutchman was contrasted to the "bad" or "mistaken" one.

As we shall see in great detail, one of my central claims in this book is that the murder of Theo van Gogh recalled the ghosts of the Second World War, including the loss of empire in its wake and the treatment of Jews during the German occupation. This helps us understand the emotions that that social drama unleashed. The accumulated historical memory, along with that of the turbulent 1960s, provided the framework through which many of the actors directly involved in our social drama understood their actions, making it necessary for a social scientist to reconstruct that framework in order to understand those actors and their actions. Two central actors, Ayaan Hirsi Ali and Mohammed Bouyeri lie outside that particular frame, but, as we shall see, they had accumulated traumas and root paradigms of their own that are in need of reconstruction. This is all by way of reminding the reader that the past shapes the present and the future. If this is one central claim, what I also hope to show in this book is that sociological analysis can be multidimensional, offering not only a thick description but also thick explanation.

CHAPTER 2

MEDIATING SOCIAL

DRAMA

Journalism gives us a simple moral world, where a group of perpetrators face a group of victims, but where neither history nor motivation is thinkable because both are outside history and context. Even when newspapers highlight violence as a social phenomenon they fail to understand the forces that shape the agency of the perpetrator. —**Mahmood Mamdani**

A social drama is a plotted narrative in which the actions of the various protagonists can be reconstructed as distinctive attempts to define the situation. Each protagonist has his or her own "ideal" plot: how he or she would have the story unfold and be interpreted. One of our tasks then must be to reconstruct the ideal plots as conceived by each protagonist, to interrogate the drama from their particular point of view, to gain a fuller meaning of the event at the level of social action. We must ask for example, what the ideal plot and ending could be from Hirsi Ali's perspective. Perhaps that the murder of van Gogh be taken as yet another expression of the "backwardness" of Islam, that it should further demonstrate the perverseness of the teachings of the Koran. Further, that the murder provoke wide public protest that could spur political action and reform Dutch policy regarding the treatment of immigrant woman, if not the reform of Islam itself. We could then interpret her actions as the attempt to make this occur. This would also provide insight into later reactions, such as her claiming not to be shocked by the murder, since it could have been predicted given the nature of Islam, and her outspoken desire to make a sequel to *Submission*, perhaps becoming herself a martyr. As contrasted to this, Mohammed Bouyeri's ideal plot might have been to have been martyred, thus making his actions part of an Islamic vanguard in a worldwide social movement. This ideal plot would have as a goal to further polarize Dutch society and ultimately to mobilize immigrant groups as part of this historical struggle.

All plots in a modern social drama, idealized or not, are necessarily filtered through mass media. This fact of modern society makes the attempt to determine interpretation through controlling performance imperative. How this was done must be studied and elaborated. But good performances do not by themselves account for actions, as these must necessarily interact with political and moral imperatives, that is, actions are guided by moral and strategic as well as aesthetic or dramaturgical motives. In this regard, the actions of individuals are similar to those of collective actors like social movements, in so far as balancing the expressive and strategic is a defining characteristic of political performance (Alexander 2006).

The symbolic terms that script social drama need also to be specified and analyzed. In Wager-Pacifici's (1986:15) consideration of the Moro affair in Italy, these include "political legitimacy, terrorism, negotiation, sacrifice, family and the State." Some of these terms will be important in our case as well, especially terrorism and political legitimacy. Such symbolic terms are useful in that they "reveal the strategic spots at which ambiguities necessarily arise" and are potentially illuminating "as they necessarily offer up for consideration alternative readings and plot moves that may have been wittingly or unwittingly suppressed," as Wagner-Pacifici puts it (1986:15). What then are the symbolic terms that script the murder of Theo van Gogh? These include Islam, fundamentalism, terrorism, immigration, and artistic freedom. Interpretation through such concepts provides an insight not only into motive, but also into alternative readings of the event. For instance, if Islam is interpreted as a backward religion, then both the making of Submission and the subsequent assassination are more easily understood. If not, then an alternative reading must be sought. One could propose, for example, that van Gogh, Hirsi Ali, and Mohammed B. were all rational opportunists, seeking to promote their respective political and personal interests.

According to Turner's model (1980:150), social drama opens with the breach of an established norm in a public arena that can be deliberate or unintended, but usually involves a highly visible or valued person. In our case, there are several possibilities that can be identified and discussed. The murder of Theo van Gogh on an open street clearly broke a norm; and while many may not have liked him, he was also a visible public personality, a representative figure. On the other hand, the making of the film Submission did not break the norms of Dutch society as previously noted, at least as they are understood formally by the law and informally by the prevailing norms governing artistic expression. In fact, a court decision rendered after the murder (March 2005) rejected the complaint filed by a Muslim association to prevent Hirsi Ali from making a sequel. In its ruling the court noted that although Hirsi Ali had tested the limits of the tolerable, there were not yet sufficient grounds to prevent her making a sequel. While it may not have been sufficient in itself to cause a breach, the film certainly contributed to the possibility. This is especially so given the response, both a formal kind as in the example above and the various expressions of public protest with followed. The initiators of the film (van Gogh and Hirsi Ali) must thus be considered protagonists insofar as preparing the next phase in the drama process, the murder. At his point another protagonist, Mohammed B., enters the scene and must also be identified and interrogated as to motive and how successfully these were realized. From his perspective, and from that of many others in the Netherlands, the film was but another indication of a separation, if not a breach, between Muslims and the rest of the population. Other perpetrators are important to identify and to include in our analysis: for example, the media and its multilayered audience and, in the near background, the enigmatic figure of Pim Fortuyn.

While a breach may appear to result abruptly, it is "the expression of a deeper division of interests and loyalties than appear on the surface" (Wagner-Pacifici 1986:65). Breach requires a striking occurrence, one "rich in symbolic presentation," but this only serves to expose and agitate deeper divisions that can then be articulated in the ensuing struggle to attribute and fix meaning. In this process aesthetic considerations and dramatic performances are connected to social and political outcomes. This marks a clear difference with theater, where different kinds of outcomes prevail. While audience engagement may be a prime concern in determining the success or failure of a theatrical performance, strategic concerns permeate politics. As opposed to artistic performances, perpetrators in social dramas must be gauged and analyzed according to political as well as aesthetic criteria. The meaning struggles that clarify perpetrators and victims should thus be seen as inherently political in that they help identify opponents who face each other in a strategic battle. At stake here is the attempt to define the situation in a particular way, one that stipulates an opponent against whom to assert collective strength. While both can have real consequences, as opposed to theater social drama can be a step in a process leading toward social polarization and deep political crisis. It is at this stage that social drama becomes cultural trauma.

Analysis of a potential breach should identify the key relationship that such a breach would interrupt. This process of identification is also central to the attempt by protagonists to fix meaning, as this type of meaning struggle involves naming and the attempt to constrain the agents of a breach, as well as affecting the latter's consequences. In the Moro affair, for example, identifying the perpetrating agents was relatively easy, as the Red Brigades took full responsibility, but establishing just who the Red Brigades were, outside provocateurs or internal criminals, was a matter of interpretation and at once contested. Designating the nature of the Red Brigades was of central importance, as, according to Turner's understanding of social drama, a breach must occur between members or groups of the same society. A breach, in other words, can occur only within an already established collective. Thus, if one can claim that perpetrators are outsiders, then one can limit or even eliminate a breach by calling for a united front of insiders (who may, of course, have internal disagreements) against those outsiders. Thus, in our present example, understanding Mohammed B.'s actions as part of a worldwide terrorist movement could potentially unite all other citizens of the Netherlands against this enemy and, on the other side, could unify Muslims either in support of him or against him. This can be considered as part of the politics of naming and also of convincing others of the significance and truthfulness of a name.

Wagner-Pacifici (1986:72) identifies three separate, but interacting oppositional pairs that defined the meaning struggle in the Moro affair: indigenous versus foreign (as in the above example), common criminal versus political criminal, left versus right.[1] If we apply this to the van Gogh murder we can make use of at least the first two, perhaps even all three. In the first place, one key social relationship that the murder disrupted was the rights of citizens to express themselves and to move freely in public. With this as a starting point there are many levels involved that must also be uncovered. At the deepest level is that of the foundations of Dutch society: who is Dutch and what if anything is Dutchness? This is something we will deal with in detail in a later chapter. More to the surface lay the question of who are the parties in opening the social drama and the breach. What was the meaning of the act that brought the filmmaker van Gogh and the assailant Mohammed B. together as protagonists? Then a more difficult question arises: what does their meeting mean and represent? Was it merely a criminal act, something not uncommon on urban streets? If only this, then there would be no breach of a basic social relationship, merely a case for the police and the courts. Or, was it an attack by an immigrant, a member of an identifiable social category on another representative person, a white Dutchman. If so, the action becomes something more than a simple criminal act, a hate crime perhaps, and a breach looms in the background. What about the identity of the assailant? If he was an immigrant, of what background and type was he and how would such a designation reflect on motive and meaning? Can the assailant's actions be explained by personality, by biography, or by something wider and deeper that needs accounting? Was the killer a member of a political group or a sect? If so how does this bear on his actions, on interpretation and response?

All these issues became central in the attempt to understand the occurrence and to fix its meaning in the various mediums and forums of public debate. Similarly, one must discuss the victim. Who was Theo van Gogh? Was he an innocent victim of an enraged assailant or himself a perpetrator? In what capacity was he attacked—as a citizen, a Dutchman, an artist and filmmaker? What bearing did all or any of these identifications have on the assault? How was he identified? Was van Gogh the real target and if not, who was and why? Answers to such questions, especially in conjunction to those concerning the assailant, are all part of the meaning struggle and help us identify the key social relationship and the breach itself. Indeed, whether or not it is proper to at all speak about a breach. Answering such questions requires an analysis of the motives of the perpetrators, including those interpretations articulated in and through the mass media and the media itself as a perpetrator in its own right.

Addressing these questions requires analyzing the shifting images, the status and the rhetorical appeals made to the "root paradigms" that motivate and support practices. As previously discussed, root paradigms are frameworks of meaning, shared narratives, or, to use a more familiar term, traditions, that are embedded in and expressed through social practices. They are formative in that they are foundations of collective identity, making a group recognizable to itself. In her analysis of the Moro affair, Wagner-Pacifici (1986:164–66) uncovered several such root paradigms, "resistance," "democracy," the "sanctity of human life" (for the fundamental right of the individual) and of the collective, and the sanctity of the state, the party, and the proletariat. We must seek to identify similar root paradigms in the Dutch case; "free speech," linked to "democracy," "free society," Western culture, and so on are clearly aspects. It may not have been mere chance that the relatively spontaneous demonstrations that followed the news of the murder focused on the principle of free speech rather than being anti-immigrant or immigration, which could have also been a theme. Free speech could unite a much larger segment of the population; it is an inclusive in a different way than the theme of "Dutchness," which would have been the root paradigm called upon in mobilizing around the dichotomy of native versus immigrant.

MISE-EN-SCÈNE

The setting is almost as important as the players. According to Wagner-Pacifici (1986:69), "The setting can provide or deprive the protagonists of a necessary symbolic arsenal." The street and the time of day added symbolic significance to the murder of van Gogh. Being killed on an open public thoroughfare in the early morning rush hour gave a meaning to the killing different from what it would have been if the same action had been committed on a lonely street in the dead of night, or in a parking lot. As the killer knew his victim's habits well, including the fact that he regularly walked his dog alone in the late evening, the choice of acting in the daytime on the street was a conscious one. The daytime assault in full public view exposed the vulnerability of any citizen in the practice of a taken-for-granted right, the right to free passage and safety in public.

Who was assaulted on that busy Amsterdam street in the morning of November 2004? Clearly, he was no ordinary Dutch citizen. The great grandson and namesake of the well-known brother of a world-famous painter, Theo van Gogh maintained a high public profile. He identified with his ancestors and often spoke publicly in the family's name, as at the opening of a new wing in Amsterdam's van Gogh museum when he addressed the queen and the nation in an ironic voice, poking fun at the occasion, the guests, and the role he was playing (Gogh 2002). Theo van Gogh's appearance was part of his persona. A robust and scruffy figure, his loud and often vulgar voice was part of a very public personality that prided itself on being loved or hated, on not being ordinary or anonymous. In a book written soon after the murder, Tomas Ross (2005), van

Gogh's friend and scriptwriter, provided readers with a long list of the latter's prominent enemies, including the royal family.[2] In so doing, Ross was contributing to the public image, and now memory, of his friend as the court jester, the insider who enjoyed playing at being outsider (Buruma [2006b], a not so intimate acquaintance, furthers this impression). Van Gogh was a champion of self-presentation and self-promotion, who learned much from previous antiheroes in Dutch public life. The photographs that adorn the books in which his articles and sayings are collected resemble those of Jan Cramer, the antiestablishment artistic rebel who mocked Dutch society in the 1960s and is now a well-respected artist. Often identifying himself as "the village idiot," Van Gogh was a well-known filmmaker and a popular journalist, whose works had a following that spread well beyond the local Amsterdam circles he frequented. He maintained a webpage and invited commentary and conversation on his antics. Van Gogh's outspokenness and provocations were known well in the Netherlands and beyond. He seemed to glow in the light of his provocations, which, as noted earlier, included comments against Jews as well as Muslims.

Determining how accomplished van Gogh was as an artist and writer and how large his audience was was part of the meaning struggle that followed the assault. This determination became important in fixing his place as perpetrator. If van Gogh could be labeled a small-scale opportunist, he could be partly blamed for the attack and the chance of a breach lessened. To characterize him as having political motives, to place his work on a left-right scale, or as a racist motivated by ethnic or identity politics would lead to a quite different account. Representing van Gogh in this way would also, perhaps even necessarily, mean attributing political aims to his assailant, Mohammed B. Such an accounting would attribute political motivation and point toward a breach in Turner's sense of the term (see Boltanski and Trevenot 1999 for a discussion of types of justification in "critical moments").

This brings us to the question of if—and if so why—van Gogh was a target? In one sense he was not, as was made clear in the note pinned to his body; the primary target was Ayaan Hirsi Ali. Yet van Gogh *was* murdered, so the question as to why must be asked. Was he killed because he directed a provocative film? That is, because he was the perpetrator of a blasphemous act, was he therefore sentenced to death? This is clearly a possible answer. Unlike Salman Rushdie (discussed in a later chapter) with whom Hirsi Ali if not van Gogh was often compared (though not in aesthetic terms), there was no official fatwa against him. In fact, after the murder at least one prominent imam, Abdullah Haselhoef of Rotterdam (whose image appears on a Pim Fortuyn book cover), criticized the decision by two regional TV stations for deciding not to broadcast *Submission*. What then did van Gogh represent beyond the film that might explain his murder? Was he the real target or was he merely a representative of something larger, that is, of Dutch identity or even Western civilization itself? If one takes seriously the note, this appears a likely possibility. On a slightly lesser scale, van Gogh's murder represents to the profession another journalist killed in the line of duty. Seen this way the killing represents the threatened right of a free press and, more generally, of free speech. As representative of a profession dedicated to free expression, van Gogh meant something significant to the killer as well as to the victim himself. From the side of the murderer, van Gogh would be a target because of his professional role, one that was fundamental to the idea of democracy. This line of argument could easily be carried to the level of Western civilization.

From the police and trial records, it is clear that van Gogh was an important target for Mohammed B. and for other Muslims in the Netherlands and elsewhere. His public statements about Islam, including the recently published collection of his newspaper articles *Allah weet het beter* (Allah knows best, 2003) made him an object of disdain and even hate long before the controversy over *Submission*. These articles appeared in book form largely because *Metro*, the free newspaper for which he wrote, began to censor his columns. One can find van Gogh's image blown through with fake bullet holes on a radical Islamic Internet page, including one with the caption "When is it your turn van Gogh?," a clear reference to the murder of Pim Fortuyn. On this basis, it might not be necessary to look any further in explaining the murder. What forces one to look deeper is the manner in which it was carried out, most especially the use of the knife and the notes. Taken seriously, these shift the search for motive, from targeted victim to representative figure and shift the narrative reconstruction from murder to assassination. Of course, the motives of the assailant might matter very little to an angry and fearful populace; and whatever the motivations, the killing of a well-known public figure by a member of an immigrant group would almost certainly have provoked vengeful response given the context. At the same time, one must also take note of the undeniable increase in the serious attacks and threats to public figures in recent times. After all, it was not only Fortuyn who shortly before was murdered; Swedish minister Anna Lindh had recently been killed, and many other European politicians had received publicly acknowledged threats to their lives. The security of public figures had become an increasing concern in Europe and elsewhere before the murder of van Gogh.

Be that all as it may, the way the murder was carried out, the heavy symbolism of the weapons and the texts provided by the assailant point us beyond vengeful murder to much broader issues. Van Gogh was a target, even if a secondary or substitute one, *because* of who he was and what he represented. Theo van Gogh represented a despised Western civilization to a young man who, though born in the Netherlands and a competent participant in its modern culture, had recently rejected it. The power and substance of this rejection will be discussed in a later chapter. First, one needs to reflect on the power of some of the symbolism invoked.

THE BODY AND MODE OF EXECUTION

At least since the Middle Ages and the legitimating role given royal blood, the physical body has played a central symbolic role in politics. As Kantorowicz (1957) reveals in a classic study, the body of the king referred to both a physical person and to the body politic, yet killing a king was not the same as killing a kingdom. In many modern political assassinations, this principle seems to apply. The murder of American leaders such as John and Robert Kennedy and the attempts on the life of presidential candidate George Wallace and President Ronald Reagan may not have been intended as attacks on the American political system or the country's "way of life." However, when one considers the assassination of President Abraham Lincoln at the end of the American Civil War by a disgruntled Southerner or of civil rights leader Martin Luther King Jr. by a white supremacist, things get more complicated. These public figures might well have been targeted as representing more than themselves. The murder of Pim Fortuyn, a new style of celebrity politician, a flamboyant figure who flaunted a gay lifestyle and who broke with many of the staid traditions in Dutch politics and many norms of Dutch society, could be analyzed in this way; so also the murder of Theo van Gogh. Though neither a prominent politician nor a representative of the state, van Gogh was clearly a public figure and, through self-identification and the projection of others, an iconic representative of a long-standing artistic as well as journalistic tradition. This tradition, embodied in such concepts as "artistic license" and codified in norms and laws protecting free expression, is one of the foundations of Western democracies, at the same time as it is a continually contested terrain. Even those who were verbally assaulted and publicly insulted, like Amsterdam mayor Job Cohen (a bitter enemy and among those on the list of van Gogh's enemies compiled after his death by Tomas Ross), defended van Gogh's right to say the things he did, or at least to be taken to court to test their legality. The violence inflicted by Mohammed B. was both physical and symbolic: van Gogh was a target not merely for his slanderous words and images, but also as a representative of Western liberal traditions that permitted and protected such outbursts. The way his body was mutilated in broad daylight and full public view only confirms this: civilization clashed with civilization in the killer's eyes and not in his alone.

Tomas Ross (2005) attempted to make sense of the plot and choreography of the actual murder by contrasting it to Fortuyn's assassination. Why would such a carefully planned murder occur in broad daylight, when there were so many other possibilities? Ross goes so far as to say that if he or van Gogh himself had written the script for this assassination, it would never have been done in this way. It would be "too obvious" and "too risky" in that its drama could be so easily ruined by an innocent passerby and turned into farce, writes Ross. But this is to miss the point. The murder had to be witnessed; it had to be in full public view, with the possibility of interruption. This was an act of violence against a principle in the name of another principle. The principles in question derive from a conception of holy war and were carried out by a holy warrior defending a particular interpretation of Holy Scripture and hoping to die a martyr in the process. That at least is what was written in the accompanying notes. This also is what was written on the body of the victim. Though it did not appear in the form of text, as did the quotations from the Koran on naked female flesh in Submission, the meaning of van Gogh's assassination was clearly written on the body of the filmmaker. Of course, the female body also plays a central role in Submission, where it is both symbol and bearer of text at one and the same time. Visible to a much broader public, lying in the middle of a busy street in broad daylight, van Gogh's body amplifies that significance when it was adorned with a text stuck through a dagger, not unlike Luther's nailed testament to the cathedral door, a reference Mohammed B. would surely not make. An ordinary knife can be seen protruding from the body of the victim, but this simple kitchen utensil became transformed into a dagger in the hands of Mohammed B., a dagger that in the eyes of some Dutch interpreters was meant to pierce not merely the heart of his victim but also that of Western civilization.

ACTORS

The assailant was less well known to the general public than the victim, but he was not anonymous during the act itself. Mohammed B. identified himself in public through his appearance. He presented himself not only as a holy warrior on this occasion, but also as representative of a distinctive social category, a member of an immigrant population that was becoming increasingly visible and in some eyes more problematic. One, probably unintended, outcome of the murder was to complete the transformation of the "immigrant" as the focus of negative attention to the narrower "Muslim immigrant." Mohammed B.'s appearance (his clothing, facial hair, and skull cap) and his choice of setting and props allowed accounts of his actions to focus on a smaller range of perpetrators. His bodily appearance as well as his actions encoded his motives and presented a preferred reading to the audience. Here the mass media became significant, as it not only helped amplify the act into an event, but also added coded meanings of its own.

How would the murder be reported? As part of a struggle to affix meaning to the assault and to control or at least effect a breach, a media-induced story line could draw on the dichotomies "indigenous versus foreign" and "common criminal versus political criminal." Was Mohammed B. acting alone, out of frustration and thus as an outraged Dutch citizen/immigrant, or was he the pawn of foreign forces much more sinister and dangerous? Similarly, were his actions to be judged as criminal or as politically motivated? There is a world of difference in a media-infused attribution of meaning. Wagner-Pacifici uses the term *defamiliarization* to describe the framing of the Red Brigades in the Italian media. The aim or at least the effect was to turn them into outsiders, to make them foreign; even though they were Italian citizens, they had become something else, a group of terrorists motivated by a foreign ideology. She interprets this as an attempt to avoid a breach. This was the case in many accounts of Mohammed B.: he may be a Dutch citizen, born and bred in the Netherlands, but he is not "one of us." Alternatively, he might well have been described as a lost or wayward son who had fallen into the hands of bad elements.

Van Gogh on the other hand was "one of us"; at least he was to become so after his public remarks about Muslims and especially after his death. He was a bit odd, but still our own, our van Gogh.[3] Fortuyn was represented in the same way. In van Gogh's case, this attribution was taken as obvious, the name and even the lifestyle fit into a recognizable tradition of cultural radicalism and iconoclasm. Even if it appears obvious, however, the media mainstream must remind its audience of all this, underscore for them whom we are dealing with and why he is important and why to attack him is to attack "all of us." In the case of Fortuyn, this reminder was not made by the mainstream media as much as by the public, his supporters who never ceased to remind the newspapers and the political establishment that while Fortuyn may had been odd, he was still "Our Pim." Van Gogh did not have the same charismatic following and may not have been a "hero," but, for the media and the political establishment, he was one of us. Van Gogh has become a martyr and hero, antihero to some, a man who died for the cause of "freedom." As discussed above, for Mohammed B. in the role of holy warrior, van Gogh represented something else, the kind of decadence that the so-called freedom of Western civilization could inspire.

What, however, was Mohammed B.'s own view of his actions, and what was his goal, his ideal plot? Now that he identified himself as a holy warrior, how would he like the story to unfold? In the role of holy warrior, the wider plot could have been the polarization of Dutch society and the radicalization of immigrant, primarily Muslim, groups, as already stated. It is also clear from the note he carried that Mohammed B. intended to be martyred, but given that he survived and was subjected to criminal prosecution, he was forced to invent the stance of a living martyr. At first, he found this best achieved through dramatic silence, by publicly refusing to recognize the legitimacy of the legal process to which he was submitted. There were at least two audiences for this act. The first was the representatives of the court and through them, and the media representations, the wider public. The second was the local and global Muslim population. Mohammed B. must have hoped his silence would speak loudly, but differently to each. Silence was the primary performative act, the attempt to define the situation, in front of different audiences, in his own way. This was the case during his first trial. In the second, when he was brought forward as a witness in the conspiracy trial of the Hofstad group, Mohammed B. changed tactics and offered a long and rambling speech about his vision of Islam, declaring that although he was "no Bin Laden," he was still proud of how he was being portrayed in the media as a holy warrior and soldier of Islam.

TARGET

The note pinned to Theo van Gogh's body announced that Hirsi Ali was the intended victim of assassination. One could assume that killing van Gogh was then merely a matter of access, since security around her made this difficult. Still one must ask why Hirsi Ali was the prime target. Was she so chosen because of her participation in the making of *Submission*, as is often reported, thus linking her fate directly with that of van Gogh? Since a letter addressed to her was placed on van Gogh's body, this seems a reasonable inference. In this case, van Gogh's body became a conduit and his murder a message addressed directly to someone else. There are other, wider possibilities however. Hirsi Ali may have been a target because of her outspoken views on Islam, for her political activism. She may also have been chosen because she was a woman, a black woman, or a publicly declared renegade Muslim. From Mohammed B.'s standpoint Hirsi Ali was a well-integrated immigrant, a successful member of Dutch society. Was personal jealousy thus involved, which would then both explain the letter and limit the confrontation to the interpersonal, or was it something more: was Hirsi Ali a symbol of successful integration in a way that Mohammed B. was not and thus an alternative model that needed elimination? If this were the case, the audience was the Muslim community and not only the "Dutch." From the point of the holy warrior, Hirsi Ali was a fallen Muslim who abandoned her roots to join the other side and thus a traitor, a "daughter of the enlightenment," as the *New York Times* called her. She was also a model and symbol of successful integration, whose success was intertwined with the abandonment of Islam.

As a member of the Dutch parliament, Hirsi Ali could almost automatically be considered a part of the establishment, and thus obviously a well-integrated constituent of the Dutch nation. However, as a recent immigrant and a black Muslim woman, Hirsi Ali could as easily be identified, and identify herself, as an outsider and a representative figure. Her own self-presentation draws on both identities. For the Dutch nation, Hirsi Ali is identifiable as a first-generation immigrant (arriving in the Netherlands as a political refugee in 1992) and the daughter of Hirsi Magan, a well-known leader of the Somalian opposition to the dictatorial government of Mohamed Siad Barre, which is also her own description (Hirsi Ali 2002:7, 2007). As will be described in more detail in the next chapter, she quickly mastered the language, became a Dutch (and European) citizen, obtained an advanced degree from Leiden University, and worked in a research position for the PvdA (Partij van de Arbeid), the Dutch Labor Party, before becoming a member of parliament for the liberal VVD. She was selected as "Dutchman of the Year" in 2004, the same year van Gogh was murdered. These are all significant measures and symbols of successful integration and assimilation, though it must be mentioned that Hirsi Ali resigned her parliamentary post in May 2006 because of allegations that she falsified her original application for political asylum. These charges were brought by members of her own party and enforced by Minister Verdonk, an important member of the VVD.

Hirsi Ali couples her rise in politics to her identity/identification as an immigrant, a black woman, and a Muslim (Hirsi Ali 2002:88). She turned these attributes into research interests and into political issues, things on which to build a career and to attain public presence as representative of a constituency and as a representative figure. Such self-identity and identification work in both directions, inward as a source of personal identification and outward as a source of social status and recognition. Such identification is also important in that it helps one to designate an Other against whom one organizes resources. In Hirsi Ali's case, this was a form of conservative Islam and those who identified themselves with and through it. Mohammed B. was Hirsi Ali's opposite, her Other. Hirsi Ali's political identity is also significant from the point of view of the left-right axis, which couples with the indigenous/foreigner axis mentioned by Turner and Wagner-Pacifici. Ali's move from the PvdA to the VVD can be interpreted as a move from left to right. She herself explains it partly in this way, as she says she found the concern with individual rights (in her case the rights of Muslim woman) more easily aligned with the liberal tradition of the VVD than with the collective interests of the PvdA (Hirsi Ali 2002:88).[4] The model of the politician as celebrity offered by Dick Pels (2004:26) in describing the place of the "crossover intellectual" Pim Fortuyn in the landscape of contemporary Dutch politics might also be useful here. Pels adds a crosscutting emotional dimension to the left-right axis in accounting for a political celebrity, a product of the media age. Like Fortuyn, Hirsi Ali is a political celebrity, but not quite the "political bohemian" or dandy in the style of Fortuyn. Successfully playing the "dandy" or the "bohemian" would not have been easy for a first-generation immigrant, especially a black woman with an elite, conservative background. Hirsi Ali became an important media personality on the basis of her political views, her photogenic appearance, and a charismatic quality quite her own. Like Fortuyn, Hirsi Ali was very clear about what she stood for and why, while appearing both courageous and vulnerable at the same time. This may well have been a product of her class background and her socialization as a member of a political and cultural elite. This clearly is a factor in explaining how she could move with relative ease in her new surroundings among the political and intellectual elite in the Netherlands.

Hirsi Ali's outspokenness and her celebrity made her very visible, yet the question of determining why she was a target for Mohammed B. still remains. Calling the Prophet a "pervert," as she had done, was certainly provocative, as was making *Submission*, but was this enough? If Hirsi Ali was the intended target of the assassin, which Hirsi Ali was it that was to be eliminated? Was she to be killed for her role in the film, for her blasphemous representation, for her alternative interpretation of the Koran and of Islam, for her model way of assimilating and integrating, or for her status as an independent-minded woman, which only amplified the rest of the possible factors? All of these are possible interpretations and offer motivation for Mohammed B. to select her as a target.

One could also ask what would have happened had Hirsi Ali and not van Gogh been killed. Would the murder of a female member of parliament have raised a different reaction than the killing of a filmmaker? Would different constituencies have been formed and mobilized in mourning and protest?

THE GHOST OF PIM FORTUYN

Though not an actual participant, the ghost of Pim Fortuyn hangs over this social drama. When his murder was first announced, it was feared by some and hoped by others that the killer would be a Muslim militant, as already noted. That someone like this would be motivated to murder Fortuyn seemed obvious. Immediately following the murder *De Volkskrant* (May 7, 2002) wrote, "Don't we all passionately hope that the perpetrator turns out to be a lunatic who comes from a family of farmers who have lived in the Noordoostpolder (a rural region of the country) since its reclamation, a blond, blue-eyed man who stands for God, Orange and Country" (quoted in Pantti and van Zoonen 2006:210).

Later, when the actual killer was identified as an "animal rights activist," there was both relief and surprise: relief that the killer was neither a Muslim nor an immigrant and surprise that he was not. With the murder of van Gogh, these anticipations were finally realized. The debate about what Pim Fortuyn represented continues unabated after his death. For many on the political left, Fortuyn was an opportunist and a media personality who was able to put his personal charisma and connections to great political use. From this perspective, those who voted for his party voted for him, not because they shared any particular set of beliefs or political ideology, but as an expression of discontent with the current political leadership. Others saw Fortuyn's success as not so much a matter of charisma, but as representing a previously untapped constituency. For the blogger Paul Treanor (http://web.inter.nl.net/users/Paul.Treanor/pim-fortuyn.html), "Dutch politics was waiting for Pim Fortuyn." Treanor, a prolific Internet author, describes Fortuyn as an ethnic nationalist and compares him to France's Jean-Marie Le Pen and Austria's Jörg Haider, both leaders of right-wing nationalist movements. The only difference, writes Treanor, is that Fortuyn is dead and "if he had not been assassinated he might today be Prime Minister." From this point of view, Fortuyn represented the same sort of nationalist sentiments that helped ground the European nation-state in the nineteenth century and that have been lurking beneath the surface in the Netherlands. Accepting this rather simplistic comparison might help explain the current focus on "successful" integration through language training and other forms of cultural competence that those following in Fortuyn's footsteps have made mandatory. The aim appears to be to ensure that something identified as "Dutch culture and way of life" is clearly identified as the dominant culture and that any enclaves representing other cultures disappear. Such a shift from multiculturalism to assimilation in immigration policy will be discussed in a later chapter. Looking at the matter this way "normalizes" Fortuyn, placing both him and the Dutch electorate more in line with the current European voting trends. In France, Austria, Italy, Belgium, and Denmark, anti-immigrant nationalist parties receive between 10–20 percent of the votes in national elections. For historical reasons to be discussed in a later chapter, the Netherlands has seen itself as an exception in this regard. At least one political leader has said that the greatest shock of the past few years was neither the murder of van Gogh nor that of Fortuyn, but the latter's completely unexpected rise to power.

In his perceptive intellectual biography, Dick Pels (2004) offers a nuanced analysis of Fortuyn and his appeal. Like Treanor, Pels places Fortuyn in the same ideological family as Haider and Le Pen, but sees clear differences.[5] While the adamant opposition to immigrants and immigration characterizes the new right generally, Fortuyn distinguished himself by his moderation. According to Pels, Fortuyn's use of a phrase like "the Netherlands is full" was meant as a demographic rather than an ideological or racist statement. It was meant, in other words, to apply to immigration across the board and not to specific groups. This, of course, says nothing about how these words might have been understood by Fortuyn's supporters, especially when one takes into account other remarks he made about Islam and Muslims in general. Rather than fitting into a European pattern, Pels's Fortuyn represents a new type of political figure, a media celebrity whose audience appeal is not easily captured by traditional political categorizations, such as the left-right divide. The political celebrity is populist in the sense of being widely popular as a personality, someone very familiar yet somehow also larger than life. The celebrities on the American political scene are more likely models than the right-wing European populists. Though not a movie star turned politician, Fortuyn appears to be the creature of an age where mass media has become increasingly important in the selection of political leadership and in the functioning of politics. The peculiarities of the Dutch political system, where small parties can play an important role far beyond the size of their constituencies, only amplifies the possibilities for media-oriented charismatic figures like Fortuyn. It is more in this sense that the Dutch populace was waiting for Fortuyn: a political outsider with a media-genic personality who could command authority without coming through the established ranks. There remains, however, the question of what the roots and the stability of this popular appeal were. Was this mainly a "Pim" phenomenon, entirely rooted in the particular person, or did his rise represent something deeper and more permanent? This question is also interesting given Fortuyn's open homosexuality and flamboyant lifestyle, traits that at least on the surface should have limited his popular appeal in the culturally conservative Netherlands.

REPRESENTATION AND ARENAS OF DEFINITION

In his analysis of the Watergate scandal, Turner (1982:74) notes that "social dramas generate their symbolic types: traitors, renegades, villains, martyrs, heroes, faithful, infidels, deceivers, scapegoats." In modern societies such symbolic types are articulated, magnified, and projected largely through mass media. Any analysis of contemporary social drama then must not only clarify the protagonists, but also the social spaces in and through which they are constituted and within which, once constituted, they act to define, set, and control the meaning or interpretation of the situation. It is in these spaces—the mass media most especially but also the debate forums provided by political parties, the parliament, trade unions, schools, churches, and other public arenas—that protagonists present themselves and map out their positions in opposition to others. Some protagonists are already present—the assassin and the victims, for example—but these and others come to the fore as symbolic types in the meaning struggle that is central to the social drama. These may include those who claim to speak for the victim (the "friends" of van Gogh, for example) and also those who speak to, if not for, the assailant (Muslim leaders, for example). They may do so in their own name or as representatives for various groups, such as political parties and religious groups and immigrant organizations. In the latter case, such groups may already be organized and institutionalized, yet those particular persons who come forward to speak in the group's name on the issue become new actors in the public eye. As the occurrence becomes an event, it can provide an opportunity for particular individuals to present themselves in a new light as public representatives. A particularly significant example can be found in the case of Amsterdam alderman Ahmed Aboutaleb, named as a potential target on Mohammed B.'s Internet list. After the murder, Aboutaleb spoke from his position in the Amsterdam city council, making forceful pronouncements in many public forums, including televised debates, where he presented himself as an exemplary Dutch citizen who, like Mohammed B. was also a Muslim of Moroccan descent (Hajer and Uitermark forthcoming).[6] In one well-publicized speech at the

Alkabir Mosque on the day after the murder, Aboutaleb advised those Muslims who did not accept the norms and values of Dutch culture to pack their bags, as there was no place for them in the Netherlands. Aboutaleb was not the only one to specifically address Muslims living in the Netherlands; as mentioned earlier, NGOs working in the city had also organized meetings in the Muslim community to help defuse the situation.

Arenas of definition also serve as arenas of defense, in that interpretative positions are not only articulated; they are also defended against those of others and against those wider forces against which many of the protagonists unite in common cause (Wagner-Pacifici 2000). For example, if the interpretive position is that of a struggle against terrorism, many actors can unite behind this particular interpretation while disagreeing as to its meaning and the proper response. In the latter case, when identifying an outside force as the root cause of the assault several of the protagonists can find common ground as potential victims and seek common defense by rallying behind higher authority, such as the police, the law, and the state charged with upholding it. In this case, articulating an interpretive position directly implies a defense; it names the problem and the solution at the same time: the problem is terrorism, and the solution calls for common action in defending "our way of life." The problem can be more limited but have similar effect, such as "an attack on artistic freedom" or "freedom of speech," calling for a defense of "liberal values," rather than an entire way of life. This was the position of many who identified van Gogh as an artist or journalist and interpreted the murder as an attack not merely as against his person but against a right guaranteed in Dutch society, or, more abstractly, in "Western" society, or, more concretely, in "Christian" society. What makes the murder of van Gogh and the reactions to it uniquely significant is that what was called upon as in need of defense were the values many in the Netherlands came to identify as distinctly Dutch, at least since the 1960s: a liberal attitude toward abortion, homosexuality, and artistic freedom. Calling such values "Christian" or even "Western" would surely raise some eyebrows not only in the Netherlands but in the rest of the "West" as well.

Identifying areas in which a situation comes to be defined is at least as important as identifying those actors who seek to impose or control that definition. After all, those persons may change, while the arenas remain more stable. What needs mapping here are not only the interpretative positions as they emerge and are articulated, but also the underlying messages, the calls for unity and strength, for calm, and for action. This was not only a meaning struggle to define the situation, but also a form of action, informing audiences of the proper modes of response and at the same time, part of the attempt to expand or to limit the potential damage, or, in terms of social drama, to deny a breach and prevent a crisis. The types of actions that are called for, explicitly or implicitly, arrest, change of law, more police, restrict immigration, better assimilation, and so on, need to mapped and analyzed. That a breach does not appear or that it does not develop into a crisis says something about the quality of the occurrence itself (its symbolic or interpretative potential) and of the society in which it took place. The occurrence may not be of the scale that could initiate a breach, that is, not "meaningful" or significant enough to evoke response at the most fundamental level of collective identity. It could be just another media event, for example, something for the six o'clock news and then forgotten. Media entrepreneurs, including energetic reporters or public officials or celebrity experts, as products and co-producers of the society of the spectacle, might do their respective best, but still fail to keep the momentum and the cameras rolling. Public attention is short lived. At the same time, Dutch society may not be as open to spectacle as other Western societies. The Dutch mass media is strongly regulated, and there is no equivalent to the daily tabloid such as Bild in Germany or the Sun in Great Britain.[7] There may not have been sufficient grist in this occurrence to allow for the rise of a new celebrity politician or sufficient basis to create a clear dichotomy between good and evil, such as that constructed between New York's firefighters and Bin Laden in the aftermath of the attack on the World Trade Center in 2001. Though media friendly, van Gogh was not the best figure to stand for "Western values" of the civilized world.

THE POLITICAL SPHERE

As mentioned previously, Dutch politics is characterized by a multiparty model with long-standing roots in confessional divisions. Although there have been as many as thirteen parties, at least since the 1980s two main blocks have been able to form relatively stable coalition governments. These blocks have been led by either the Christian Democrats on the center-right or the Labor Party (PvdA) on the left. The PvdA was formed in 1946 as a merger of social democrats, left-liberals, and social policy–

oriented Protestants. It became a mass party in the 1970s under the dynamic leadership of Joop den Uyl who headed coalition governments with newly formed left parties between 1973 and 1977. In those years, the party recorded its highest number of parliamentary seats, winning 53 out of 150 in the lower chamber. Formed out of a coalition of three Christian parties (Dutch Reform, a Protestant party, and a Catholic party) in 1980, the Christian Democratic Appeal (CDA) has been successful in countering the power that the left accumulated during the 1960s and 70s. As such, it has successfully managed to modernize the traditional confessional politics that had dominated the Dutch politics until at least the end of the Second World War. The CDA won 43 seats (out of 150) in the elections of 2002 and 44 in 2003; in both cases they formed the cabinet and claimed the prime minister post. In 1989 the PvdA and the CDA formed a governing coalition. It is still fair to say that left-right cleavages continue to be modified by religion in a characteristic and defining way in Dutch politics. Muslims in the Netherlands have organized themselves through a variety of local and national organizations, but they have thus far remained content to work through the existing political parties (for an account of these organizations, see Hussain 2003).

The elections of 2003 and 2004 are central to the unfolding social drama surrounding the murder of Theo van Gogh. The murder of Pim Fortuyn should also be understood in the context of these elections. The relatively stable coalition politics that characterized Dutch politics after the formation of the two mass parties (CDA and PvdA) was shaken by the emergence of locally based citizen-initiative groups that transformed themselves from local pressure groups into national political parties in time for the election of 2002. The first of these, Leefbaar Nederland (Livable Netherlands) was formed in 1999 out of the joining together of similar groups in two cities, Hilversum and Utrecht. At the head of their list of candidates for the 2002 election was the sociology professor, writer, and publicist Pim Fortuyn. The addition of this charismatic public figure in November 2001 gave the new party an increasingly positive response in public opinion polls, making the move from local to national politics that party leaders had wanted seem more possible. However, after a controversial interview in the De Volkskrant on February 10, 2002, in which he voiced sharp criticism of Islam and laid out plans for the more forceful integration of immigrants and changes in the Dutch constitution, Fortuyn was dismissed by party officials. He quickly set out to form his own political organization. With the help of a network of influential supporters in the professional and business community, the new party called Lijst Pim Fortuyn (LPF) was in place for the May elections (Paul Treanor provides the names of these supporters and also a biography of those fifty candidates who appeared on the list). The list of fifty candidates was composed largely of people without previous political experience, further strengthening its populist appeal. The party's program emphasized tougher action against immigrants who did not assimilate into Dutch culture, stronger measures to fight crime, less bureaucracy in government, a reduction in teacher shortages and a shortening of waiting lists for hospital treatment. Most of these ideas are familiar from similar parties around Europe, the significant difference here was the dynamic figure of Fortuyn. In a flurry of highly publicized appearances, Fortuyn denied accusations of racism with comments such as "I have nothing against Moroccans, I've slept with many of them." In focusing on immigrants and immigration policy, Fortuyn did not advocate deporting those already in the country or the closing of Dutch borders. He did however propose a quota to prohibit Muslims from entering the country and revoking the article in the Dutch constitution that prohibited discrimination, if that would allow one to better tackle the problem of Muslim assimilation into Dutch culture. Fortuyn was assassinated on May 6, 2002, the week before the election.

Leaders of the LPF thought there were others involved and circulated rumors about those they believed were responsible, from the radical left to the political establishment and the mass media itself. The LPF also proceeded to stand in the elections but decided to wait in naming a new head. The party won a spectacular twenty-six seats to become the second largest party in parliament. When a new leader was announced, the party joined a coalition government with the VVD and the CDA. It placed several of its members in the cabinet headed by CDA leader Jan Peter Balkenende. Only a few hours after being installed by Queen Beatrix, chaos erupted when one of the newly appointed ministers was forced to resign. Through photographs transmitted on the television channel RTL-4, it was revealed that Philomena Bijlhout—a former local television reporter and mother of two, who was newly appointed as state secretary for emancipation and family affairs—had lied about her involvement in the Surinamese militia in the 1980s.[8] A native of Suriname, Bijlhout had never denied her participation in the right-wing militia headed by Desi Bouterse, implicated in the "December Murders" of oppositional politicians in 1982. The photographs taken in 1983 showed Bijlhout in the uniform of this group. Bijlhout had previously claimed that she had left the organization at an earlier date. In accepting her resignation, Prime Minister Balkenende called the event "a sad drama." Balkenende rebuilt a coalition composed of the CDA, VVD, and D-66 (Democracy-66), a small left-liberal party formed by radical students in 1966. This government was in power during the murder of van Gogh, but fell in June 2006 because of the controversy surrounding the citizenship of Ayaan Hirsi Ali. At the time it was predicted that a new government would form with the LPF replacing D-66 as originally planned in 2002, but the CDA and the VVD managed to form their own government without either.

THE MEDIA AND THE PUBLIC SPHERE

The stature of those involved and the dramatic nature of the occurrence brought immediate media attention to the assault. The foreboding in the air was enough to send local residents rushing to the scene, even when the first reports mentioned a killing in a central neighborhood and nothing more. After the initial reports, Radio Netherlands broadcast conflicting accounts of how the murder was carried out, by shooting or stabbing; many of the details, however, were already made available, including eyewitness descriptions of the murderer, a man dressed in a traditional attire (which actually turned out to be mistaken). A "pamphlet" was also reported as stuck to van Gogh's chest. Radio Netherlands' Internet version from the day of the murder reports "a nation in shock" and contains messages from Queen Beatrix and Prime Minister Balkenende calling for calm. The prime minister was quoted as identifying van Gogh as "a champion of freedom of expression," a viewpoint repeated by Boris Dittrich, a leading member of D-66, who had made the same remarks regarding Pim Fortuyn after his murder. Amid the calls for calm, van Gogh was being cast as a champion in the struggle to maintain Western values in a threatening situation.

Four hours after the murder, a televised press conference was organized with the recently appointed head of the Amsterdam police district, the city's mayor, and an official from the ministry of justice; this was later in the day followed by a press conference organized in the heavily immigrant neighborhood where Mohammed B. grew up. The victim was well known by the time the press conference began, and interest turned to the assailant, who was identified at this press conference only as "another bicyclist." When asked for more information about the assailant, especially if the person was previously known to the police authorities, the justice department representative replied, "No, the perpetrator was previously unknown to the us," something that he later denied having said when it was exposed as untrue. This appeared to be a conscious attempt to define and control the situation by declaring the murder a spontaneous act carried out by a single individual without a criminal record. It later emerged that the assailant had been under surveillance by the federal intelligence agency (AIVD), but this information was not yet public knowledge. Even Mayor Cohen, who condemned the "cowardly act" and took the opportunity to announce a demonstration that evening in support of the victim and his family, apparently did not know this as he stood in front of the microphones and cameras. This public denial later became a central piece of evidence in the conspiracy theories that continue to circulate about the murder. The DVD that accompanies *Prettig Weekend* (Pleasant weekend) (Jong 2005), one of several quickly produced books about the murder, features several takes of this denial, implying that sinister reasons lay behind it.[9]

Later in the evening of November 2, a large crowd gathered on Amsterdam's Dam Square, a traditional gathering place since the 1960s. This semiofficial event was attended by van Gogh family members, who asked the crowd to "make as much noise as possible in support of freedom of speech" (Agence France-Presse [AFP], November 2, 2004). In his remarks, Mayor Cohen called van Gogh a symbol of free speech, declaring that " freedom of speech is a foundation of our society and that foundation was tampered with today. . . . Theo van Gogh picked fights with many people, myself included, but that is a right in this country." According to the AFP, these words carried added weight because "in his final column van Gogh even likened Cohen, who is Jewish, to a collaborator with the Nazi regime at the time of the German occupation of the Netherlands in World War II." Representing the government, the immigration minister Rita Verdonk declared, "We stand at a crossroads: do we follow the spiral of alienation, polarization, fear and hate . . . or do we make a stand and say 'no more' " (as reported by AFP France). Also present in the crowd were immigrants, including a woman who identified herself as a "Muslim and a Moroccan" who carried a placard proclaiming "Muslims against Violence." While this rally ended peacefully, another in The Hague was followed by the arrest of twenty people for "inciting hatred and shouting discriminatory and racist chants" (AFP).

On November 9 the formal funeral service for van Gogh was broadcast live on Dutch television. Part of the service included family and friends telling stories about the filmmaker, his "playful nature" and his love of provocation. According to a report distributed by the Associated Press (November 9, 2004), "About 150 people gathered at the De Nieuwe Ooster Crematorium. Hundreds more watched on a screen outside. Mourners left flowers, cigarettes and beer at a makeshift monument where the 47-year-old filmmaker . . . was killed."

In her account of the role of funeral oration in the "invention of Athens," Loroux (2006) suggests a linkage between the functional and the symbolic in a public ceremony of this nature. She writes that "the community turned the honor paid to its most valorous men to its own account, since in doing so it expressed its cohesion and greatness, solemnly attested in the face of the universe. Homage to the dead and celebration of 'the entire nation' went hand in hand, and the civic spirit found its own reflection on every side; that the dead was matched by that of the living, who come to the *demosion sema* to learn a lesson in patriotism while listening to the orator" (Loroux 2006:49). Van Gogh was an unlikely hero, as Mayor Cohen had pointed out earlier, but his death, as reaffirmed at the funeral, helped demarcate and reinvent a collective. With the aid of mass media, this collective was made visible for all to see. Those viewing it or who chose not to could imagine themselves as either inside or outside its bounds.

Steps to be taken in response to the murder were being discussed simultaneously in the media and the halls of government. On November 7 *De Telegraaf* editorialized,

> There needs to be a very public crackdown on extremist Muslim fanatics in order to assuage the fear of citizens and to warn the fanatics that they must not cross over the boundaries. International cash transfers must be more tightly controlled, magazines and papers which include incitement should be suppressed; unsuitable mosques should be shut down and imams who encourage illegal acts should be thrown

out of the country. This should also apply to extremists who have dual nationality. They have no business here. In addition, the range of extremists to be kept under surveillance needs to be expanded.

On the same day, the more liberal De Volkskrant stated that "Muslims have to learn, in a democracy, religion, too, is open to criticism—this applies to Islam no less than to Christianity. Theo van Gogh, in this respect, always purposefully went to the limits of decency. Many have regularly had reason to feel hurt or offended by him. In a democracy, those who want to defend themselves against this can go to court. Any other curtailment of free speech is inadmissible." The Algemeen Dagblad advised Muslims to take to the street and demonstrate their condemnation of the killing and "cleanse" themselves as a community. "There has to be a time when voices from the Muslim community must say a massive 'no' to this kind of madness. A mass protest made by Dutch Muslims could be the symbolic beginning of a needed cleansing of the self." (All translated quotes are from news.scotsman.com, November 7, 2004). The Volkskrant and the Algemeen Dagblad asked Muslims in the Netherlands to show signs of solidarity with the wider Dutch community, requesting that representatives come forward and speak out on behalf of the group. De Telegraaf also treated Muslims as a collective, but viewed this collective primarily in negative terms, as something to be managed and controlled, and perhaps even isolated and excluded from the larger community. Here notions of collective responsibility dominated the debate.

The days following the murder were filled with reportage that widened the interpretive frame, from the actions of a lone individual against a single person to something much broader. Minister of Home Affairs Johan Remkes called the killing "a direct attack on our democratic legal order," and Justice Minister Hein Donner thought someone holding "an extreme religious ideology" might have been responsible. Both officials called for measures to tighten security to "protect critics of Islam" and Dutch citizens generally. At this point, the murderer was acknowledged as someone "known" to police authorities. Journalists inquiring about what this meant were given hints of a conspiracy, that there were others under suspicion. Now that the attempt to limit interpretation to the actions of one man proved unstable, police authorities released information that "the Netherlands is home to some 150 potential Muslim extremists." (All of the preceding quotations are from reports on Radio Netherlands Internet service, November 5, 2004). Dutch police then announced the arrest of seven suspects charged with participation in a criminal organization with terrorist aims and terrorist conspiracy. These persons would become known as the Hofstad group, of which the accused Mohammed B. was described as a peripheral figure, "not a member of the core group."

That same day, November 5, Radio Netherlands broadcast an interview with Hans Jansen, professor of Islamic studies at Utrecht University, who stated that it was unlikely that any terrorist network was involved, and that the sweeping arrests made by police authorities "just rounded up the usual suspects that had to be arrested anyway . . . and they (the authorities) may have thought the timing was right . . . and that it would probably impress the newspaper reading public." According to Jansen, it was still an open question if the murder was the act of a "lone wolf" or someone acting in concert with others. If the latter turned out to be the case, he thought it more likely that "five or six or ten young men met up, talked together, got very excited, and at a certain point in time—as has happened in other cases years ago and has been described to the greatest detail in literature—in their excitement, they then go and look for a cleric, they ask his permission, and if they obtain it, they start committing these unpleasant acts." Rather than hunt for a terrorist cell, Jansen thought it more profitable to look locally for a Muslim cleric, lawyer, or spiritual adviser who would give the necessary permission. In his view, if the assassin "wants to pose as a super-Muslim, he probably obeyed the laws of Islam . . . and then it is really very important to find the expert on Islamic law who gave him permission to commit this act" (Jansen 2004).

Such interpretation would disappear in the wave of highly publicized police raids and the clamor created by remarks by political leaders including Gerrit Zalm, the finance minister representing the VVD. In response to questions from journalists as to whether a jihad had broken out in the Netherlands, Zalm declared that the country was "at war with Islamic fundamentalism." These remarks produced the banner headline "We Are at War" in leading newspapers. Several Internet commentators linked these remarks and the media response directly to the wave of attacks on Muslim institutions that followed over the next few days. The remarks and the ensuing violence led to a furious debate in the parliament, and Zalm toned down his message.[10] A dramatic shift had occurred, however. From this point on, interpretation of the killing of van Gogh was dominated by theories of conspiracy that transformed a local act of murder into an event of world-historical proportions.

As November progressed, conspiracy theories abounded as Dutch newspapers confirmed reports that police authorities were seeking Redouan al-Issar, also known as "the Syrian" in conjunction with the murder.[11] De Telegraaf and Algemeen Dagblad identified this man as having lived in Germany since 1995 and as having applied for asylum in the Netherlands in 1998. Al-Issar was further identified as a "self-proclaimed preacher of radical Islam and was in touch with the group in Amsterdam of which the presumed killer of Theo van Gogh was a member." There was now a group, given the name Hofstad group by the police, and not just a single person responsible. Radio Netherlands interviewed Fred Burton, "of US intelligence and the forecasting company Stratfor," who saw clear links to other terrorist activities. "When you look at the train of events that has unfolded with the assassination [of van Gogh], then I am struck by the similarities to what—I believe—was the first act of the 'holy war' in the United States. . . . I think perhaps you have an autonomous cell here, with tentacles that have spread, and with potential links to Casablanca as well as potential links to the March 11 attacks in Madrid." From Burton's "30,000-foot point of view," there is no ambiguity and there are no spontaneous acts of overly enthusiastic youths, but rather "the actions of a cell, which were very similar to the methodology of the Madrid cell . . . when you look at the methodology and relate that to past events, this certainly appears to be an al-Qaeda type methodology."[12] This story was followed on December 3 by some background on "the Syrian."[13] The story line about the murder was now stabilizing around what could be called the dominant interpretation: that Theo van Gogh was murdered by an Islamic radical who was part of a terrorist group with probable links to an international network.

NARRATIVES, FRAMES, AND DISCOURSES

In summarizing Dutch newspaper accounts of the murder of Theo van Gogh, Hajer and Maussen (2004) identify three significant interpretive frames: (1) an attack on free expression; (2) part of a clash of civilizations, the war on terror and the Islamic holy war; (3) an example of failed integration. They cite Mayor Job Cohen's remarks at the demonstration where he commented on van Gogh and free speech. One could also point to the continual use of van Gogh's first name as a sign of familial inclusion: he was one of us and although we quarreled, as members of the same collective, we intuitively recognize each other. Similarly, the idea of free speech points beyond the person, the body or spirit of the dead van Gogh, to a principle, free speech, around which many could unite, even if the representative person was no true exemplar of the principle. In all these examples, the identification of the murdered van Gogh with a cause and a deeply held value seems to be a common theme. One can surmise that the aim was to include as many elements as possible under the umbrella of the abstract principle of free speech combined with a firmly held belief.

The second frame, the clash of civilizations or war frame is more polarizing; it implies fixed identities at war with one another. Here a line of demarcation is more clearly drawn between generalized perpetrators (radical Muslim extremists) and victims (Dutch civil society). Minister Verdonk however, drew a connection between the two when she implied that the Muslim community in the Netherlands had a different relation to democratic principles like freedom of speech than the average Dutch citizen (quoted in Hajer and Maussen [2004:1]).

In the third frame, failed integration, the polarities revolve around the "success" and "failure" of Dutch immigration policies regarding the integration of immigrants, most particularly those identified as Muslim (about 6 percent of the Dutch population, 13 percent of the population of Amsterdam). Some politicians were cast as being "soft and naïve" in regarding the possibility of accommodating the Islamic faith in a modern, liberal society. This frame locates the discussion on a political, rather than cultural continuum. As in the clash of civilizations, however, the identity and motivation of the assailant carries heavy symbolic weight. As the apparent model of successful integration turned murderer, Mohammed B. was said to embody policy failure. The perpetrators in this account are liberal politicians and the victims are again the Dutch public, who were misled, in the double meaning of that term.

In a related content analysis of four leading Dutch newspapers on the day and the first anniversary of the murder, Pantti and van Zoonen (2006) locate three distinctive discourses: (1) constraint and solidarity, (2) anger, and (3) shock and sorrow. Rather than frameworks of interpretation, they are concerned with public expressions of emotion and uncover these discourses through identifying "key descriptors of feelings." Thus, "restraint and solidarity" is connected to calls for calm and linked with sympathy for the victim and empathy with his family. Similarly, "anger" is associated with public displays of rage and linked with the desire to name those responsible and to exact revenge, while "shock and sorrow" is connected to public expressions of grief and commemoration. As opposed to Hajer and Maussen, Pantti and van Zoonen intertwine discourses and practices. They suggest that discourses reflect political styles and interests: calls for restraint are made by those in positions of authority and connected to performing an authoritative role in crisis situations. We can then interpret the public statements of the prime minister and mayor of Amsterdam as following scripts learned after the murder of Fortuyn and role models from political leaders in other countries, as they called for calm and expressed sympathy for the family of the victim. In this sense Prime Minister Balkenende was "performing authority" (Hajer and Uitermark forthcoming) when in his first public statement after the murder he said, "In great horror I heard of the shooting of Theo van Gogh. Our thoughts and compassion are with his family, his friends and his colleagues" (quoted by Pantti and van Zoonen 2006:209). Rhetoric was apparently not enough, as Balkenende would soon be criticized for what was viewed as his failure to keep the country together. The statement clashed with those of other members of the cabinet, such as those who had declared that the "country was now at war." Often the brunt of Theo van Gogh's anti-Semitic statements, Amsterdam's mayor, on the other hand, was very visible at public memorials and commemorations and received compliments for his efforts. The nation was here called together with pleas for collective solidarity with the fallen, one of "us," and the larger family of the nation was called upon through the smaller family of the victim. Let this bring us together, not tear us apart. The nation as fallen in time of crisis was one of the deeper root emotions called upon here. The position of Muslims in this trope was either unstated or assumed: they are one of us and here to stay. This was most explicitly voiced by Cohen, who was featured in the international press for his efforts. As for the established Muslim organizations, their leaders reacted in similar ways with calls for "calm, moderation and mutual respect" (Pantti and van Zoonen 2006:209), also fitting for their role in the Dutch system of collective representation. The exception was perhaps Amsterdam alderman Aboutaleb, as was discussed above.

The discourse on anger was seen as improper for political leaders, a sign of irresponsibility, as shown in the example of the minister of finance. However, those with right-wing credentials had little difficulty in aligning themselves with the strong feelings expressed by a significant section of the Dutch population. The concept of *volkswoede* (mass rage) had already been used after the murder of Fortuyn and was thus readily available. At that time it was applied to and expressed by Fortuyn supporters against the media, as much as other central institutions of the society. In describing angry crowds that attacked journalists, Pantti and van Zoonen (2006:210) quote a May 11, 2002, *Trouw* article: "A man is fuming when he sees the cameras. 'This is your fault too,' he shouts. 'You created this, you saw this coming.' " In the immediate aftermath of the Fortuyn murder, angry crowds burned cars in front of the state offices in The Hague and shouted threats directed at the politicians inside, especially those of the ruling PvdA. Public displays of emotion after the van Gogh killing were more attentive to the artistic sensibilities of the victim and the theme of freedom of expression. There was first a noisy and then a silent demonstration as expressions of the right free speech, which van Gogh was said to embody. Anger was permitted, but it was to be expressed in symbolic ways, thus combining emotion with restraint, with respect for the victim and his family, as well as the idea of legally protected, but also constrained, freedom of expression. The fact that family members as well as political leaders took part in these demonstrations may have contributed to this, as well as the urban roots and class background of those involved in the protests.

Pantti and van Zoonen link together the murders of Fortuyn and van Gogh in their analysis of the discourse on "shock and sorrow." The two events appear to have a cumulative relation to one another that also affects the level of feeling, raising it to an indication of the relative health of the nation. The sorrow expressed here was not so much for the victims and their families, but for the nation itself, the shock being that such things should not happen here, not in our country, "our Netherlands." Another call could be made to unify the nation in sorrow, but the shock of two political murders in close association with one another, brought about a feeling that something had changed in the nation. A new sense of anxiety for the future emerged. This has resulted in a new discourse about the meaning of Dutchness, the grounding values that made the nation, the subject of a later chapter. This analysis of the media frames and discourses is extremely useful in understanding how the murder of van Gogh was transformed into an event. To the more traditional forms of discourse analysis identified above, I have added a performance perspective as filtered through the concept of social drama. What remains to be done is to gauge any wider significance the event might have. For this we will need to look more deeply into the central actors and into recent Dutch history.

ENDINGS

Either on his own or as part of a group, Mohammed B. killed Theo van Gogh on the morning of November 2, 2004. The killing was carried out on an open street with a knife as well as a pistol. In this, Mohammed B. not only consciously linked his actions to what he understood to be ancient ritual; his actions also, consciously or not, combined the ancient and the modern, the Dutch and the Moroccan. He rode a bicycle to meet his victim and shot him before applying his kitchen knife and cleaver. Such details however gain significance only as part of a plotted narrative: the desire to strike a blow against Western culture in the name of radical Islam. The happy ending to this narrative was to be his own symbolic death, a martyr to the cause and an inspiration for others to follow. All this is revealed through the mise-en-scène, the props and the scripted actions as well as messages he left behind. What still is unclear is whether or not this murder was part of a larger conspiracy in which the killing of van Gogh was only a subplot. Mohammed B. saw himself as part of a wider social movement, Radical Islam, but whether or not others in that movement saw him and his act in the same terms remains unclear. The trial that followed the murder, in which the members of the so-called Hofstad group were tried as co-conspirators seemed merely to assert rather than prove this. It left many questions unanswered. In order to probe deeper and to seek some answers to these and other questions, we need to look more closely at the key actors and the historical factors that helped shape their actions and their understanding of them.

CHAPTER 3

PERPETRATORS AND
VICTIMS

This chapter will offer an in-depth answer to the question of who the actors are, taking them one by one. The common theme that unites them is not only the narrative of the event, but also their roles as exemplary agents in search of recognition in a changing Dutch society. Most directly through the social drama of the murder, but not only there, these actors/agents came to represent something to themselves and to others: heroes and villains, perpetrators and victims, who either built on or sought celebrity in a media-saturated age. How they were represented and what they represented in that media is, of course, important, but so is how they represented themselves, their self-representation in the struggle for recognition. Shifts in a narrative can come not only from the actions of agents, but also from material objects. In our case, the name, social background, dress, and mode of killing all shifted the narrative, from murder to ritual murder and helped move the story from a crime to conspiracy and war.

MOHAMMED B.

In the previous chapter, we dealt with Mohammed B. in his role as murderer of Theo van Gogh. Here we will look deeper into his biography as a means of finding motives for his actions. Since this account necessarily is based on official documents and other published sources, it grounds itself in the dominant narrative outlined in the previous chapter. At the time of the attack, Mohammed B. was twenty-six years old and unemployed. Born in the Netherlands to immigrant Moroccan parents on March 8, 1978, he held dual citizenship. His father, Hamid, was a manual laborer who emigrated from Morocco to France where he worked on rebuilding the Paris métro before moving to the Netherlands in 1965. Hamid Bouyeri settled in Amsterdam and was employed as a cleaner and dishwasher at nearby Schiphol Airport. He married Habiba Amyay in 1967; it was a union arranged through relatives in Morocco. The couple lived apart (she in Morocco and he in the Netherlands) until 1977, when they had sufficient funds to unite in the Netherlands. They settled in Amsterdam on Domselaerstraat a few blocks from where Theo van Gogh would be murdered. Mohammed B. was born one year later. They moved to Hart Nibbrigstraat in another part of Amsterdam soon thereafter. In all the family would comprise eight children (some accounts say five), the youngest born in 1987. Mohammed was the second child, but the eldest son and his mother's favorite (Chorus and Olgun 2005:42). When Habiba Amyay died of breast cancer in 2001, she was buried in the rural area of Morocco where the family maintains a second home. There was a constant flow in familial relations between rural Morocco and urban Amsterdam.[1] Mohammed B. spent the summer months of 1999 driving around the region (Buruma 2006b:196), more the tourist than the resident. The family spoke Tamazight, the Berber language; the little Arabic Mohammed B. spoke he learned through the Koran lessons he attended at a local mosque. Tamazight was the language at home, but, except for a small circle of close friends, Dutch was the language of the street.

Mohammed B. attended neighborhood schools and was considered a promising student in a class where 40 percent of the students were the children of immigrant parents, the majority of those from Morocco (Chorus and Olgun 2005:43). As opposed to most of his immediate peers, Mohammed B. went on to higher secondary education, graduating in 1995. His teachers report a bright, shy pupil who was interested in all the "normal" things that can be expected of a boy his age. He had a newspaper route and considered himself a "labor party man." While at school Mohammed B. was active in community affairs, working at a neighborhood youth center where he assumed something of a leadership role. In 1994 the center was torn down and replaced by a migrant center, serving the needs of adults rather than youth, something that he and others resented. Later accounts claim the effect was to turn the young people out on the streets in both a physical and psychological sense and to deny Mohammed B. a positive source of identity. In the spring of 1998, street disturbances broke out in the area around August Allebeplein where Mohammed B. hung out. Hundreds, mainly Moroccan, youths battled with the police. It is not known whether or not Mohammed B.

took an active part in these events, but in his own accounts he placed the blame for their occurrence on the local authorities for closing the youth center.

Deciding to further his education, Mohammed B. studied accounting and business information technology at the InHolland College, a professional training institution. After five years of schooling, he left without finishing a degree. In later reconstructions, former classmates recall changes in attitude and the sudden appearance of beard and skullcap, noting that Mohammed B. became an outspoken critic of the social behavior of other Muslim students, especially regarding alcohol consumption. In one telling recorded incident, Mohammed B. threw objects at the television screen and harassed other students in a school café in June 2000. They had been watching the European football championships, and he became agitated when the Netherlands defeated France. The fact that he had been supporting the French team and not the Netherlands, when one can assume that most others in the room were, is perhaps also a sign of growing alienation. The French team had been publicly criticized by the extreme right for the number of immigrants wearing the national colors, while the Dutch team was widely reported to harbor racial tensions. Rooting for the national football team is one form of public patriotism not only permitted, but encouraged in the Netherlands and many immigrants show their sense of being an outsider by vocally rooting for the other side. By Mohammed B.'s own account, a significant cause of this change in behavior, from the upwardly striving son of immigrant parents to alienated and angry rebel, was the death of his mother, after which the study of Islamic texts became more important than his school work and gave new meaning to his life.

Throughout, Mohammed B. remained active in neighborhood affairs, meeting with local authorities about building a new youth center. When these plans were stymied, he became "frustrated and angry." The "white world" failed to "take him seriously"; he felt "betrayed and let down. His suppressed anger start[ed] transforming into aggression. This led to several confrontations with the police" (Benschop 2005:8). In 1997 Mohammed B. was fined 500 guilders for striking a policeman in an Amsterdam snack bar, an incident that would later prevent him from securing work as a security guard at Schiphol airport. In the spring of 2000, police were called to the family home when Mohammed B. refused to permit his seventeen-year-old sister to leave the apartment as punishment for having an affair with a neighborhood youth. He took charge, he recounted, because he felt his father was too lenient, reflecting his role as the eldest son. In the most serious confrontation with the police, Mohammed B. was arrested for threatening a policeman with a knife in a city park, after he had confronted his sister's former boyfriend. He spent two and a half months in prison. By the time of Mohammed B.'s release, in the fateful month of September 2001, his father was disabled from the years of hard physical labor; then in December, his mother died of breast cancer.

Mohammed B. had other encounters with the police, including one a little more than a month before the murder of van Gogh. On September 29, 2004, he was arrested for aggressive behavior after being stopped for fare-dodging on public transport. In his pockets, police found a list of names and telephone numbers and a last will and testament. These were turned over to the federal security police (the Algemene Inlichtingen- en Veiligheidsdienst or AIVD) and added to its files on Mohammed B. Many of those who appeared on the list of names would later be identified as part of a terrorist network that, allegedly, included Mohammed B.[2] The months spent in prison proved to be crucial to his conversion to radical Islam.

Despite or perhaps because of these frustrations and confrontations with authority, Mohammed B. remained engaged in community affairs and helped set up a self-help organization for local youth. Benschop describes how, during this time, Mohammed writes "columns in the neighborhood newsletter and starts a computer club for young people. . . . with the support of the neighborhood association . . . Mohammed and two friends draw up a solid plan for a new youth center. . . . the plan is named Mondriaans Doenia, the World of Mondriaan, after the name of the neighborhood street where the center is to be located" (Benschop 2005:9). The request for a subsidy was sent to The Hague, where it was denied. This occurred in early 2002. In December 2002 there was another meeting with the ministry at which, as Benschop relates, "Mohammed explains his plans. But he explodes when afterwards a female policy official asks him how he knows his plan will work. He throws his arms in the air and yells: 'Are we so clever or you so stupid' " (ibid.).

Following this second rejection, Mohammed B. began writing articles on web pages that were highly inflammatory, suggesting a radical change of attitude. Using the pseudonyms mentioned earlier, he composed lists of people to be condemned to death, including the Moroccan king, long an enemy of Islamic radicals. Even if viewed as pranks, these acts reflect a forceful change in rhetoric and reference, from angry immigrant youth to holy warrior. The rhetorical style was continued in the suicide note he carried in his pocket on the day of the attack. If these texts reflect his state of mind, Mohammed B. was in the process of transforming his personal identity by early 2003.[3] Around this time, his apartment on Marianne Philipsstraat became a meeting place for what would be called the Hofstad group.

BEYOND THE INDIVIDUAL: THE NEIGHBORHOOD AND THE CITY

Mohammed B. spent his formative years in the neighborhood around his family's apartment in the Overtoomse Veld section of Amsterdam. This is an area with a highly concentrated immigrant population, filled with what the Dutch call "allochtons" a word taken from the Greek (allo=other, chton=earth), identifying those who live among us, but are not of us. On the "wrong side of the motorway," Overtoomse Veld is dominated by gray concrete apartment buildings built after the Second World War to house Dutch workers and their families. It is now largely populated by immigrants from Muslim countries. It is locally known as "saucer city" because of the larger number of satellite discs visible on balconies and windows, which enable residents to view television stations from their native countries. Of all the registered immigrant groups in Amsterdam, Moroccans have the highest percentage of unemployment at 31 percent according to figures from 1997, a figure affected by the high rate of unemployment of Moroccan women (42 percent) (Mollenkopf 2000:213). According to more recent figures, this has not changed. A 2005 government report points to nearly 60 percent unemployment for all Moroccans between the ages of fifteen and sixty-five, nationally. The same report shows a significant rise in the number of Moroccans with a "middle-class" occupation, yet goes on to speak of the formation of an "underclass" forming among second- and third-generation Moroccan and Turkish immigrants. ("Nederland als immigrantiesamenleving," is cited in Hirsi Ali 2004c:67. The report is available in English summary as "Ethnic Minorities and Integration" in Gijsberts 2004).

Any sense of collective identity emerging out of this urban environment will almost necessarily build on a sense of difference, a feeling that is reinforced through language, food, clothing, and, especially, religious practice. Along with the extended family, the local mosque and religious schools are core institutions of identity-formation in this neighborhood, reinforcing kinship and friendship ties. The shared Islamic religious heritage may help to mitigate ethnic differences, such as those between Berbers and Arabs, while not entirely eliminating them. Many of those living in this neighborhood have roots in Morocco, and it is relatively common for families to send their sons back and forth as part of their education. Some, like Mohammed B.'s family maintain property "back home" in a Berber community in the Rif Mountains of Morocco, reinforcing a sense of living in two worlds. While Morocco may be a source of common identification, there are old divisions between Arabs and Berbers reflected and reproduced in Overtoomse Veld. From the viewpoint of an outside observer, this may be an allochthon neighborhood, or, more specifically, a "Moroccan" neighborhood. Internally, however, there are finer distinctions that affect individual identity and collective identification and, more importantly in our case, the formation of friendship networks. But one of the effects of the murder of van Gogh may well be the lessening of these divisions and a focus on commonalities rather than differences.

In a series of interviews carried out one year after the murder at one of these schools, located near Mohammed B.'s apartment, a journalist found clear evidence of feelings of solidarity with Mohammed B.'s "predicament": how to deal with someone who slanders one's faith (*NRC Handelsblad*, November 2, 2005). Views ranged from "one must do something" to "punishment should be left to Allah," but identification with the issue was clear and was apparently a topic of discussion at the school, an indication of that institution's role in identity- as well as opinion-formation.

The larger "Dutch" society makes itself felt in this neighborhood through schools and community centers, where teachers and social workers are important agents, and, of course, the police and local politicians are as well. Depending on the circumstances, the individuals filling those roles can be viewed with comradeship or suspicion, as intrusive or welcome outsiders. An example of the latter can be found in Mohammed B.'s reaction to the visits made to his family by social workers, which were seen as intrusions into familial authority, and his contrary reaction to teachers, which were (one can speculate) positive. One social worker I spoke with, one of the last to meet with Mohammed B. before the murder, recounted how impressed authorities were by the latter's intelligence, but also found him angered and frustrated by the simple-mindedness of the tests and procedures he was forced to endure in order to secure financial assistance and by the bureaucratic mentality that mandated them. My interest, however, is not so much how residents of relatively segregated urban neighborhoods view state and local authorities, as with how this segregation affects friendship circles and how these can affect attitudes and practices. For example, how are these authorities perceived by the residents? As "our" authorities or as those representing an alien community? Do the residents perceive themselves as Dutch or as allochthon? And how do these authorities view them?

This, of course, is something that has interested social scientists and those concerned with social policy. In a perceptive article on the evolving discussion of the politics and policies of integration in the Netherlands and elsewhere, Uitermark et al. (2005) describe the new "diversity" policy that currently frames the actions of politicians in the city of Amsterdam. As opposed to earlier attempts to form representative organizations for each ethnic group at the national level, the new policy "aims to recognize ethnic diversity as such" (2005:635) in a more local and decentralized manner. The focus is on the quality of immediate results, rather than the formation of stable ethnic organizations and leadership, and envisions ethnic identity as more fluid and as only one of the many elements that combine to form the contemporary, urban individual. Such changes in policy outlook might have played a role in denying Mohammed B.'s application for his youth center, in that his plan might have been perceived as too rooted in an administrative policy that was no longer in vogue. It appears clear that at the local level, Dutch policy concerning immigration is much more malleable and open to accommodation than the current discourse implies, though shifts are occurring as will be discussed in the next chapter.

The debate surrounding the meaning of the murder of van Gogh has amplified and in some sense polarized this discourse. Within this discourse, Mohammed B. and Ayaan Hirsi Ali are important actors as symbols or representatives of alternative positions on immigration and identity. In choosing to limit his identity through conversion to radical Islam, Mohammed B. fused ideology with ethnicity and rejected both integration and a multifaceted modern identity. For him, the term *integration* took on a theological meaning, integrating oneself with the spirit of Islam

(Chorus and Olgun 2005:57). This shift would have made Hirsi Ali seem as a well-integrated immigrant even more of an enemy and a threat: she represented a real alternative in the struggle for recognition and immigrant identity. Hirsi Ali's position may have hardened as well, turning a liberal pluralist into an "Enlightenment fundamentalist" (Pels 2005).

In geographic terms, the Amsterdam intellectual subculture in which van Gogh participated was not that far removed from that of Mohammed B. and their paths are likely to have crossed many times. They would hardly have taken notice of one another, however. Mohammed B. and Theo van Gogh may have occupied the same geographic space, but they lived in different worlds. As the epigraph from Descartes at the opening of chapter 1 suggests, Amsterdam, with its relatively small but dense population, has long been known for its tolerance of difference and idiosyncrasy. From its place as a center of world commerce, and its role as a "global city" in the seventeenth century, tolerance has been a cornerstone of its self-conception. More than this, tolerance toward other cultures is institutionalized as part of the local political culture and is an essential part of commercial transaction and public social intercourse. Currently, the notion of tolerance is part of the tourist niche Amsterdam has created for itself in the latest phase of globalization (Nijman 2000:41). In terms of urban geography, the commerce in goods has followed international trends and moved to the outer suburbs of the city and especially to the airport area; commerce related to "tolerant" tourism, having to do with sex and drugs, occupies the central city, a space it shares with other forms of tourism, such as that related to art and music. Here two distinct age and status groups mix rather uneasily, the young, primarily male and working class, with the older, more middle class interested in high culture. Nijman suggests that the meaning of tolerance has shifted over the centuries while still remaining a central norm in Amsterdam: from a respect for cultural difference based in the desire to buy and sell commodities, to a more stylized version aimed at selling the city itself. In this account, the effect has been to turn parts of the city into a "theme park," where a restrictive and even repressive form of tolerance can be practiced, a tolerance designed to attract and appeal to specifically defined demographic groups to the exclusion of others. Though older, van Gogh would fit easily into this group with its notions of tolerance, while Mohammed B. would probably feel himself excluded.

Why did Mohammed B. turn to radical Islam? In his own account, he refers to his mother's death as initiating a "search for truth" (Chorus and Olgun 2005:69). Rather than just personal troubles, however, the anger and frustration he exhibited might be indicative of a rather typical attitude and view of authority that marks second-generation immigrants off from their parents. Kepel (2000:196) describes this new generation of "young European adults of Muslim origin" in this way: "Unlike their parents, who were unfamiliar with the laws and cultural codes of their host countries and whose worldview had been formed during the era of colonial domination, the children were fully aware of their rights and quick to voice their complaints and tackle the institutions of the countries whose languages they spoke and whose citizenship they either possessed already or were about to claim." To the extent this is correct, the generation of which Mohammed B. was part had a clearer sense of itself and had a different sense of where to place the blame for their frustrations than their elders. This change, however, is not merely a generational effect; it has something very much to do with wider changes within the consciousness of Muslim immigrants to Europe from the 1990s onward, something that will be discussed in more detail in a later section.

One of the experts called upon in the police investigation of the murder, the Islamist Ruud Peters, also suggests a generational struggle between an older, largely illiterate generation whose Islam was primarily ritualistic, and a younger, more textually oriented generation for whom Islam was a major source of identity and inspiration (Chorus and Olgun 2005:70). Mohammed B. explained the killing of van Gogh as one motivated not by anger but by faith. In fact, he struggled to find textual justification for killing a non-Muslim in a non-Muslim country. He found it in the "pure Egyptian Islam" he began studying, primarily on the Internet, after the death of his mother, as he began his search for a higher meaning to life. The works of the secular Egyptian intellectual Sayyid Qutb and the Indian-Pakistani Mawlana Mawdudi (discussed below), which he downloaded (causing some to speak of "Internet Islam"), helped provide that justification. Mohammed B. also had the help of a mediator, a significant other, in facilitating his conversion. Abu Khaled, "the Syrian" mentioned in the previous chapter, appears to have been that person. Mohammed B. apparently met Khaled at the Al Tawheed mosque early in 2002 and became an avid student of his radical preaching. It was from Khaled that Mohammed B. would have learned the value of martyrdom and from whom he would have sought advice and justification for the murder of Hirsi Ali and van Gogh (Chorus and Olgun 2005:65, 198). It is also suspected that Khaled supplied the pistol used in the murder of the latter.

A young Surinamese woman who converted to Islam and who had contact with those close to Mohammed B. described the conversion process (from the point of view of the facilitator) to the Dutch police in the following terms: the first step is to win the confidence of the person and then to speak authoritatively about Tawheed (Unity, the oneness of Allah, one of the bedrocks of Islam) and to condemn all secular authority, politics, politicians, and the royal family.[4] Once this delegitimation is achieved, one slowly replaces secular with sacred authority, which it is proclaimed, actually practices what it preaches. In this process, changing behavior is as important as changing ideas in an endeavor that is as political as it is religious. Boycotting goods associated with the United States and Israel were things that Khaled stressed along with his religious teaching. The use of film and video was an important part of the conversion process, films showing the atrocities done by American soldiers in Iraq, by the Israeli army in Palestine, photos from the Abu Ghraib prison in Iraq and the war in Bosnia (Chorus and Olgun 2005:209). Films downloaded from the Internet were a very important part of Mohammed B.'s reeducation; he and his friends spend hours watching such films, and he viewed *Submission* in this manner. They downloaded the film from the Internet and thus missed the studio debate that accompanied the original broadcast.

In addition to accounting for a growing sense of alienation and a significant other to guide the conversion process, it is important to consider the more general condition of being a second-generation immigrant. Dutch social policy defines an "immigrant" as anyone having at least one parent born outside the country, and by this definition Mohammed B. doubly qualifies. After surveying current research on the topic of second-generation immigrants, Mollenkopf (2000:201–2) lists four outcomes that may affect their assimilation, making it more difficult than it is for their elders: negative neighborhood effects, unfavorable labor-market niches, biased treatment by public institutions, and "oppositional" group identity. The effect of growing up in a neighborhood segregated by ethnicity and income can both stigmatize and provide a negative stimulus for assimilation and social mobility.[5] In fact, the last factor suggests it can encourage the formation of an "oppositional" identity, which may influence school performance and opportunities on the labor market in a negative way. Both of these might also influence how others, including authorities, view the individual from that background and neighborhood. Important also in the Dutch context, Mollenkopf points out, is the relative lack of opportunity for niches in the labor market, an unintended outcome of the top-down steering of the welfare system. As opposed to market-driven economic integration in countries like the United States, immigrant groups in the more tightly regulated Netherlands have fewer opportunities to create and then control small business niches such as groceries, bakeries, and other small businesses. All of these factors are important in considering the fate of Mohammed B., a second-generation immigrant in a city with a shifting labor market, a welfare system in transformation, and increasing neighborhood segregation. Stressing social factors such as these can be contrasted with explanations—for example, those of Ayaan Hirsi Ali (2004a) and Thomas Sowell (1981)—that emphasize cultural factors, such as religion, something to be discussed later on.

Another source of explanation comes from the burgeoning literature on radical Islamic terrorism. Sageman (2004:97), for example, offers the following in explaining why those he studied might turn to the radical form of Islam: "The lack of spiritualism [in modern culture] was keenly felt. Underemployed and discriminated against by the local society, they felt a personal sense of grievance and humiliation. They sought a cause that would give them emotional relief, social community, spiritual comfort, and cause for self-sacrifice." Like those recruits described by Sageman, the actions of Mohammed B. were not those of a marginalized person seeking to restore a perceived traditional order. Mohammed B. acted as a modern individual, yet one living between two worlds, the more traditional world of his parents and the street-wise world of urban youth. Whatever frustration he might have felt at not being fully integrated into Dutch society (however one might interpret that) came after he had absorbed some of the fundamental values and practices of urban life. He played football, smoked and drank, and enjoyed the clubs and nightlife, while at the same time defending his younger sister's honor in the traditional fashion of the eldest son. He was a serious student in a secular school with dreams of social mobility for himself and his community.

These are modern ideals. It was perhaps the frustration arising out of attempts to combine traditional and modern ideals that caused him to look somewhere else for recognition.

Mohammed B.'s Muslim upbringing, benign as it might have been, conditioned that search; yet had he been born twenty years earlier, he might well have turned to another form of radical politics. The existing political culture, as well as personal experience must be taken into account when explaining behavior and not simply the "frustrations" and disappointments of an individual or even a community. Frustration, after all, is something that must be interpreted. In a context permeated with ambiguity, radical Islam provided a source of authority and perhaps "psychological reassurance in a world in which areas of relative security interlace with radical doubt and with disquieting scenarios of risk" (Ruthven 2004:86). In alleviating the ambiguity that is the modern condition, a thin Muslim identity might turn thick, just as a fallen Christian might be born again as a true believer. Radical Islam might fit with and help resolve certain ambiguities in the life of a second-generation immigrant of Moroccan background raised in Amsterdam in the late 1990s. In this sense, it is different from previous efforts at reform or revival within Muslim culture (see Kamrava 2006 for a thorough discussion). This difference stems as much from an altered historical context as it does from changes in doctrine. What makes the contemporary context different, among other things, is the ready availability of alternatives (Ruthven 2004:198–99). Not only could Mohammed B. choose from a variety of lifestyle alternatives in Amsterdam; he was already living one. The conversion to radical Islam in this sense represents the conscious choice of a resource and shield against the real and available temptations of modern urban life. Following Riesebrodt (1993), who compared "fundamentalisms" in the United States and Iran, we can say that Islamic fundamentalism is a protest against the perceived attack on patriarchal principles.[6] As an ideology, it may resonate with differently situated individuals; as a form of militant activism, it appeals primarily to young males, and in Europe to young, urban males with relatively high levels of formal education (Pape 2005). It resonated with Mohammed B. at a particular point in his life and at a particular time in its own historical development, which occurred within the context of the explosive atmosphere in the Dutch public debate.

How do we explain this? At the individual level, radical Islam in its contemporary guise is macho and militaristic, as well as millenarian. It promises virgins in the afterlife; one goes out in flames as a holy warrior, transforming masculine fantasy into something holy and sacred, which is something potentially more meaningful than the escape and entertainment of much of the contemporary popular culture aimed at young men. As Richardson (2005) puts it, radical Islam is aspirational and inspirational rather than practical; activists find appealing what she identifies as its three R's: revenge, renown, and reaction. Put more positively, radical Islam offers a sense of dignity and clear purpose in a context where they may not seem readily available or may even be denied. Mohammed B.'s decision to push his father aside, taking over the role as male head of the household, could be interpreted through a traditionalist framework, but it can also be seen as an assertion of authority within the personal sphere by someone denied recognition elsewhere. According to Riesebrodt (as quoted by Ruthven 2004:104), "What fundamentalists cannot prevent in the way of structural transformation they attempt to impose symbolically." In addition to being a generational conflict around patriarchal authority, this household struggle might well have been a sign of another sort of identity transformation. As analysts like Riesebrodt have pointed out, radical Islam offers the means to assert authority and to master at least some segments of an uncertain social environment. As a symbolic practice, it offers a means of gaining respect not only within the family but also in the neighborhood, and if one could perform a heroic act, one could gain recognition and respect of a much wider scope. In today's mass-mediated world, it could bring recognition on a global scale.

The desire for recognition and respect is universal, and success in attaining the respect of others is difficult under any circumstances. This is made even more difficult when one lives between worlds with widely different norms and values. This is not uncommon and surely not restricted to young Muslims living in the West. Young black American males face similar difficulties when they seek to combine street-wise norms and values with middle-class notions of success. In some ways, the black Muslims, especially as exemplified by the iconic figure of Malcolm X, created a role model and an institutional framework for achieving this balance.[7] Mohammed B. was raised in another form of Islam, yet one he sought to combine with the urban street codes of contemporary Amsterdam. When this failed or at least became frustrating, he turned to the pure and simple world of messianic religion and its modernized version of martyrdom.[8] This earned him as well a new standing in the neighborhood, where young people began referring to him as "the Taliban" (Chorus and Olgun 2005:61).

RADICAL ISLAM

According to the historical narrative presented by Gilles Kepel (2000), radical Islam or Islamism emerged in the political vacuum created as Marxist socialism began to lose its hegemony in framing anti- and post-colonial politics in the Third World and elsewhere at the end of the 1960s. This process accelerated in the Middle East in the 1970s, when a re-juvenated Islamic ideology challenged the postcolonial nationalism that had dominated in countries like Egypt. The writings of Muslim intellec-tuals like the Egyptian Sayyid Qutb and the Pakistani Mawlana Mawdudi (sometimes spelled Maududi) began to assert much wider influence, a process that culminated in the Iranian revolution of 1979, led by Ruhollah Khomeini (Kepel 2000:23).[9] Prior to this, Islam had largely been a state religion serving to unite both ruling elites and a pious population; its primary "political" role was to maintain an orderly social life, not to be a source of mobilization or a motor of social change. This offered religious clerics a stabilizing role in the service of a state-sanctioned and sanction-ing Islam. It was this role and interpretation of Islam that secular, radical intellectuals opposed to secular-nationalist regimes like Nasser's began to challenge through readings of sacred texts. In short, their interpreta-tions placed Islam above the state and its institutions, challenging not only their legitimacy but also the role of clerics as the only legitimate interpreters of the sacred.[10]

On this basis, there began to emerge dissident sects calling for the development of "authentic" Islamic political culture in which the Koran would be the constitution. In her autobiography, Hirsi Ali (2007) re-counts a similar process involving her father's political activities and also her own youthful interest in radical Islam. As these movements became more influential, it was no surprise when nationalist leaders struck back. Qutb was executed by Nasser in 1966, and other members of his Muslim Brotherhood were forced into exile in Saudi Arabia. Important for us here is that these developments eventually grounded a new social movement rooted in a politicized Islamism with universalistic claims, a doctrine that Qutb and his followers had first begun to articulate.[11] In addition to providing the key conceptual innovations discussed below, Qutb's thirty volumes of commentary on the Koran, written while in prison, individualize Islam through turning sacred scripture into a manual for action. As Ruthven (2004:38) puts it, "Qutb's understanding of Islam was almost Kierkegaardian in its individualism: his 'authentic' Muslim was one who espouses a very modern kind of revolution against the deification of men, against injustice, and against political, economic, racial and religious prejudice." This would also fit well with a modernized version of martyrdom, where individuals could act in the name of religion and claim that their actions were expressive and representative of a community. Martyrs never act as individuals, whether or not they are incorporated into actual networks or groups: they always act in the name of a community, real or imagined. Martyrdom is the representative act of a "representative" individual, who acts in the name of a community. In its modernized Sunni version, this martyrdom includes an exhibitionist element in that the martyr gains this worldly recognition through the act (Khosrokhavar 2005).[12] It is this triangular relation, intertwining protagonist, victim, and audience, that makes it so available to performative analysis.

Key concepts developed out of Qutb's Koranic commentary that are important for our analysis of the assassination of Theo van Gogh are *jahiliyya* and *takfir*. In its modern usage as a condition or being in the world, jahiliyya identifies a form of paganism and ignorance, whereby members of a society so characterized are no longer viewed as Muslims, even when they may claim to be (see Armstrong 2006:105 for a full account). It was this term that Qutb, based on passages in the Koran, applied to Nasser and his ruling party in Egypt. Once one possessed a means of distinguishing between claims and reality, a next step was to label these "false" Muslims as takfir, those who are impure and who should thus be excommunicated from the community of true believers. The effect, as Kepel (2000:31) puts it, was that "one who is impious to this extent can no longer benefit from the protection of [Islamic] law. According to the consecrated expression, 'his blood is forfeit,' and he is condemned to death." As the Koran strictly forbids the killing of Muslims, this was an important conceptual innovation. It legitimated the assassination of Nasser's successor, Anwar Sadat, in 1981, and it would later be applied to Salman Rushdie and Ayaan Hirsi Ali. In the first instance it was aimed at Nasser himself, though he was quick to see its potential, jailed Qutb and others in the Muslim brotherhood, and died peacefully in office. Another important conceptual contribution was made by Mawdudi, whose book *Jihad in Islam* was first published in the 1920s. Mawdudi promoted "Islamization from above," by which he meant from heaven. It is also he who added the concept of jihad, holy war, to the other pillars of Islam, making it the duty of believers to aggressively oppose enemies of their beliefs. As with Qutb's conceptual innovations, this helped to turn religion into an ideology, a guide to political as well as social practice. It also furthered the individualization of Islam by transforming it to Islamism. Mohammed B. downloaded texts by Mawdudi and Qutb from the Internet (Chorus and Olgun 2005: 72).

While doctrinal changes are significant in explaining the possibility of radical Islam, the Iranian revolution and the powerful figure of Ruhollah Khomeini helped actualize it by providing a bridge between intellectuals, the wider middle class, and the larger population. The Iranian revolution showed not only that Islamism could be a mass movement but also that it could be a successful mass movement, capable of uniting widely diverse social groups under one banner.[13] In addition to these changes and the transformation of the role of the clerisy, Khomeini made another very significant contribution to the development of Islamism when, just before his death in June 1989, he issued a fatwa, or religious decree, calling for the assassination of Salman Rushdie, which will be discussed in a later chapter. According to Kepel (2000:185), this act had many levels of motivation and meaning. It was meant to condemn a heretic, of course, but it was also a weapon in an internal struggle to control the meaning of Islam, a struggle between conservative Saudi Arabia and radicals like Khomeini, whose "bold action contrasted strongly with the powerlessness of Riyadh [the Saudi capital] and its international networks to prevent the book's publication" (2000:185). Issuing a fatwa against a citizen of Great Britain also extended the range of Islamic jurisdiction, to include Europe and all the rest of the globe. As previously practiced, Islamic doctrine limited the jurisdiction of a fatwa to the geographic domain of a specific Muslim prince. "At a stroke, dar el-Islam was made universal, and its politics was expanded to include Muslim immigrants to the West, who became the first hostages and the actors in a worldwide struggle for control of Islam" (ibid.). The West was now included as part of the Islamic domain, where Islamic law could be applied and its justice carried out.

In the path laid out by Khomeini, the radical Islam personified by Osama bin Laden put theology to work as dramatic political practice. The attack he helped organize on the World Trade Center in New York resonated with frustrated and angry Muslims around the globe. Its broadcast images provoked celebration in Rotterdam, as well as other cities in the Netherlands, something that received a good deal of attention in the Dutch media. Those same images unified, at least for a period, Western democracies behind an American-led "war on terror." The pictures of Muslim youth celebrating the fall of New York's Twin Towers appeared to shock many Dutch citizens as much as the attack itself. These mediated events served to articulate and further polarize two groups, the Dutch, who represented Western values, and the Muslim immigrants, who would rejoice at the collapse of those values. As the symbolic figurehead of a political movement using religion to legitimate acts of violence, bin Laden is as important in our account of the politicization of Mohammed B. as Qutb and Mawdudi. He specifically pointed to the Netherlands as a center of radical Islam, and his broadcasts would have helped Mohammed B. in his (later) search for meaning and, more specifically, for legitimating the murder of van Gogh. In a statement broadcast in February 1998, bin Laden and a cohort of radical Islamic leaders calling themselves the World Islamic Front declared jihad on the United States. The statement said in part, "To kill Americans and their allies—civilians and military—is the individual duty incumbent upon every Muslim in all countries . . . This is in accordance with the words of God Almighty: 'Fight the idolaters at any time, if they first fight you'" (cited by Charles Glass, "Cyber-Jihad," *London Review of Books*, March 9, 2006, 18). These words proved significant for they provided Mohammed B. with the justification for the murder of a non-Muslim in the defense of Islam. They would also prove important in that they provided the opportunity to feel oneself part of a world-historical movement, dramatically orchestrating a sense of importance and purpose, especially when infused with religious force.

To signal his conversion, Mohammed B. switched allegiance from his local mosque to one known for its radicalism and its international cliental. (According to one source, he was excluded from his local mosque because of his growing radicalism.)[14] It was here he met Abu Khaled, mentioned earlier. He altered his appearance and changed his eating habits, broke with some of his friendship circles and sought new ones that more closely reflected his changing beliefs and habits. He took on new names like Abu Zubair, at least on the Internet chat pages and blogs he participated in. Mohammed B. became, in other words, a "keyboard terrorist" and virtual jihadist before he became one in reality. Nilufer Gole (200:95–96) calls this a relatively common path. She describes it as follows: "After moving from their small provincial towns to cities, they [the new rebels] encounter, during their years in high school and university, the works of authors who set up the landmarks of contemporary Islamist ideology. . . . One common feature of these authors is their effort to redefine Islamic 'authenticity' in a manner that is no longer apologetic before Western modernity. This new critical stance in relation to Western modernity marks the principal difference between the new generation of Islamists and those of the nineteenth century . . . all of whom tried to accommodate Islamic values with modernity." This search for authenticity in Islam is supplemented with the idea that the sharia, or religious law, "provides a comprehensive and organic system for the regulation of all aspects of human life—individual, social and political—in accordance with God's will" (Guazzone 1996:10). The difference in our current case is simply that Mohammed B. was born into this double world and did not have to move from one to the other in any physical sense. The ideology came to him over the Internet and other mass media, as much as through the person of Abu Khaled. Mohammed B. is not alone in this, of course, but one must still look at individual biography to explain why he was attracted to radicalism and not everyone else who was similarly located in his social stratum and milieu.

At this individual level, one can view Mohammed B.'s conversion to radical Islam as a lifestyle choice. As Geert Mak (2005c:33, my translation) puts it, "Radical fundamentalism is not only a reaction to modernity; it is a product of modernity." The city of Amsterdam, if not Dutch society more generally, can be described as cosmopolitan, a global city in the sense that a number of ways of life blended together in a form of coexistence if not mutual interaction. Muslims mixed in public places with Christians, Jews, and atheists like van Gogh. At the same time, there were levels of commitment to and belief in this cosmopolitan public culture. One could be an outspoken proponent, continually testing its limits, such as van Gogh or merely a casual participant. One could also be a marginal outsider merely passing through or a strong opponent looking for a proper way to express opposition. Radical interpretations of Islam are fairly new to the Netherlands and became more attractive after September 11, 2001, to a relatively small number of individuals who have only recently become visible to the general public. This form of politicized Islam had previously existed primarily on native soil, as part of nationalist movements in the countries of the Middle East and South Asia. In Mohammed B.'s case, it offered another way to live within Dutch society, one that permitted various levels of commitment here as well. Following the analysis cited by Pels (2005:46), the argument has been made that radical Islam offered a "masculine," patriarchical alternative to the "feminine," democratic values of the dominant Dutch culture. Hirsi Ali (2004a) goes even further when she associates such values with Islam generally. The murder of van Gogh meant many things to Mohammed B., especially the killing of an infidel, an event that he could hope would spark others to action. It was also important, however, as marker of a new way of life. The description Ruthven (2004:38) applies to Sayyid Qutb may be applied to Mohammed B. as well: "His was the paradigmatic case of the 'born-again' Muslim who having adopted or absorbed many modern or foreign influences makes a show of discarding them in his search for personal identity and cultural authenticity." While Qutb, the reflective intellectual, could confine his transformation to the discursive, Mohammed B., chose another form of action. Radical Islam provided the framework and van Gogh the target. From this perspective, the murder of Theo van Gogh was an important step in Mohammed B's conversion process. It gave him a stage on which to perform his conversion before the widest possible audience. Once he had done that, there could be no turning back.

RADICAL ISLAM AND MUSLIM MIGRATION

The issue of Muslims in the Netherlands will be discussed in more detail in the next chapter and only be introduced here. As a force within European society, radical Islam was made possible by migration flows, including the movement and concentration of political exiles, as well as by new communications technologies that permitted individuals to live in several worlds simultaneously. Thus it was possible for individuals to adopt and practice several "identities" in one geographic location where "identity becomes a personally reflective (and reflexive) project that is organized and expressed through often elaborately managed lifestyles" (Bennett 2003:144; see also Sen 2006 on multiple identities and Ramadan 2004 on modern Muslim identity).

Muslims in the Netherlands lived a more or less "hidden existence" until the latter part of the twentieth century (Rath et al. 2001:27, Cherribi 2003). The first groups came from colonies like Indonesia and then, after the Second World War, from the Moluccan Islands. A major shift occurred with the first waves of economically motivated "guest workers," primarily from Turkey and Morocco in the late 1960s. These immigrants were actively recruited by the Dutch government, with the latter being forced to seek labor agreements with the countries involved in an attempt to impose some order. From 1968 onward, the flow of immigration between countries was formally regulated by mediation services (Lucassen and Penninx 1997:55). In addition to the increasing numbers during these years, Lucassen and Penninx also note a "striking" shift in their geographic origin: "from the towns in the most developed parts of the country to the less developed rural districts" (59). As to the total Muslim population, Rath et al. estimate the number at 50,000 in 1971 and around 100,000 by 1975 (Rath et al. 2001:28). Writing in 1991 Shadid states that "Turks and Moroccans constitute the two largest groups with about 160,000 and 120,000 persons respectively" (1991:359). He also notes that while "Muslim," these groups are far from homogeneous, in that they represent a number of different schools and traditions within the Islamic faith. Such differences, however, tend to diminish in periods of polarization. Added to the Turks and Moroccans are about "25,000 Muslims from Suriname, 9,000 from Indonesia, 6,000 from Pakistan, 2,000 from Tunisia and 1,500 from the Moluccans." Rath et al. (2001:28) put the total number of Muslims in the Netherlands in 1992 at 414,000.

The growing numbers of Muslim immigrants and their concentration in urban centers underpinned a shift in their relation to and perception by Dutch society.[15] This can be noted from a shifting focus of Muslim voluntary associations. Even in the 1980s Muslim organizations showed little concern for Dutch politics (Graaf 1985); by the 1990s, however, a noticeable shift had occurred (Rath et al. 2001:89, Hussain 2003).[16] From the side of the immigrants, it meant that these individuals were governed by Islamic law while living abroad, opening the possibility of conflict with the laws of the host country. For the primarily male first waves of immigrants, it might have been possible to assume a temporary or thin identity as a temporary resident or guest. To wear the clothes proper to a migrant working class, to be "one of the boys," participating in shop talk and even the after work drink while still maintaining one's primary or "thick" identity as a Muslim. With the extension of Islamic law to include Europe, this was made more complicated, a difficulty that was compounded when extended families and religious authorities entered the picture in a concrete way. The possibility, and responsibility, to maintain a Muslim way of life became greater, and more public, even if one remained only a temporary guest in everyone's eyes, including one's own. Modes of dress as well as behavior could become a public issue where they had not before, except on a small scale as in the case of bus drivers wearing traditional headdress. Women could be expected to be veiled and children to be educated according to Muslim codes and strictures. There was also a growing sense of identification as an "immigrant," with a sense of responsibility as well as the ascribed negative connotations from the native population. Hirsi Ali, for example, would be accused by some Muslims, including Mohammed B., of "forgetting her roots" and of joining the "other side" (Buruma 2006b:143).[17] In addition to this, the common phenomenon of the "settler's mentality" also developed, whereby those arriving earlier feel a sense of superiority to the newly arrived "greenhorns." These layered differences created tensions on individual as well as collective or ethnic levels.

Rath et al. (2001:42) trace this process as one of institutionalization, pointing, for example, to an increase in the number of mosques and clergy, the legalization of ritual male circumcision to include Muslims, the ritual slaughter of animals and the existence of Muslim butchers, the possibility to take a formal oath on the Koran instead of the Bible, and the number of Muslim religious festivals in the Netherlands.[18] According to Cherribi (2003:196), "In the Netherlands, the Muslim women checkout cashiers at the upscale major supermarket chain Albert Heijn wear a specially made scarf with a corporate logo." Such institutionalization was in part encouraged and subsidized by the Dutch government. Partly as a means of combating the influence of radical Islam, Saudi Arabia and other Muslim countries have also contributed funding for the construction of mosques in Europe and elsewhere. According to Cherribi (2003:195–96), the Gulf States are funding "the construction of one of the largest mosques in northern Europe, on the outskirts of Rotterdam, which will be known for having the tallest minaret in Europe." It should be noted that mosques do not have to be formal structures, but as with African American religious activity, Islamic religious services can be held in storefronts and abandoned factories and similar buildings. This fact led Shadid (1991:361) to say that it was not possible to know the exact number of mosques in the Netherlands, though he estimated the number at 300, "of which 155 are for the Turkish and 105 for the Moroccan community." In a comparative study published four years later, Shadid and Koningsveld (1995:26–27) put the number at 380, explaining that this was an estimate based on information provided by Muslim umbrella organizations. Rath et al. (2001:100) estimate the 1994 figure at 380 and put the density ratio at "one mosque for about every 1,250 Muslims."

Whatever the exact number, with this dramatic increase, religion and clerics could play a more central role in the lives of Muslims in the Netherlands, who by the 1980s were no longer temporary immigrant workers, but had formed distinctive communities that had come to stay. Added to this were the housing and immigration policies of the host countries, and the attitudes of the populace, including those of the immigrants themselves, all of which influenced the development of segregated neighborhoods, helping create concentrated populations where the sharia could be more easily applied. Conditions for the second and third generations with Muslim roots are clearly different from those of the first generation of immigrants. In 1982, Dutch regulations regarding the preparation of meat where formally amended to allow for the ritual slaughter of animals according to Islamic law.[19] In 1986, the supreme court of the Netherlands recognized that imams should be permitted the same rights as ministers, priests, and rabbis, and, later, imams were given the right to serve as spiritual guides in prisons and in the military. There are now courses for training Muslim religious leaders in the Netherlands, but currently the majority of imams are recruited from abroad (Rath et al. 2001:85). Muslim holidays, however, are still not formally recognized in the Netherlands.

While the number of mosques in the Netherlands might be difficult to gauge, Muslim schools are more strictly regulated. Article 23 of the Dutch Constitution guarantees the right of religious groups to found their own schools and appoint teachers. It also "guarantees equal financial treatment of private and state education: both are funded from the public purse according to the same criteria" (Rath et al. 2001:71). The first Muslim primary schools emerged in 1988, and in 1994 there were twenty-nine, this out of a total of 8,139 primary schools in the Netherlands (Rath et al 2001:82). Currently there are about forty state-subsidized Muslim schools in the country, and a much larger number of religious classes that are connected to mosques. Hirsi Ali has made the existence of Muslim schools into an issue in her campaign for assimilation. In this, she has taken up earlier arguments made by Dutch politicians at least since the early 1980s that permitting Muslim schools would only increase social segregation and create ghettos (Rath et al. 2001:107).

GLOBALIZATION

A good part of the literature on global culture and the effects of globalization has focused on a new form of cosmopolitanism, the hybrid individual with a weakened territorial identification. For example, Jan Nijman (2000:34–35) discusses cultural globalization as a product of "the increased access and exposure to mass communication media and international travel," which "results in the growing importance of people's individual identity as distinct from their territorially-based group identity." This has been interpreted as largely progressive, as a counterbalance to nationalism. It is possible to see radical Islam as a reactionary current in this same development, a new form of nonterritorial collective identification that is made possible by the flow of information and people and in which cities like London and Brussels became nodes. This is not merely a matter of numbers. According to Nijman, immigration flows to Amsterdam were greater in previous centuries than they are today, and current migration, at least since the 1990s (migration linked to decolonization and the need for industrial workers) has little to do with economic opportunities in the city itself and more with family reunification of previous waves of immigration. In this sense, the radical Islam adopted by Mohammed B. is as much a product of globalization as it is of any religious tradition, even as it is spread from place to place through traveling clerics and mediated texts and images (see Roy 2004 for the effects of globalization on modern Muslim identity). In order to explain why Mohammed B., in particular, converted, one must combine biographical with wider contextual factors. In many ways, Mohammed B. was a typical second-generation Muslim immigrant in search of recognition and respect, caught in a time and place where opportunities for social integration were shrinking and where an attractive alternative appeared on the horizon.

As will be discussed below, Mohammed B. appears not to have acted alone when he murdered Theo van Gogh. At his trial, evidence was presented suggesting that he was a member of an organization that the authorities named the "Hofstad," or court city, group; as already noted, accounts differ as to his role and status within it. On the one hand, there were meetings held at his apartment, which would seem to give him a prominent status. On the other hand, others in the group had a longer history of involvement with the radical Islamic movement. Some had received formal military training, while others had at least made the attempt to participate in international militant actions. The killing of van Gogh might well have been part of an initiation rite for someone whose most intensive encounter with radical Islam came via the Internet and in the mosque.

After his arrest, police recorded the following testimony from one of their informants: "The murderer of Theo van Gogh in Amsterdam was a criminal Moroccan who had been introduced in Amsterdam to a group of Muslim extremists. He belonged to an extreme group that meets in the El Taweed mosque in Amsterdam. In Muslim circles this mosque is known as extreme and it is reported that connections exist with Al Qua'ida. This extreme group knew beforehand that this boy would kill Theo van Gogh. He had also gotten permission to do this. The perpetrator of the murder intended to, after having committed the murder, be killed by police bullets and thus become a martyr and end in heaven. Months before the word had spread that extreme Muslims were busy collecting money to kill Theo van Gogh and Ayaan Hirsi Ali" (quoted in Benschop 2005:36).

It was in part this testimony that led to the suspicion that the assassination was not the act of a single individual. It also raises in a different way the question of what the murder meant to Mohammed B., the "boy" referred to in the testimony above. Of course, this term, jongen, could just be a colloquial expression and not a reference to status, specifically, that of a young person who needs to prove himself. If it refers to status however, it would not only point out the relative position of Mohammed B., but also cause one to reflect on the meaning of the assassination itself. As previously discussed, van Gogh was not the prime target, but it is also clear that he had grossly insulted Islam and in that sense was a legitimate target. The assassination might also have been a test of commitment and a search for recognition within the group and within this world, as much as for the promised rewards of martyrdom in the next.[20]

At the level of personal identity and group identification the Internet has replaced other media and forms of virtual representation and become central to what has historically been a long tradition among migrant and immigrant groups. As Sherry Turkle (1995:10) points out, "In the story of constructing identity in the culture of simulation, experiences on the Internet figure prominently, but these experiences can only be understood as part of a larger cultural context. That context is the story of the eroding boundaries between the real and the virtual, the animate and the inanimate, the unitary and the multiple self, which is occurring both in advancing fields of scientific research and in the patterns of everyday life." The Internet and other forms of digital media, including the disc and the cell phone, have contributed to the possibility of an anticivic sphere in the heart of civil society.

There exist a number of chat pages used by and popular with immigrant youth in the Netherlands, some of which are further specified by ethnic or national origin. One, Marokko.nl, conducted a user poll before the murder of van Gogh, raising the question "Will Hirshi Ali [sic] end up just like Pim Fortuyn"? Out of 171 replies, 115 answered in the affirmative. The terms "Internet fundamentalist" and "keyboard terrorist" have been coined on the basis of interactions on these websites. In this sense, the Internet not only facilitates protest, but also creates it, by creating a new virtual reality within which protest is performed and new roles as well as ideas are tested and tried on. This also conceivably helped create a climate of aggression that made political assassination appear legitimate and even necessary: "We have seen how radicalized Islamic youngsters used the Internet to hatch their networks of hatred and disseminate their hostile message. This gave rise to a climate for violent jihad, in which the murderer of Theo van Gogh could be recruited. A climate in which Mohammed B. and his friends of the Hofstad group could be trained to attack personal targets. . . . and political targets, such as the house of parliament and the decadence of the Amsterdam Red Light District" (Benschop 2005:99). As some extreme right-wing groups followed suit, the Internet became a battleground in which extremes on both sides could try to shout each other down in a quickly escalating cascade of rhetoric. This was another way in which to drown out the middle ground of reconciliation.

A general point regarding new forms of organizing protest and opposition in contemporary society can be highlighted here. Following Benschop (2005) and Bennett (2003) and others, one can make a case that the Internet provides something more than a resource for groups and organizations involved in political activity; the Internet may well create conditions of and for political protest at the same time that it facilitates it. According to Bennett (2003:143), "Digital communication networks may be changing the political game in favor of resource-poor players who, in many cases, are experimenting with political strategies outside of conventional national political channels such as elections and interest processes." While Bennett is primarily concerned with the global justice movement, his discussion of new forms of organizing protest can be applied, with modification, to radical Islamic groups. According to Benschop (2205:105), "Terrorist networks consist of semi-autonomous local cells that are self-supporting to a great extent. . . . 'polder-jihadists' are not organized according to a tight or formal pattern, but rather as a loose network of friends and acquaintances, who feel connected by a shared Islamist doctrine and way of living. The Hofstad group was in fact a nomadic movement of 'angry young muslims' and muslimahs with extreme and violent convictions." Even if accurate, there is an important distinction to be drawn between a network and a group, where the latter implies a collective presence, a dynamic personal interaction between members. While the alleged Hofstad *group* may have had wider contacts with a global network, linked together by a radical ideology, it was the interactions of the group that radicalized the individual member; the ideology and the network were more a resource in this process.[21]

Social scientists have long been interested in networks and how they function in group formation and collective action. Some recent attention has focused on self-organizing networks that are local, nonhierarchical, and friendship based. Such networks have both organizational and ideational aspects that loosely link them together. An anonymous "expert" cited by the *New York Times* (October 7, 2005) claimed, for example, "The threads between the London, Madrid and Bali attacks are not organizational. . . . They are threads of the mind." For others, it would be more correct to say that a new organizational form is emerging in contemporary conflicts as a means of coordinating collective action. Recent studies have pointed to what are called "all-channel" networks, nonhierarchical organizing structures that are replacing older bureaucratic forms. All-channel networks are those "in which every node is connected to every other node" on a horizontal rather than a vertical plane (Arquilla and Ronfeldt 1999:193).[22] Something similar might be at work in the murder of Theo van Gogh.

Through its youth centers and mosques, as well as significant individuals, the Amsterdam neighborhood in which the alleged group's core membership lived might well have been linked to wider national and international networks. Such linkages, however, were likely more virtual than real, in the sense of building on direct, face-to-face individual contact. The driving force here was ideology rather than personality although significant individuals like Abu Khaled probably served as catalysts. An explosive form of radical Islam provided an emotional bridge between individuals and a communicative thread between nodes. Mosques were one of the conduits, as they have long been noted as crucial sites by all sides in this conflict. For example, "De politieke Islam" (Political Islam), the report produced by the Dutch secret police (the BVD, predecessor of the AIVD) in 1998, named mosques as central to "the integration process." At this point in time, social integration was the official aim of immigration policy, and mosques were identified as playing a "crucial role" in this process. The report pointed out that mosques in the Netherlands were political arenas, something that has also been recognized by "foreign powers" and those interested in resisting integration and in promoting alternatives, including active resistance (see Benschop 87). This point of view was further extended and elaborated in a 2001 report "Terrorisme aan het begin van de 21ste eeuw" (Terrorism at the beginning of the 21st century). The title is significant because in the wake of the attacks in New York "terrorism" became a prime concern. At this time, the threat of terrorism was seen as coming primarily from outside the country, and local mosques were singled out as conduits. The 2001 report identified a potentially dangerous spiral: failing integration, strengthened segregation, increasing polarization, and violent confrontation. Following the murder of van Gogh, new laws have been recommended to deal with radical clerics ("hate imams") and troublesome mosques ("hate sites"). In addition, Muslim schools have also been pointed out as sites of conservative cultural transference and possible hindrances to integration, if not sources of radical Islamic fundamentalism. Hirsi Ali has made the existence of such schools a prime concern in her campaigns.

There is an important difference between a network and a group, in that the latter implies a collective presence and a dynamic interaction, while the former does not and can merely be a formal construction. While the term "Hofstad group" is a name applied by the police and the mass media, it may well refer to something real, a loosely structured group formed out of neighborhood ties, based on friendship and youth and religious organizations that was given more coherence and purpose through the Internet. The Internet provided a space for discovery as well as communication. It opened up a virtual world of politicized religion, which could then be actualized through being shifted from the neighborhood mosque to another, which then afforded access to new people and ideas. Ties were relatively weak and resources relatively poor, and there existed no formal organization or leadership; yet individuals could form allegiances, coordinate activities and most importantly reinforce each other's beliefs. A group without a formal structure, coherent ideology, or name was formed.

The tension between the loose ties of contemporary terrorist groups made possible through the Internet and the close ties that are necessary to sustain the level of commitment to carry out an act of terror and martyrdom should be reflected on. While the former supplies the necessary links to the global movement, the Internet contacts, and educational instruction (ranging from religious instruction to how to build a bomb), the latter supplies the intense social contact, the interpersonal support, and collective ritual practice to maintain a high level of commitment. As Sageman (2004:120) puts it, "During the wait for heavenly rewards, a religious revivalist community sustains its members with strong social and emotional benefits, which give a general sense of direction to their lives and opportunities for involvement in a cause."

With examples taken from research into earlier terrorist groups, the German RAF, Italian RA, and the Egyptian ILO, Sageman (2004:133) offers a perceptive analysis of the steps toward conversion to radical jihad. His general proposition—that "social bonds came first, ideology followed"— is too mechanical if strictly applied, however. Better to view this process as an interactive dialectic. One of his insights is highly relevant in the present case: that the Western ideal of social mobility, something that marks the majority of terrorists in his study, may well have had the negative effect of distancing these prospective terrorists from family and friends and paradoxically increasing their sense of isolation when mobility was frustrated. Regarding the Egyptian Islamic groups, he writes, "Their mobility had distanced them from their original families or friends, and when they were socially isolated in a big university city, they found a family substitute in the MG (Muslim Group). There was a progressive isolation from society at large and complete absorption and commitment to the new group. This total commitment was carried out with zeal and joy and included personal sacrifice for Islam." Sageman is referring to individuals whose mobility was geographic as well as social, in that they moved from smaller towns and villages to university towns. This was not the case for Mohammed B., whose mobility was social and geographic only in the minor sense of moving from one urban neighborhood to another.

While from the point of view of network analysis there are clear parallels to be drawn between the extreme left- and right-wing groups of the 1970s, there are clear differences as well. In his interviews with imprisoned suicide bombers, Khosrokhavar (2005) discovered a deep sense of guilt and shame that characterized those who chose Islamic martyrdom in what he describes as a subculture of death.[23] For those living in Europe, the sense of guilt and humiliation was intensified by the difficulties of attempting to live a "pure" Muslim life in a world shaped by nonbelievers. In addition, the marginalization one felt in these surroundings was multiplied by what Khosrokhavar calls "humiliation by proxy," where alienation led to empathetic identification with the perceived humiliation inflicted on Muslims around the world. Television played an important role in this process, where one's own sense of marginalization was less dependent on actual life chances, such as being a relatively well-educated person living in Europe than on identification with oppressed others (including non-Muslims) around the globe. Here again, similarities with the extreme left in the 1970s might be drawn; what is distinctive in the current case is the reinterpretation of humiliation and alienation in religious terms. In Mohammed B.'s case, as with others in the so-called Hofstad group, these others included Muslims in Kosovo and Chechnya, as well as Palestinians and African Americans. This implies that one must go beyond "material" factors in any discussion of integration and assimilation. Like Mohammed B., many of those interviewed by Khosrokhavar were "middle-class" when measured in classical terms, but still experienced the world through a veil of guilt and humiliation, where a sense of "no future" in the present world was predominant. All of which lent itself to a search for recognition and a better life in the next world. One's own death and the death of responsible and representative others were then easily legitimated through heroic martyrdom.

From the point of view of the official policy, Mohammed B. is an example of successful integration and multiculturalism, at least until his conversion. For critics of Dutch multiculturalism, his case is proof of the wrong-headedness of this policy, proof that it was doomed from the start. From his point of view, Mohammed B. might well be an exemplar of another form of integration, into a global oppositional network. If his actions are viewed as part of a wider Islamic social movement, then his aim in the assassination of van Gogh should be interpreted as an attempt to inspire others to revolt and, in typical terrorist form, to eliminate the middle ground by further polarizing the debate on integration.

AYAAN HIRSI ALI

The issue of free expression in the service of cultural liberation is central to Ayaan Hirsi Ali's self-presentation. In her often articulated biographical statements (in contrast to Mohammed B., Hirsi Ali has a very available and worked-out biographical narrative), she presents herself as someone who has struggled to liberate herself from the past, from the constraints of patriarchal, religious tradition (for the most complete biographical statement, see Hirsi Ali 2007). This self-presentation is structured in the form of an emancipatory narrative, from submission to collective norms to liberation as an autonomous individual, a form very much rooted in the Enlightenment, as articulated in Kant's notion of individual autonomy and intellectual maturity. Her version stresses breaking with "backward" religion in moving from darkness to light, a path she advocates for other Muslims and for Islamic religion as such. More like Voltaire than Martin Luther, Hirsi Ali sees herself as a leading voice in a churchless religious reformation. Her historical narrative is also embedded in an evolutionary theory, in which certain "cultures" are more advanced than others, a perspective taken from Norbert Elias rather than Darwin and Herbert Spenser. From this position Hirsi Ali poses and answers the question: "Why have Muslims fallen so far behind the West"? Her answer is founded in the shortcomings she finds in Islamic religion.

Hirsi Ali was born Ayaan Hirsi Magan in Mogadishu, Somalia, in November 1969. Her father, Hirsi Magan, a well-known educator and a leader of the Muslim opposition to the dictatorial, secular government led by Mohamed Siad Barre, was in prison when Hirsi Ali was born. By her own account, she met her father for the first time at the age of six. Her mother was the second wife in this traditional Muslim household, where the tension between oppositional politics and the clan-based tradition was strongly felt by Hirsi Ali and her younger sister. Both clearly identified with an absent, but modern father more than with their strict and always present traditional mother. In one telling anecdote, Hirsi Ali recalls how her father's fancy Italian shoes were more appealing than her mother's bare feet. "We told our father we didn't want to be girls. It wasn't fair that we weren't allowed to go out with him and do all the things that Mahid [their brother] could. Abeh [their father] would always protest, and quote the Quran: 'paradise is at the feet of your mother!' But when we looked down at them, our mother's bare feet were cracked from washing the floors every day, and Abeh's feet were clad in expensive shoes" (Hirsi Ali 2007:50).

Hirsi Ali's parents separated when she was a teenager, and her father married again and raised another family. She presents herself as an outspoken family rebel, yet one who could still maintain a warm and loving relationship with her often absent father. The women in the family, most especially her grandmother, are presented with ambiguity, as strict enforcers of tradition, organizing, for example, the children's genital mutilation against the wishes of her then absent father. While her mother appears helpless and unable to cope with the pressures of enforced exile, the ever-present, tyrannical grandmother seems strongly independent by comparison.

Because of Hirsi Magan's militant political opposition, the family was forced into exile in 1976, first moving to Saudi Arabia and then Ethiopia and finally spending ten years in Kenya. Hirsi Ali was six when this process began, and her early formal education occurred in Muslim schools in these countries. She describes herself as a devout and even radical Muslim during this period, wearing traditional dress, including head covering, with honor. She recalls that as a schoolgirl in Kenya she voiced the opinion that Salman Rushdie deserved to die for slandering Islam in his *Satanic Verses* (Linklater 2005), though in her autobiography this is not mentioned except for a recollection of observing a burning of Rushdie's book and some reflective comments on the real value of such a symbolic act. "I felt estranged, somehow very uncomfortable. I wondered if it wasn't silly to have bought one copy of this book to burn it; after all the money would still go to the author (Hirsi Ali 2007:118). Yet, she writes, she believed Rushdie deserved to die, as did anyone who had insulted the Prophet. Influenced by a revived Muslim Brotherhood, she sought out Somali religious leaders who had studied in Mecca and Medina (Chorus and Olgun 2005:92–93). Like Mohammed B., Hirsi Ali read and drew influence from the texts of Mawdudi and Qutb. Until the early 1990s, she considered herself an adherent of radical Islam.

As represented in various autobiographical accounts, Hirsi Ali's questioning of inherited, clan-based tradition began at an early age, connected in large part to internal family dynamics and her encounters with different religions and cultures due to the many moves the family was forced to make. The most significant event, however, came in January 1992 when her father returned home from the local mosque in Nairobi to announce her marriage to a clan member from Canada he had met for the first time a few hours previously. Complying with her father's wishes, she was married six days later in a formal Muslim ceremony, which required neither her presence nor her signature (Hirsi Ali 2007:176). Soon thereafter her new husband returned to Canada, with the promise that she would soon be able to follow. This was actually Hirsi Ali's second marriage, as she had earlier married another Somali man she had been attracted to, but the marriage could be annulled since neither her older brother nor her father had been present or given permission.

The trip from Nairobi to Canada was routed through Frankfurt and it was there she took the opportunity to flee, first to Düsseldorf to the home of a clan member and then to the Netherlands. This was primarily for pragmatic reasons: there were no visa requirements for those traveling from Germany, as opposed to Great Britain or the United States, her first choices, which did have them. After two days Hirsi Ali was on a train to the Netherlands, arriving at the Amsterdam central station on July 24, 1992. Three days later she applied for political asylum at the refugee center in Zeewolde. On the application she gave the name Ayaan Hirsi Ali, the name of her grandfather, instead of Magan, her father's name—a fact that, together with other factual misrepresentations in her asylum application, would later threaten her Dutch citizenship and create the controversy that would cause a government to fall. Hirsi Ali lived at the refugee center for nearly a year and, not allowed to do paid work, took Dutch lessons and volunteered as an interpreter and consultant, helping other immigrants in their dealings with Dutch society, including at abortion clinics and women's centers. She worked as an interpreter (first using her knowledge of English and "asiels," the pidgin language of the camp, and then Dutch when she became proficient). It was here, she recounts, that she became aware of the problems faced by Muslim women living in Europe. Hirsi Ali recounts this awakening in various articles and books (Hirsi Ali 2004a, 2006, 2007), using them to build and support her case against Islamic culture. While at the refugee center, Hirsi Ali marked off steps in her own conversion process: she removed her head scarf, cut her hair, and learned to ride a bicycle. The most significant step however, occurred when she wrote to her father explaining what she had done, thus making the meaning of her actions clear not only to him but also to herself. There would be no easy return.[24]

Hirsi Ali left the refugee center to enroll in Dutch language courses, sharing a flat with another refugee. She worked for short periods in local factories, cleaning floors and packing cookies, so that she could attend school in the afternoons. This allowed her, she writes, to meet another class of Dutch people and to experience firsthand the informal ethnic segregation practiced in the workplace. "It was mutual xenophobia: the Dutch thought the Moroccans were lazy and unpleasant and the Moroccans said the Dutch stank and dressed like whores" (Hirsi Ali 2007:221). At the same time, she insightfully projects her clan-based worldview onto the local Dutch culture, seeing how the "Dutch" interact in clanlike ways to ensure and reproduce group solidarity as well as difference. In describing the Dutch model of pillarization, for example, Hirsi Ali writes: "These pillars operated just like clans. For generations, Dutch Catholics and Protestants went to separate schools, hospitals, clubs, shops; they even had separate channels on TV and separate radio stations. As late as 1995, in Leiden, the pillars at least partly defined who you were and who you knew, as the clans did in Somalia" (Hirsi Ali 2007:238).

After trying her hand at the various educational opportunities offered her, and taking college preparatory courses, Hirsi Ali eventually studied political science at Leiden University, where she received an advanced degree. After graduation, she worked as a researcher at a foundation associated with the Dutch labor party (PvdA). Her research focused on the problems of integration of foreign, primarily Muslim, women into Dutch society. Her policy recommendations, such as calling for closing the forty-one Muslim schools in the Netherlands and amending the Dutch constitution to prohibit separate schools and other institutions and thus alter the foundation on which "pillarization" had been built, led to some conflicts with the party leadership.[25] This conflict, she recounts, eventually led to her accepting an offer from the right-liberal vvd to stand for parliament on their platform of individual, rather than collective rights. Once elected, the opportunity to become even more visible as a parliamentarian representing the rights of Muslim women presented itself.

The role and place of women in Muslim culture and Islamic religion has become Hirsi Ali's leading cause. It is the foundation on which her argument against the possibility of full integration for immigrants from Muslim backgrounds rests. In newspaper articles and interviews, Hirsi Ali stresses three characteristics as distinguishing Muslims from other immigrant groups. These three elements are (1) the autocratic nature and hierarchical structure that shape Muslim social relations, (2) the patriarchical attitude that structures family relations, and (3) the group mentality that shapes personal identity for both men and women. All three she writes are legitimated through the Koran and, when this is seen as the direct word of God, are impossible to challenge or change. All three are said to prevent integration, especially for Muslim women, because they impede reflective thinking and individual autonomy. Their cumulative effect was to make reformation the only alternative, outside of total segregation or deportation.

Hirsi Ali made the transition from marginal refugee to member of parliament and highly visible public intellectual in a remarkably short period. In the same process (if we accept her own account), she moved from radical Islam to Enlightenment agnosticism and finally to atheism. This is a conversion at least as remarkable, perhaps even more so, than that experienced by Mohammed B., though in the opposite direction. Significant persons in the later stages of this conversion were academics, writers, and intellectuals like Paul Scheffer, Paul Cliteur, and Leon de Winter. The step to atheism was guided by the philosopher Herman Philipse, whose *Atheistisch Manifest* (The atheist's manifesto) provided her with a clear-cut alternative to her previously strongly held religious belief. This is acknowledged in her preface to the book's second edition. While this group of close friends was influential in Hirsi Ali's intellectual development, they were unable to influence her making the film *Submission*. All advised against it, primarily for the harm it would bring to Dutch-Muslim relations and to her personally (Chorus and Olgun 2005:114).

Just as one must move beyond individual biography in understanding Mohammed B.'s conversion to radical Islam, one needs to include the social context in understanding Hirsi Ali's conversion to Enlightenment skepticism and, especially, in accounting for her becoming a member of parliament and a very visible public intellectual of international reputation. By remarkable coincidence, both Mohammed B. and Hirsi Ali completed their Dutch high school qualifications in the same year, 1995 (though she was nine years older). Hirsi Ali moved on to classical university study and Mohammed B. to a more practically oriented polytechnic curriculum. This difference can in part be explained by gender- and class-based perceptions of available opportunity. Both Mohammed B. and Hirsi Ali, however, appear to be motivated by a desire to help their similarly situated but less fortunate peers, as well as by personal ambition: in her case immigrant women and in his immigrant youth. Both were unusual when compared to their immediate counterparts. Hirsi Ali was, by her own account, one of the very few formally educated female refugees at the asylum center; Mohammed B. one of the few youths from his neighborhood to move beyond occupational training.

The opportunity to stand as member of parliament for a right-of-center political party is not open to just anyone, and certainly not to someone working for a left-leaning labor party. Being a forceful and attractive black woman, a Muslim with a critical stance toward Islam, and a recent immigrant who was fluent in Dutch most likely played a role in both situations, being hired as a researcher specializing in immigrant issues and standing for election with the same representative potential. The time was ripe for someone with these social and personal characteristics, or at least those making the selections thought so. This was especially so in the case of political representation.[26] Once elected, opportunities to be publicly visible only multiplied; being an elected official also meant having to negotiate one's statements to fit party policy, but on this particular issue things were mostly resolved: the notion that Islam was a backward religion and that it was the responsibility of individual Muslims to free themselves fit well with VVD ideology, as Hirsi Ali herself readily acknowledges.[27] As an elected member of parliament, Hirsi Ali considered herself a spokesperson for Dutch immigrants, one who "regularly advocate[s] the emancipation of immigrant women" (Hirsi Ali 2006:165). The prime audience for her written works, however, appears to be the nonimmigrant Dutch population and the wider "Western" public.

The role and place of women in non-Western society has long been a political issue in cross-cultural confrontations. In the French-Algerian war, it was a central part of the ideology justifying French colonialism; in the immediate aftermath of the Iranian revolution, women's position in society was a core issue for the new Islamic regime; and it plays a role in current Middle-East policy of the United States. At least in the West, the liberation of women is an issue around which left and right can potentially unite because it can be couched in universalistic terms. While Hirsi Ali's public positions on these issues are not unique (her positions on Islam build on writings by Bernard Lewis, D. Pryce Jones, and Samuel Huntington, as she acknowledges), the fact that they are so forcefully voiced by a young black women with her well-publicized background makes them all the more powerful in the current explosive context.[28]

Unlike Mohammed B., Hirsi Ali never lived in an immigrant neighborhood: she never really had the time to develop an identity as an immigrant in the Netherlands. The perception of her as such is ascribed by others, including significant individuals among the political elite who sought her out to represent their party. As noted earlier, some of the anger against her voiced by those with immigrant backgrounds stems in part from just this lack of authentic and authenticating experience. The designation "immigrant" appears rather to have been something of a nom de guerre, taken on in political and cultural struggles, a form of cultural capital to trade upon. This does not necessarily imply opportunism or cynicism on her part. It was a role made available to her and she adapted to it early on when serving as an interpreter, the go-between, the representative and spokesperson for others. This helped prepare her for the rather typical intellectual role she would later adopt: a spokesperson putting into words what others were said to only feel and not properly express. "Immigrant" thus has a positive connotation in this context, while "integration" meant being able to speak in public, to be heard and seen, as a representative figure, a public person speaking in the name of an oppressed group. However, as was expressed to me in interviews with members of her party, Hirsi Ali adopted the habit of the classical intellectual, speaking to and for those she chose to represent, rather than with them. From a rather different angle, Mohammed B. chose the same role.

Regarding the possibility of integration, Hirsi Ali has taken a middle ground between critics who see in Mohammed B.'s actions confirmation of the failure of Dutch policy and those who argue for a more flexible form of multiculturalism. She writes that integration takes time and must be viewed as a "civilizing process" in the sense described by Norbert Elias, a long historical process of social learning.[29] Ali appears almost to be speaking directly of Mohammed B. when she writes that "the majority of native Dutch citizens have had more than a hundred years to develop modern values, they live in another world than the recent immigrant from the Rif mountains"(2004a:68). It would seem that one could oppose Ali's positions from two different vantage points: on the basis of form, the position taking of the outsider intellectual claiming to speak for and to represent others, and from the point of view of content, that is, her substantive positions on Islam and Muslim culture. The first can be relatively easily dismissed as it applies to anyone speaking in the name of others; critics would do better to challenge the content of what she has to say. In her writings and speeches, Ali often refers to a "pure" Islam, which can be found in the words of the Prophet Muhammad and in sacred texts, such as the Koran. For her, *Submission* represents a truth about Islam, which was the point of the Koranic texts on the naked female bodies, revealing how two "truths" intertwined: the oppression of woman as legitimated through the word of God. Her aim, she says, was not to be provocative for its own sake, but rather to present what was true. "It can be that I provoked, but what I said was true. . . . I made six thorough Koran readings while in America and can point to the texts" (Chorus and Olgun 2005:170), but "my intention was to challenge Muslims, through thought-provoking texts and images, to think carefully about the extent of their own responsibility for their deprived circumstances" (Hirsi Ali 2006:155). This is an intellectual speaking, for whom the written word has a deep authority and for whom textual interpretation and citation are the basis of meaningful action. This is also something that harks back to her radical Islamic past and that links her to Mohammed B.

The contrasts and continuities between Hirsi Ali and Mohammed B. are worth exploring on another level. Each may be said to be reacting in distinctive ways along lines constituted by the Orientalism/Occidentalism divide. As made famous by Edward Said, the term *Orientalism* was meant to capture the many ways in which the "East" has been conceptualized as an Other by the West, rather than referring as it had previously done to a field of study. In *Occidentalism* Buruma and Margalit (2004) attempt to capture the opposite, that is, how the "West" has been conceptualized by the East. As Said, Buruma, and Margalit portray it, Orientalism and Occidentalism have produced sets of assumptions and representations of their respective Other. In Orientalistic terms, the East is mysterious and dangerous. Hirsi Ali's depictions of Islam as backward and primitive resonate with many because they draw on Orientalistic representations and fears. Further to the right, radical Islamists are depicted as the natural expression of this dangerous Other. To those eyes, Mohammed B. only substantiates these fears. On the other side, for the Occidentalist, the West is irreligious, greedy, and decadent. It is led by Jews and the United States, a view reproduced in Mohammed B.'s notes, providing both motivation and justification for his action, lifting his murderous deed to a world-historical level and making him not a criminal, but a hero, not a murderer, but a holy warrior in a worldwide struggle of light against darkness. From that perspective, *Submission* and its coproducers embodied the Occident, and the murder of Theo van Gogh constituted a performance of the clash of civilizations.

In May 2006 a television documentary covering the stages of Hirsi Ali's career revealed that she had presented false information when applying for political asylum in the Netherlands. Although she had been forthright about this in many published accounts, Hirsi Ali felt compelled to once again recount the story of her arrival in the Netherlands in a televised interview. This public disclosure in the midst of a struggle for leadership within the vvD, in which her friend and ally Rita Verdonk, the minister of immigration, was a prime candidate, caused a new political uproar. Since she had been campaigning on a tough approach to immigration, including the treatment of asylum seekers, Verdonk felt compelled to revoke Ali's Dutch citizenship, a decision she was later forced to rescind. The coalition government that had been in place since the time of the murder of van Gogh eventually fell in the aftermath of this controversy surrounding the citizenship and political career of Ayaan Hirsi Ali. In the fall of 2006, Hirsi Ali arrived in the United States to work at the American Enterprise Institute, where, according to George F. Will, a conservative American journalist who interviewed her, "she is where she belongs, at last" (*Washington Post*, September 21, 2006, A25).

THEO VAN GOGH

In his perceptive article on the politics of tolerance in the Netherlands after the assassination of van Gogh, Peter van der Veer (Veer 2005:1) says of the victim, "He was fat, purposefully unkempt, antiauthoritarian, satirical, and immoderate in his language—in short, a personification of the Dutch cultural ethos since the 1970s." Very succinctly, that sums up van

Gogh's public persona, while at the same time linking it to a formative generational experience. If Paris became the center of radical European politics with the near revolution of 1968, Amsterdam was at the center of the cultural revolution that swept through Europe in the 1970s. Like Copenhagen and other major European cities, Amsterdam became for many young people an alternative symbol to what was perceived as the staid, middle-class conservatism of their parents. This was a different Amsterdam from the one in which Mohammed B. was to grow up. The large wave of immigrant guest workers was only just beginning, and the largest influx was from the relatively privileged strays of a Western youth culture. Along with the world-famous red-light district (which would become a symbol of all that was wrong with Western culture and an alleged target for the Hofstad group) and the cafés and bars in the myriad of local neighborhoods, the monument in Amsterdam's Dam Square was a gathering place for youth from around the world.

Van Gogh was born in 1957 and grew up in solidly middle-class Wassenaar, an exclusive suburb of The Hague, where his father was employed by the federal police authority. Though he grew up in the affluent and secure atmosphere of the late 1950s and early 1960s, the memory of the Second World War and the German occupation was very present. Ian Buruma (2005:2) writes, "Like most people of his and my post-war generation in Holland, Theo van Gogh was marked by stories of the Second World War, when the majority of Dutch people minded their own business while a minority (about a hundred thousand Jews, out of an estimated hundred and forty thousand) were taken away to be murdered. Van Gogh's family . . . was exceptional. His father fought in the resistance, as did his uncle, who was executed by the Germans." During his youth, the family visited this gravesite every year on the fourth of May, the traditional day of remembrance. Van Gogh often referred to the war in his writings. "The jackboots are on the march again," he wrote of the Islamists in Holland, "but this time they wear kaftans and hide behind their beards." As has already been mentioned, he compared Amsterdam's mayor Job Cohen to a collaborator during the German occupation. Theodor Holman (2006), one of van Gogh's closest friends, has written that the remembrance of the Second World War shaped his entire artistic production and also that of van Gogh. Holman's parents spent part of the war in a Japanese concentration camp, an experience they presumably shared with their son. Like the postwar generation in Germany that turned their collective anger against their parents for their alleged or real support of the Nazi regime, their counterparts in the Netherlands reacted against what they perceived as their elders' passivity and silence during the German occupation. As will be further discussed in the following chapter, it was only in the late 1950s and early 1960s that a substantial public discussion about that period took place.

Along with the German occupation, the 1960s themselves were another resource and reference formative for the generation to which Theo van Gogh belonged. According to van der Veer (Veer 2005:11), the sixties marked a turning point in Dutch culture that "was deeply connected to a shift in the social location of religion." Especially among the young, many felt that they had at long last freed themselves from religious constraint and the pillars that had defined Dutch political culture since the founding of the republic in the 1500s. The Labor Party was at the peak of its power and newer, left-leaning parties, like D-66, were making an assertive appearance in Dutch politics. The secularization promised with modernization seemed to have finally arrived. That this might today be threatened by an insurgent Islam is an apprehension that van der Veer points to in his understanding of the strong public reaction to van Gogh's murder. From this perspective, the person of Theo van Gogh symbolized the right to criticize and even mock the most sacred objects and his murder the threat of a religious revival in public life.

In many ways van Gogh was perfectly placed to absorb the antibourgeois, anticlerical revolutionary atmosphere that ran through significant parts of Dutch society during his teenage years, especially after he moved to Amsterdam in the turmoil of the mid-seventies (Ross 2005:28). In an unusual (for his background), though hardly radical move, van Gogh joined the Labor Party at the age of sixteen. More in line with that background, he studied law at university, but dropped out to work as a stage manager, before turning to filmmaking. He directed his first film (Luger) in 1982 and eventually made more than twenty-five motion pictures, several of which won significant awards. Now, after his death, four of his films will be remade with American actors. Van Gogh also produced advertisements and television programs, including the remake of Romeo and Juliet called Najib en Julia, about a Moroccan pizza delivery boy who falls in love with a Dutch girl. It was shown on public television over a five-week period and is currently being used in schools as part of a program to promote integration. Van Gogh wrote columns for the free newspaper *Metro*, and when these became too controversial he continued on his own Internet page and then published collections of his writings as books. The last of these is entitled *Allah weet het beter* (Allah knows best), a collection of his columns from 2002–3. In an interview about this book, van Gogh defended his right to say what he pleased, stating "my use of language is part and parcel of my message" (English translation from the Militant Islam Monitor.org site, September 2, 2004, *www.mili tantislammonitor.org/article/id/269*). In April 2004, just a few months before his murder, van Gogh staged a well-publicized performance addressing the issue of free speech and the Muslim community in the Netherlands. Dressed as an "Imam," complete with false beard and headdress, van Gogh represented the "conservative" Islamic position in a scripted "debate" against the liberal position, here represented by Finance Minister Zalm. The staged event was televised and widely reported in the mass media. Though some labeled him a "nihilist" (Boomkens 2004), van Gogh considered such provocations "functional," claiming that even the most vulgar voice only enlivened the dull Dutch scene. His intention, he often said, was to warn not merely against what he saw as the impending threat of Islam, which he called "the Fifth Column which is trying to hinder our free way of life," but also against a placid and complacent Dutch political culture. The latter point was something with which other, less outspoken, Dutch commentators seemed to agree (Brinks 2005).

Van Gogh was, in other words, someone very conscious of his role in public life. He was relatively successful in his chosen profession of film producer and something more than the bigoted, foul-mouthed village idiot he often referred to himself as. That may have been a role he cherished, but it was not one he invented out of nothing. The Amsterdam counterculture and art scene provided a well-established social space within which to test and create such a public persona. Van Gogh was adept at using mass media to amplify his views and had relatively easy access through his own productions and through his network of well-placed contacts. He also had many role models to draw upon. One of the most notable was that of Jan Cremer, whose memoirs (*I, Jan Cremer*) received worldwide attention. What shocked Dutch readers at least as much as the open sexual lust in that book was the personal pronoun in the title. It was not considered proper in the postwar Netherlands to speak of oneself with such self-assuredness. The focus on oneself struck an older generation as narcissism and arrogance. One look at Cremer's author photo is enough to recognize the pose and posture that van Gogh later assumed. There were also films and filmmakers that helped make visible the Amsterdam scene, and van Gogh followed a trail that had already been blazed. According to Buruma (2006b:96), van Gogh's favorite film was Stanley Kubrick's *A Clockwork Orange*, but the Dutch director Paul Verhoeven was a clear mentor. Verhoeven's first film, *Business Is Business* (1971), was a semidocumentary of Amsterdam street life as seen through the lives of two prostitutes, and *Turkish Delight* (1973), in much the same way as *I, Jan Cremer*, brought Amsterdam brashness to the world stage. This was a career path that van Gogh had marked out for himself, but his timing was off. Unfortunately for him, he chose the wrong sort of vulgarity and misjudged his audience.[30]

As has become even clearer since his death, van Gogh moved in a circle of well-placed, media-oriented literary and visual artists, many of whom had access to the nationally based means of cultural production. This is a circle that has little trouble making itself heard and seen. The name van Gogh was not a hindrance in this; on the contrary, it was a resource—it offered immediate access and recognition. Theo van Gogh was a symbol even before he opened his mouth or put his pen to paper. He merely turned up the volume. If we are to make sense of his actions and what he represented to himself and to others, we need to place him securely within the Dutch art and intellectual scene, at least as it has developed from the 1960s onward. The sixties bohemian attitude has trickled down into contemporary Dutch culture generally and is often identified as one its characteristics, a form of anything-goes directness. Jews and Muslims only provided Theo van Gogh with weapons to attack his prime target, Dutch middle-class conservatism.

SUBMISSION

In addition to the initial shock it caused, the murder of van Gogh greatly affected the intellectual and artistic discourse in the Netherlands; it has become a point of reference. The murder helped articulate and solidify distinctive positions that had been forming at least since the remarkable rise of Pim Fortuyn, when a discursive field began to solidify around the polarities of a clash of civilizations and, more directly, Dutch identity versus Muslim identity. In the media debate and in the public demonstrations of solidarity and protest that followed van Gogh's murder, loose coalitions formed around issues such as the right to free speech, the meaning of Islam, and the internal threat of terrorism. The positions and the personalities of Hirsi Ali and Theo van Gogh were important in this process, though they formed just part of a complex constellation of factors. The possible long-term consequences of this ongoing discursive struggle will be treated in later chapters; here I will restrict myself to the film *Submission* and immediate aftermath of the murder of van Gogh.

The production and broadcast of the film and the possible motivations of Hirsi Ali and Theo van Gogh raised issues that further fractured public discourse. The film forever paired what on the surface looked like a very odd couple, a slovenly bohemian rebel—male, white, and happily overweight—with a delicate, fashion-conscious, upwardly mobile, black woman. What they shared, however, was a desire for an audience and a taste for provocation. Who were they, beyond name and image? For some they were opportunists, who used an explosive issue to gain further celebrity at the expense of Dutch norms of religious tolerance, while slandering Muslims and the Islamic religion in the process. For others they were courageous individuals who defended the right of free expression, while tackling issues that had been taboo but in sore need of discussion. There were many positions in between. Analysis can begin first of all by asking why a film of this nature should be made in the first place. While not so interesting regarding van Gogh, this question is especially relevant for Hirsi Ali. She was already very visible and successful in the literary and political realms. Her written work was widely read; she had public presence and, perhaps even more important, a central place in parliament and public life generally. In addition, she had already received a number of threats on her life. Why, then, make a film with such an explosive context? Hirsi Ali and van Gogh were cognizant of the dangers involved; they knew what they were doing. From her statements, it is clear that Hirsi Ali wanted to reach out to another audience; she sought a public beyond the intellectual and political circles in which she already moved. Her intended audience, she claims, was Muslim women living in the West, those who probably did not read her books or follow parliamentary debate. Not as restricted by language and education, a short televised film (even on public television) might reach both a wider audience and deeper into the one she already commanded. Hirsi Ali was also interested in visual media as means of communicating a political message, her web page displays the tattooed and painted bodies of women, and she had contact with the exiled Iranian artist Shirin Nesat, whose photographic images of Islamic women are powerful and provocative. Film is a more popular and potentially more powerful medium than the written word, and it carries the potential of a wider audience, especially when it is short and shown on television. Part of the answer, then, is that Hirsi Ali wanted to be an artist, as well as an intellectual. Although in places she has claimed her aim was not to provoke, her intentions were largely polemical and political: to make a piece of political art that would provoke a designated audience (Hirsi Ali 2006).[31] As she later told Ian Buruma (2006b:177), "If you want to get a discussion going, and needle people into thinking, you must confront them with dilemmas." A film visualizing sacred texts on naked female flesh with highly charged voice-overs about rape and other forms of violence seemed a likely way to do that, especially given the sensitivities and the taboos of the targeted group.[32]

Van Gogh, on the other hand, was a successful filmmaker and did not need to make another film to prove that, even if he did remain on the margins of the Dutch film industry.[33] Rather, his intention was to make a comedy, a short and funny film with a provocative message about Islamic fundamentalism (Chorus and Olgun 2005:154). The shorter the better, thought van Gogh, and he would later, probably with a touch of irony, call Submission his best film. Hirsi Ali preferred to think of it as tragedy; her idea of provocation was not to make people laugh at themselves through the antics of a jester, but, as quoted above, to confront them with an intellectual and moral dilemma. The dilemma here was that of how to reconcile oneself to a religion, or a culture, that according to her not only condoned but also justified violence against women.

At least between themselves, Hirsi Ali and van Gogh agreed that the film should be provocative about Islam, but they disagreed over how this could be achieved. She wanted to shoot the film in a mosque to further the provocation; he wanted full shots of naked female bodies. They compromised on a studio location, because it offered him more control, and on showing only the top half of the female body. Hirsi Ali wrote the screenplay and did the voice-over; she also selected the woman for the roles. They were all relatively young and dark-skinned, though not all were Muslim. Attractiveness and skin tone appear to be the key signifiers guiding the selection. The bodies of the women had to attract the eye of the viewer, impressing the audience with their beauty, vulnerability, and virtue, at the same time as their dark bodies signified race and sex. Hirsi Ali also selected the music, played by soft flutes, presumably to signify the East. The title, which she chose, was highly symbolic and double-edged. "Submission" is a literal translation of "Islam," carrying the implication that one must submit to the word of God. The film makes it clear that women must also submit to the will of men, who are God's earthly representatives. Islam in Hirsi Ali's representation is a worldview and a system of patriarchal oppression. The battered female bodies in the film are thus expressive of a way of life, not merely of a cruel personality or criminal act. Male violence against women has been a major theme in contemporary debates; Hirsi Ali sides with those who place the blame on "culture"—not on men per se, but on a way of life. In this case, what is at issue is a way of life legitimated through religion.

If the aim was to be provocative, Hirsi Ali and van Gogh certainly succeeded. Though very short and shown to a presumably limited high-brow audience, *Submission* provoked a ferocious debate in the Netherlands and throughout the world. It added to Hirsi Ali's reputation as the Dutch Rushdie and made her into a celebrated "daughter of the enlightenment," with numerous awards, an American publicist, and book-signing tours. It also got van Gogh killed, which probably will secure his place in history. The murderer of van Gogh also achieved a form of celebrity recognition, if not the martyrdom he apparently desired. In a sense, the social drama reached a successful, if not a happy, ending. But did the film manage to reach a wider audience? Did it reach Muslim women and in the way Ali intended? Judging from the public debates that have followed, one can surmise that the film succeeded in engaging at least some Muslim women in the debate, though perhaps no more than had previously been the case. What it more surely achieved, however, was to keep the *issue* of Muslim women in the public eye. The making of *Submission*, the murder of van Gogh, and the celebrity of Hirsi Ali have ensured that the issues of gender and sexuality will be central to any discussion of Islam and the West.[34]

This chapter has focused on the self-presentation of the key actors of the social drama. The search for recognition in a changing Dutch society was something that brought Mohammed B., Ayaan Hirsi Ali, and Theo van Gogh together in the actions that culminated with the murder on November 4, 2004. They were united not only by the narrative that took shape out of the events of the day, but also by their own desire to be seen and recognized. As things unfolded through the rhythms and routines of the mass media, actions became stories and actors characters in a wider narrative of global and historical proportion. Their personal desire for recognition was now securely in the hands of forces over which they had little, if any, control. Before turning to possible outcomes, we need to discuss first some of the already existing frameworks through which the social drama might be interpreted.

CHAPTER 4

THE CLASH OF CIVILIZATIONS:

A MULTICULTURAL

DRAMA

In 2000 I was called a "filthy Turk." After 2001, and the rise of Pim Fortuyn, it was a "filthy foreigner [allochthon]." After Hirsi Ali, it was "filthy Muslim."—**Funda Mujde**

An essay by Paul Scheffer in the NRC *Handelsblad*, the prominent evening newspaper, in January 2000 unexpectedly crystallized a growing uneasiness in the Netherlands concerning the immigrant population in its midst. Carrying the portentous title "The Multicultural Drama," the article warned that current immigration policy, or rather lack of one, had created an underclass whose assimilation into Dutch society was unlikely. Scheffer pointed to a recent government report that predicted that by 2015 there would be more than 2 million "allochthon" in the Netherlands, or about 12 percent of the population and that they would soon compose about 50 percent of the inhabitants of the four largest cities. These immigrants, he stressed, would not come from the United States or Sweden, but from Turkey, Morocco, Suriname, and the Antilles. While Scheffer's intention was probably not to arouse the fears of an anxious Dutch populace, to the contrary he mentioned the anxiety felt by alienated Moroccan youth in Dutch cities, his article spurred a furious debate on immigration policy that has yet to abate. The fact that the author was identified with the intellectual left appeared to add force to his message.[1]

At a higher level of abstraction, and from the opposite side of the political spectrum, Samuel Huntington's provocative notion of a "clash of civilizations" helped solidify this discourse on immigrants and immigration policy that had been dormant at least since the early 1990s. Huntington's phrase was introduced in the Dutch media in 1995, but really came into use after September 11, 2001, and the media-fuelled performance of Islamic fundamentalism. Like Scheffer, Huntington offered a dramatic conceptualization that had the power to simplify and give coherence to a complex phenomenon. Huntington's basic claim was that in the twenty-first century conflicts between nation-states will be replaced by conflicts between civilizations.[2] The struggle would not merely be an economic one between the haves and have-nots, but a cultural one between Western and Eastern civilizations, more specifically Christianity versus Islam. The idea that Islam might constitute a distinctive civilization, it could be thought, might well explain why immigration policy was failing. Even if they were not all "fundamentalist," Muslims were fundamentally different, making their assimilation at the very least problematic. How this framework of interpretation was constructed and what exactly it might mean will be discussed in more detail below. As the debate progressed, it became clear that a multicultural drama had evolved into a clash of civilizations.[3]

When it first appeared in 1997, Pim Fortuyn's *De Islamisering van onze cultuur: Nederlandse identiteit als fundament* (The Islamization of our culture: Dutch identity as foundational) received relatively little notice. Contemporary reviews identified the author as "an ex-professor, ex-student politician, ex–left wing social democrat" (*Volkskrant*, February 14, 1997) and, more simply, as a "publicist." In the aftermath of the unprecedented media coverage of the attack on the World Trade Center in New York, a second edition appeared, with a new chapter on the significance of that event and a "critical response" by Imam Abdullah R. F. Haselhoef, identified as a "spiritual adviser." The cover photograph featured a "Western"-clad Fortuyn and an "Eastern"-clad Haselhoef seated closely face to face with the phrase "The word as weapon" connecting/separating them. The selection of Haselhoef and his positioning on the cover of Fortuyn's book carried added irony in that the imam had recently made forceful public comments about homosexuals, declaring, among other things, that they be condemned to death, "providing that at least four eyewitnesses could attest to the act of sodomy" (Ireland 2004:139). In this new context, Fortuyn's book met with great success. It also helped clarify the alternatives between multiculturalism and assimilation that were at the core of what now was a very heated debate.[4] Fortuyn's argument presumed and helped solidify the idea that Islam represented a civilization, one that threatened Dutch national identity. As part of Western civilization, Dutch culture was represented as a coherent whole with four fundamental elements: individual over collective responsibility, the separation of church and state, mutual respect between the sexes, and the same between children and adults. It was assumed that Islam, as another civilization, had different views on these matters, no matter that Haselhoef argued the opposite. Less than a year later, Fortuyn was murdered, and the urge to engage in public dialogue was dramatically threatened. As opposed to sustained dialogue, a process of positioning and polarization that had begun in earnest after 9/11 gained more momentum.

Theo van Gogh and Ayaan Hirsi Ali were both shaped by and active agents of this process. While van Gogh could be more easily dismissed as the village idiot, as a member of parliament and a former Muslim Hirsi Ali especially was important in solidifying the clash of civilizations framework, which itself was given new force in the emerging "war on terror" after 9/11. For her part, Hirsi Ali claimed that Islam was at the root of the issue of integration; immigrants, now meaning Muslims, could not be integrated as long as they identified themselves as such and adhered to Islam. Following Fortuyn and van Gogh, Hirsi Ali labeled Islam a "backward civilization." Assimilation to "Western" values was thus the only possible way forward. From this perspective, *Submission* was an intervention within a polarizing discursive field; as such, the film helped visualize the clash of civilizations. After van Gogh's murder, the clash became a war, with the filmmaker an early casualty, while his killer, a failed martyr, was, from the other side, transformed into a prisoner of war. For her part, Hirsi Ali continued the campaign on the political and intellectual battlefields. Words had indeed become weapons.

The murder of van Gogh thus occurred in a context where phrases like "clash of civilizations," "Islamic fundamentalism," and "the war on terror" were freely circulating and these were important in explaining how the murder was interpreted. The American presidential elections, occurring at the same time, were an additional reference point and source of phrasing. No less symbolically important than the assassin's choice of weapons in the murder was van Gogh's own clothing. Because he planned to attend a public forum on the coming American elections, van Gogh wore red, white, and blue suspenders as he cycled to work the morning of November 4, 2004, the national colors of both the United States and the Netherlands. As noted previously, the day following the murder high-level Dutch officials and the leading newspapers declared the country to be at war. In this highly charged context, there seemed to be no middle position, one was on one side or the other, for Western values or against them.

In the months and years following the murder, Hirsi Ali continued to articulate the clash of civilizations confrontational approach, even as many in the leadership of her party, and elsewhere, softened their position. This included some leading members of her own party who now joined those encouraging development of a "Dutch Islam." In the midst of a struggle for party leadership, Hirsi Ali published a full-page polemic in the *Volkskrant* (April 8, 2006) under the headline "Confrontation, Appeasement" complete with the infamous 1938 photograph of British prime minister Neville Chamberlain waving a letter signed by Adolf Hitler and proclaiming "peace in our time." The highly symbolic photograph added to the textual message: Europe and the Netherlands cannot afford once again to be caught sleeping, as if it were the task of the Dutch to alert the world to impending danger. Calling forth the ghosts of Chamberlain and Hitler and at least implicitly identifying Islam with the fascism, Hirsi Ali called for strong Churchillian leadership in the new war of civilizations. Images from the Second World War weigh heavily on the Dutch imagination, and, like van Gogh, Hirsi Ali has learned how to make use of them. In the immediate context, Hirsi Ali's message seemed to be that her party and Dutch society in general needed the strong leadership offered by Rita Verdonk, the current immigration minister, who had become a symbol of toughness on immigration issues and who was then involved in a struggle for leadership of the VVD. One month later, Minister Verdonk would revoke Hirsi Ali's Dutch citizenship (as mentioned previously) on the grounds that she had offered false information in her original application for political asylum.[5] Immigration had clearly become more than an issue; it was itself now part of a social drama of major proportion.

IMMIGRANTS AND IMMIGRATION POLICY: FROM MULTICULTURALISM TO ASSIMILATION

As much as it was polemical and dramatic, Scheffer's article was also performative in suggesting there was no immigration policy or policy discussion in the Netherlands. Scheffer would have his words do things: while insisting there was no immigration policy, he was actually out to change the one that existed. Far from having no immigration policy, the

Netherlands had been a model for Europe from the 1970s onward. Along with Sweden, the Netherlands was an early proponent of multiculturalism, and it is this policy, rather than the lack of one, that was the brunt of Scheffer's polemic. The "Dutch Model" was forged in the 1980s, but a central plank was laid already in 1979 in the form of an "Ethnic Minority Policy" that specified funding for the "most important" ethnic minorities (Turks, Moroccans, Southern Europeans, Moluccans, Surinamese, Antillians, and Roma or Gypsies) to allow them to organize advisory bodies for the purpose of self-representation (Vasta 2007). This form of corporatism followed an already established Swedish initiative, whereby ethnic minorities were added to the list of "representative groups" that, in addition to individual citizens, were thought to compose society. Individuals representing "their" ethnic group or "immigrants" generally were then admitted to governing bodies and given the mandate to voice the opinion of that group. Such advisory bodies continue to exist in the Netherlands, but are accorded less authority (Uitermark et al. 2005). Also, similarly to Sweden, the Netherlands initiated a policy of "home-language" study, which gave ethnic minorities the possibility to educate their children in their native languages, alongside their training in Dutch, and support was given to radio and television programs in these "most important" minority languages. While some of this was the result of newly formulated multicultural policy, much of it stemmed from the much older tradition of pillarization, the system of social segregation that legitimated state subsidy for private religious education. What was different however, was the fact that the earlier model was built around worldviews, while the new division rested on ethnicity, something that contributed not only to their "difference" but also to affirming an ideal of Dutchness. It was this tradition that has allowed immigrant groups to vie for funding for religious schools, which Muslims also have done in the recent past. This has evolved into a basic value conflict, the right to religious education versus the desire for cultural integration and assimilation, an issue on which Hirsi Ali has taken a strong stand. Under the earlier versions of the Dutch model, the basic value conflict was less of an issue than it is today, especially as Islam has been deemed an alternative civilization and not just a religion. This shift in interpretation and designation, from religion to civilization is crucial to understanding the emotional context in which the murder of Theo van Gogh occurred.

Until recently, then, Dutch immigration policy was guided by a vaguely defined multiculturalism that offered ethnic minorities the right to maintain aspects of their native culture. The unspoken goal was that this would make their integration into Dutch society smoother, and that they would not continue to live separate lives.[6] That was the point of having representative bodies. As early as 1989, however, a government report on immigration policy pointed to problems with the type of multiculturalism being encouraged, stating that more emphasis on integrating immigrants was necessary (Geddes 2003:116). In the early 1990s came the first call for a more "realistic" look at the immigrant population. This was articulated by Frits Bolkestein, the leader of the VVD and later mentor of Hirsi Ali, in an article in the *Volkskrant* (September 1991) carrying the headline "The Integration of Minorities Must Be Openly Discussed" ("Integratie van minderheden moet met lef worder worden aangepakt") (Prins 2000:25). Written in the context of the Iranian revolution and the fatwa against Salman Rushdie (discussed in the next chapter), the immigrants that most interested Bolkestein were Muslims.[7] This was also one of the first articulations of a "Dutch way of life." Then, in 1998, there were signs of a more active engagement, when it was made obligatory that newly arrived immigrants receive up to 600 hours of language instruction, civic education, and career counseling. Most of these initiatives came from the conservative side of the political spectrum, primarily from the VVD, the party to which Hirsi Ali would be recruited. The left continued to define successful integration primarily in economic, rather than cultural terms. If it supported such initiatives as Dutch language instruction, it was from the point of view of helping immigrants in the labor market.

It was this "soft" multiculturalism that Scheffer targeted. What he considered "soft" was the apparent concern with labor-market integration and by implication the hands-off attitude toward culture and private life. This attack on multiculturalism, which some call a "new realism" (Prins 2000) and others "civic nationalism" (Geddes 2003:117), opened the way for Pim Fortuyn, who successfully transformed a discourse into a national political platform and himself into a celebrity. What began as an intellectual discourse and then became a populist political platform had now moved into the mainstream and opened a debate of the basic foundations of Dutch society. The murder of van Gogh was an important catalyst in this process, and public intellectuals like Ayaan Hirsi Ali were central carriers.

Migration flows to the Netherlands can be described in historical phases.[8] Lucassen and Penninx (1997:87) distinguish three: from the seventeenth century to the end of the republic and the founding of the kingdom in 1815 "when the Netherlands was an immigration country *par excellence*"; from the nineteenth century until 1970, when migration was limited and nationality was defined by the nation-state; and, finally, from the 1980s to the present, when new waves of migration and an "internationalization of immigration policy in the context of the European Union" are defining characteristics.

Some of the earliest migrants in the first phase were groups suffering religious persecution elsewhere, such as Protestant Huguenots fleeing France (between 50,000 and 60,000 settled in the early Dutch Republic) and Jews from Portugal and Spain (between 10,000 and 20,000), as well as Westphalian Germans (Dieleman 1993:118). The most significant migrations since then occurred after the Second World War, as the Dutch lost important parts of the colonial empire it had acquired from the seventeenth century onward. When Indonesia became independent in 1949 after a long struggle against Dutch and allied forces, about 250,000 people had to be repatriated to the Netherlands, many of them of mixed ethnicity. A much smaller, though ethnically significant group arrived from the Moluccan Islands, primarily ex-soldiers who had fought alongside the Dutch in Indonesia. In the 1970s, smaller groups arrived in the Netherlands from colonies in South America and the Caribbean.

Apart from postcolonial migration, more recent immigrant flows have more to do with economic than political factors, though refugees seeking asylum are still important to consider. For our purposes, the most important economic migrants were those recruited from Turkey and Morocco in the 1970s. By 1989 there were 176,500 immigrants of Turkish origin and 139,000 of Moroccan origin living in the country (Dieleman 1993:122). The numbers had risen to 357,911 and 314,699 respectively in 2005 out of a total population of 16,294,847. When looked at as a whole and in the current vernacular, "the 2005 population is composed of 13 million autochtonen, 1.6 million non-Western allochtonen (primarily Turks, Surinamese and Moroccans) and 1.4 million Western allochtonen" (Schenk 2006:12).[9]

As important as their number, the painful forced return of Dutch citizens and their supporting cohorts from former colonies in the East Indies was highly significant to Dutch collective identity. Though formal assimilation of these Dutch citizens went relatively smoothly in the 1950s, the process of postcolonial migration is still something difficult for many to speak publicly about. The numbers are significant; as Lucassen and Penninx (1997:39) put it, "In a period of thirty years, from 1945 to 1975, 273,000 more people from Indonesia settled in the Netherlands than left the Netherlands for Indonesia." In addition to those repatriated from Indonesia, there were groups returning from New Guinea, when the Dutch were forced out in 1962 and from Dutch Guyana (Suriname) in the 1970s and the Antilles and Aruba. These postcolonial migration flows are still a source of ambivalence in discussions of Dutch national identity and add an underlying emotion to any current debates about immigration and immigration policy. Already in the 1950s, when the repatriation of people from the Dutch East Indies was occurring, there were fears expressed about perceived threats to Dutch culture and society: how would these "darker" and "racially mixed" people be assimilated?[10] These fears were revived in the 1970s with the dramatic hijacking and hostage taking carried out by Moluccan youths. Yet the first wave of economic "guest workers" were more than welcome as cheap labor recruited to do the jobs others were unwilling to do.[11]

This began to change with the oil and energy crises in the early 1970s. The crises were not merely a Dutch problem, but along with other restructuring they greatly affected the need for the type of labor that immigrants from Turkey and Morocco had originally been recruited to do. By the time their unemployment rates began to climb, these "guest workers" had brought their families with them and were living in increasingly segregated neighborhoods in the urban conglomerate known as the Randstad in the western part of the country. The making of an underclass marked by color and creed was in formation.

Why have "immigrants" been transformed from welcome guests to a social problem? The statistical "facts" are not in dispute. Are factors like high unemployment, youth crime, and school drop-out rates sufficient to explain not only the concern but also the "failure" of integration policy? Is this "failure" explained by "low human capital," rooted in the "backwardness" of Islamic religion or Muslim culture, as Hirsi Ali would have it? Or, as Vasta (2007: abstract) suggests, does the explanation lie in a "pervasive institutional discrimination and the persistence of a culture of racism" in the Netherlands. The answer concerning significance lies only partly in these numbers and in the changing conditions of the labor market and any institutionalized racism. Much of the explanation lies, first of all, in the visibility of "immigrants" who will not or cannot become Dutch, those who refuse to become "like us." Another part of the answer lies in who or what "they" represent. As Scheffer noted in his article, these are not immigrants from Sweden or the United States. When they are defined as being part of another civilization, those with Muslim backgrounds are significant beyond their numbers, especially when they are clustered together in segregated neighborhoods and wear distinctive garments in public places.

While religious tolerance may have been a founding ideal, the Netherlands has an equally long history of religious segregation and social indifference, generally known more favorably as pillarization (Lijphart 1966). It also has its own Mason-Dixon line, the Maas River, which not only separates north and south but also the Calvinist and Catholic traditions. In his history of Amsterdam, Geert Mak presents some horrific tales of the methods used by the Catholic elite in the city to repress the emerging Protestant sects in the 1500s. This, of course, was before the foundation of the Dutch Republic, but ever since the end of the war with Spain in 1648 and the nation's emergence, the country remains divided between a predominantly Protestant north and Catholic south, though Mak (interview, April 2006) also remarks that, at least currently, Dutch Catholics are very Calvinistic. The traumatic experience of occupation during the Second World War and the rebuilding process in its aftermath helped forge social solidarity through common suffering and purpose, yet the old religious divisions remained largely in place. Following the war, there was a Catholic resurgence in Europe generally, and the centrality of Christian parties in postwar reconstruction at first pushed Catholic voters to the left (Judt 2005:80) and then, with the emergence of the Cold War, to the right. The fear of atheistic communism was so strong that Dutch Catholics who voted for the newly formed PvdA faced excommunication (ibid.:228). Those growing up in the 1950s who experienced the first sensations of consumer culture and the rise of the secular Labor Party (PvdA) still recall living in largely segregated communities, either Protestant or Catholic (Veer 2006). It is not uncommon even today to hear southern Catholics say that they feel uncomfortable in the North, and when an English speaker refers to the Netherlands as "Holland" this adds to their unease, as the name refers to the northern provinces alone.

Segregation along religious lines is thus nothing new to the Netherlands. In fact, the integration of Catholics into Protestant Netherlands has for some become the model of successful integration that should now be applied to Muslims (Vasta 2007). On the other side, some have compared the current fear of Muslims with that felt toward Catholics in previous centuries (Casanova 2005). Until Pim Fortuyn, there was little political exploitation of immigration issues, though his idea that "the Netherlands is full" in fact has a rather long history. What was new, and widespread especially after 9/11 and the officially declared war on terror, was that one could now speak openly in public about the immigration "problem." This marked a decided shift from the 1980s, when it was still considered a "taboo" (Vuijsje 1986). As mentioned above, Frits Bolkestein was the first major Dutch political leader to pose the issue of a potentially troubling relationship between the Islamic minority and the non-Islamic majority in the Netherlands. His central point was there could be no accommodation or compromise with the liberal principles that he claimed as foundational to Dutch society. This left two alternatives: allowing Muslims to form their own pillar or to force assimilation. This is essentially where the issue stands to this day. Bolkestein's own position was to recognize the Muslim minority as forming a separate but equal part of the Dutch community. The public debate that followed Bolkestein's article lasted more than a year before it quietly disappeared until 2000, when Scheffer opened up the issue once more with his multicultural drama. This lack of public discussion did not mean that nothing was happening beneath the surface in Dutch society.

FRAMING ISLAM AND MUSLIM IMMIGRANTS

As mentioned in the opening chapter, a survey carried out in 2005 found that 51 percent of native Dutch citizens "admitted to unfavorable views towards Muslims." This was slightly higher than in Germany and significantly higher than in the United States (Haan 2007:2). Public attention to the presence of Muslim immigrants had been slowly growing. In the months following Scheffer's newspaper article, a conflict concerning the use of school classrooms for prayers by Muslim students received some media attention. At the end of the year 2000, an opera included as part of a series of performances meant to highlight multiculturalism in Rotterdam was cancelled when "Moroccan artists had to withdraw under the pressure of certain Muslim circles, which considered this play staged around one of Prophet Muhammad's wives unacceptable" (Meuleman 2007:5). This was soon followed by a debate concerning the wearing of headscarves at work after a woman was refused a position as a court clerk when she stated her intention to wear a scarf on the job (Cherribi 2003:196–97).

With the clash of civilizations providing the interpretive frame, the Dutch discussion concerning immigration policy became more focused on Muslim immigrants and their assimilation, most particularly those from Turkey and Morocco. Moroccans especially were singled out as a particularly troublesome group. In a much reported incident, two teenagers beat a man to death in October 2002 after he commented on their motor-scooter driving habits. One of the perpetrators was of Moroccan descent. When the boy's parents were interviewed on national television in their native language and appeared to explain the killing as the will of God, it caused a fury of attention. As Stengs (n.d.:8) writes, "The entire picture of the parents, unemployed, unable to speak Dutch after having lived in the country for decades, and their 'unworldly' perception of the cause of [the victim's] death, led to immediate political conclusions and actions: the Dutch integration policy was declared bankrupt and more severe policy measures initiated."[12] Since that event, other incidents involving what Stengs calls "senseless violence" have occurred, including one widely reported case in January 2005 in which a woman whose handbag had been snatched backed her car into her attacker and killed him. The purse-snatcher was a young man of Moroccan background, and the furious reaction to his death by neighbors and friends only enhanced the media coverage. Moroccans appear to be closely associated with violence and considered "dangerous" in the popular consciousness, and the fact that many are Muslims has not gone unnoticed.

Studies of the crime rates of ethnic groups in the Netherlands have been a taboo area (Haan 1997). However, those that have been carried out, such as the one by Junger and Polder (1992), reveal a lower percentage of native Dutch involved in comparable categories. Junger and Polder's study of arrest rates among youth in three ethnic minorities—Moroccans, Turks, and Surinamese—were higher among Dutch youth, with Moroccan youth having the highest arrest frequency (34 percent). While they offer a range of explanations as to why this might be the case, such figures as well as those showing higher rates of unemployment and use of the social welfare system, contribute to the image of Moroccans as a "problematic" ethnic minority. Speaking with authorities at youth detention centers, however, one finds an "over representation" of Moroccan boys in their care, but also an "under representation" of Turkish boys and of Moroccan girls. The Moroccan boys appear to have made the most impression on the public imagination.

Besides criminality and listless hanging out, another aspect of the popular image of Muslims (especially those of Moroccan descent) is that of clannishness and collective traditional control rather than the individualism that is taken to be characteristic of modern society and, according to Pim Fortuyn, a key aspect of Dutchness. The stereotypical image of Muslims as that of a religious collectivity tightly bound by tradition and watched over by a religious leadership is nuanced by gender and age distinctions. Hirsi Ali has both built on and reinforced such images, while at the same time claiming to fight against them. Writing about what she identifies as "the world of Islam," Hirsi Ali (2006b:47) speaks of "the Islamic identity," claiming it "is based on groups, and its central concepts are honor and disgrace, or shame. The relevant groups, in order of size, are the family, the clan, the tribe, and, ultimately, the community of the faithful (umman)." While males are viewed as dangerous, clannish aggressors, females are viewed as passive victims in need of support. Muslim woman generally are seen as uneducated, tradition-bound, and oppressed by a patriarchal culture. There are some age distinctions in these images, with younger women, especially those born in the Netherlands, given more potential to adjust to modern society. And if Hirsi Ali does have an audience among Muslim women, it is most likely within this age group.

Another issue of stereotyping and contention concerns presumed attitudes toward homosexuals and homosexuality. In May 2001 a televised debate about Dutch Muslims, Islam, and homosexuality was broadcast on a popular debate program. Shown on a major network, it featured interviews with Moroccan youths in Amsterdam, some of whom made aggressive remarks and a prominent Dutch imam who, when unexpectedly asked about homosexuality, called it an infectious disease (Prins 2000:39; see Cherribi 2003:204–5 for another viewpoint). A great public outcry and media discussion followed. A producer for the program later said that after this segment was aired they received more letters, including hate mail, than for any other. In one of his newspaper columns, van Gogh defended the imam's right to express his opinions in the name of free speech. Hirsi Ali has added what she sees as the Islamic stigmatization of homosexuality to many of her speeches and interviews, though no mention is usually made of the views of some Christian groups.

In this framing process individuals and groups are placed together into categories that simplify and highlight certain features. This is the nature of stereotyping. The many layers and divisions among Muslim immigrants are thus erased. In an early study of Muslim immigrants in the Netherlands, Shadid (1991) listed several distinctive Muslim sects within the broader ethnic distinctions, such as those between Turks and Moroccans. One of the effects of such categorization, whether it is formally done by authorities or in the vernacular language of the media and the street, is that those placed in the categories are treated as a collective and may even be encouraged to react as one. When inhabitants from Turkey and Morocco are treated as "Muslims" and as "immigrants," they may well take on these characterizations, and join together even as they strongly resent the comparisons. In fact, Verkuyten (1991, 2002) has shown that processes of self-definition among ethnic groups form in opposition to other ethnic groups in the society, including the "Dutch." These studies conclude that the lower the status of an ethnic group, the more likely they are to maintain a strong sense of ethnic identity. With Moroccans appearing lower on the Dutch scale, one could assume that Turks might greatly resent being categorized together with them. Dutch Turks appear to share something of the dominant culture's view of Moroccans, at the same time as they view themselves as very different, especially concerning the distinction between what is traditional and what is modern (Horst 2006). Moroccans, on the other hand, are forced to confront their ascribed status and the associated stereotypes every day. Berbers, who make up the vast majority of immigrants of Moroccan descent, become Moroccans and are parceled together with Arabs, as well as with Turks and others with whom they share a religion. It happens to be the case that they are primarily Sunni Muslims. In this mix of ascribed identifications, religion might well be taken on as something that unites a collective otherwise stratified and distinct. Secular Muslims might become religious in part because they are so identified, and religion might well offer a sense of positive identity and social recognition in a context where that is denied in other spheres.

The effect of such framing is to position Muslims within an already existing discourse, as part of a civilization that is clashing with another. Moroccans are dually placed, first, as part of this "civilization" and, second, in an ethnic hierarchy, where they are at a lower rank than Turks. The latter status positioning is interesting to look at in national comparison, for just across the border in Germany, one might find an opposite ranking, with Moroccans having a higher standing than Turks.

FRAMING DUTCHNESS

An unspoken aspect of the discourse on immigrants with Islamic backgrounds is how Dutch identity is being represented. This is another side of a meaning conflict where various parties struggle to define a situation through constructing representations of an Other, an outsider against which to constitute themselves as a group. As is often the case, this is an asymmetrical struggle, with some having more power than others, measured in terms of access to the means of representation, as well as money and other resources. This points to the importance of well-placed agents, whom some would call cultural entrepreneurs, individuals in a position to articulate and piece together the frameworks of meaning and interpretation and spur collective identity formation. In the current case, framing Muslims as problematic immigrants is bound up with articulating an idea of its opposite, Dutchness. This needs exploring. Further, in discussing framing processes one should take into account the political and social context in which such framing takes place, including the wider cultural reservoir that serves as a resource of narratives, symbols, and images from which one can draw. The framing process is much more than discursive because deeply felt emotions are bound up with cognitive aspects, as those symbols and story lines one draws upon from the reservoir of collective representations are laden with emotional meaning.[13]

Until this current confrontation with Islam, the Dutch discourse on national identity had been muted. Many explain this by an appeal to history: the traumatic experience of German occupation by ferociously nationalistic Nazis resulted in a situation where it became aberrant to express anything that resembled nationalistic sentiments. A grade school principal noted that there was no standard textbook to teach Dutch history, that each school could more or less make its own choice. He explained this as a residue of the Second World War, going on to say that the only form of national identity that could be enthusiastically displayed was support for the national sports teams. A similar phenomenon exists in Germany and Italy. It is not uncommon to deny there is anything like Dutch national identity. This is especially so, since articulating patriotic sentiments has been taboo and denying their existence is part of the same process. The denial of patriotic emotions and of strong collective identity is something that Fortuyn (2002), a key figure in articulating a collective identity as well as in identifying the Other, found problematic and claimed as a weakness in the face of what he described as the onslaught of Islam. As others including Samuel Huntington (2004) would do later, Fortuyn sought to remind "the Dutch" of who they were and what they stood for. The current government has carried this further through introducing mandatory tests for aspiring immigrants, which may potentially be applied to those already in the country.

WHAT IS DUTCH?

Rather than a formal process of becoming a citizen, being Dutch connotes a sense of collective belonging, identification with an imaginary collective, that is more deeply felt than carrying a passport or an ID card. Like other small, centrally located European nations, the Netherlands attempted to find its identity in resisting the cultural as well as political domination of its neighbors. As Mathijs (2004:3) writes in discussing films of the Low Countries, the Dutch were caught between "historically dominant cultures: the British to the west, the French to the south, and the Germans to the east." In the struggle to free itself against Catholic Spain, the emerging Dutch nation could turn this oppositional struggle into something positive: the opening phrase of the Dutch national anthem contains the words "We are of Germanic stock." As the new nation was founded, however, identity was largely local, more linked to family, village, and province than anything else: "Place of birth was the most important criterion by which newcomers were distinguished from the native-born in the early days of the Republic (Lucassen and Penninx 1997:87). The fact of being a republic rather than a monarchy, as were many of its neighbors, was also important in framing early national identity (Israel 1998). Religion was a central feature, however, and also a significant factor in the social cleavages that both united and distinguished the native-born from outsiders. Personal wealth and family status were key indicators of social position within the religious groupings.

According to Schama (1987:69), the meaning of Dutchness stabilized after the war of liberation fought against Spain and the founding of the republic in 1648. "Dutch patriotism was not the cause, but the consequence, of the revolt against Spain. Irrespective of its invention after the fact, however, it became a powerful focus of allegiance," with "Calvinism, humanism and commercial pragmatism" (1987:67) as its core sources of inspiration. Calvinism promoted sobriety and restraint, yet, as Max Weber also pointed out, it could accommodate riches and material strivings. Mak (1999:76) also claims Calvinism as an ideological sustenance in the rebellion against Spain, as it provided "the ideal banner under which the good fight could be fought . . . the parallel between the Children of Israel and the people of God in the Low Countries by the sea was unavoidable. It was a message that was to be repeated and reinforced in thousands of works of art and tens of thousands of writings and sermons until well into the seventeenth century." Calvinism not only grounded a rebellion against established authority; it also provided an ethic to guide daily life, as it permitted combining individual freedom with an ethic of restraint in much the way Weber has described the Protestant ethic. For Mak (1999:77), this evolved into a "typically Dutch way of using the law, a modus operandi governed by civic opportunism: the state is entitled to prosecute a crime, but it is not bound to do so, especially if the means of prosecution is deemed to be worse than the crime—as, for instance, in the case of prostitution, or the use of soft drugs" (77). Similarly, Hirsi Ali calls upon a Dutch "frame of reference" (2006a:57), a system of norms and taken-for-granted expectations that characterize everything from dealing with conflicts to styles of leadership and politics. In the arts and crafts there exists a long history of referring to "Dutchness" to mark distinctive ways of making and doing. In the graphic arts, for instance, it is common to speak of a distinctive Dutch style and to offer illustrative examples.

While themes of rebellion and heroic political struggle and those emphasizing home and family have competed in ideas of Dutchness, Schama (1987:15–50) depicts a Dutch "moral geography" based on reclamation, of individuals as well as land. He recounts a narrative that featured trial by water as a means of reclaiming individuals for society in which floods and the flooding of lands were formative of a sense of collective belonging in the years that preceded Dutch independence from Spain. Here humanistic ideals of community were linked to Calvinist notions of the divine providence of a chosen people. "The making of new land belongs to God alone for He gives to some people the wit and the strength to do it," as Andries Vierlingh, a sixteenth-century hydraulic engineer expressed it (cited in Schama 1987:35). Responsibility for one's self and for others in the struggle against the sea battled against internal social distinctions grounding a specifically "Dutch" conception of the relation between the individual and the collective. According to Schama (1987:35), these were the grounding ideals (some, like van Boxsel [Boxsel 2004], would rather call them myths) of the new nation: "compounded in their determination not to yield to foreign tyrants what had been laboriously wrested from the sea were the historical title of ancestral reclamation, and the moral title awarded those whose work had created the land, and the scriptural title that survived against the flood was a token of divine ordination." It is here perhaps that one can locate the origin of the distinction between autochthon and allochthon, those who are part of us and those who never will be.

It was the Catholic philosopher Erasmus who introduced the concept of tolerance (also, some claim, an Islamic virtue) to the Dutch discussion as a result of his dialogue with Martin Luther, the Protestant leader. The reality in which their exchange took place, however, was not very tolerant. During the Catholic Inquisition, 877 death sentences were handed down in the Netherlands, and Mak catalogs some terrible examples of religious intolerance during the Eighty Years War (1568–1648). When Protestants fled north in the early 1600s, they were treated as inferior and as uncouth. Calls for understanding and tolerance came from the pulpit, however. As one preacher declared in the Old Church in Amsterdam in 1614, "And that is to be lamented most, that those from Brabant and Flanders who have fled to Holland because of the persecutions, to seek refuge here, have brought their arrogant manners here with them. . . . You Hollanders, though having a more arrogant manner than yours may look good on a Brabanter, should not imitate this arrogance, but should keep to your modesty and humility" (cited in Lucassen and Penninx 1997:123). However, the Dutch Republic became a haven for those persecuted elsewhere, including philosophers like René Descartes and John Locke. The freedom of the press in the republic also allowed works by Jean-Jacques Rousseau and Thomas Hobbes to appear in print (Lucassen and Penninx (1997:22–

24). The humanist tradition, represented by Erasmus, and the Enlightenment by Spinoza are often pointed to in discussions of Dutch identity.

From the early nineteenth century onward, the idea of the Netherlands as a Christian nation composed of virtuous and pious citizens, a moral as well as political community, formed a central theme in discourses of national identity. To this was later added the idea that the Dutch identity also grounded a national mission: to be a moral guide to other, larger and more powerful, nations. As a "small people but a great nation," the Dutch could build on their humanist traditions and be exemplary to their more power-hungry neighbors. As Dudink (2002) shows, these ideals were set uneasily alongside those which found a source of national pride in the colonial empire; however, it was possible to reconcile them by claiming that the Dutch ruled their colonies in a very different manner, one that was humane.

Unifying notions of Dutchness, however rooted they may appear, are bound up with internal tensions and ambiguity as well as conflict. One of the main lines of contest in Dutch political history from the nineteenth century onward has been that between Christian groups and liberals. "The first wished to base the state and its politics on the Bible and on Calvinist dogma (the Catholics, who joined the Liberals to free themselves from the discrimination to which they had long been subject, later formed an alliance with the Protestant parties). The second, who were heirs of the Enlightenment and in some respects of the principles of the French Revolution, wanted a secularized neutral state" (Von der Dunk 1967:171). Such splits can still be found today in the controversy surrounding debates on immigration.

To the extent one believes that Calvinism and Christianity more generally are central to being Dutch, one would worry about a perceived invasion of Muslims and feel threatened by veiled women and the number of mosques being built. These are fears that Fortuyn, a Roman Catholic, enflamed. Fortuyn's triad of Dutch identity—the separation of church and state, the notion of equality between the sexes, and that of the relative equality between adults and children—has been extended by his followers to include "Judeo-Christian and humanist" traditions, something some would like to see added to the Dutch constitution.[14] This follows from similar attempts to have the phrase included in the European Union's constitution. One of Fortuyn's main claims is that the Dutch and the West generally have become indifferent to "their own culture." This indifference he traces to the end of the Cold War with the fall of the Berlin Wall in 1989 and with that the loss of any distinctive opposing force, communism, against which to define one's own identity. Islamic fundamentalism now provides such a force and thus an opportunity to reestablish the values that define the "West" and within that context to revitalize the meaning of being Dutch.[15] It is important to remember that as the "iron curtain" was descending in the early postwar years, battle lines between East and West were also being drawn; at that time the East meant the Soviet Union and its satellites and the West meant the newly forming NATO alliance. Religion or the lack of it was also a central feature of this divide, as the "Judeo-Christian" West fought against the "godless communism" of the East. As late as 2004, when a new European constitution was being discussed, newly included former communist states like Poland, Lithuania, and Slovakia, tried to include the phrase "Christian" in the document (Judt 2005:767). The Dutch politician Geert Wilders, follower of Fortuyn and former close ally of Hirsi Ali, attempted to make a similar addition to the Dutch constitution.

While not so outspokenly locating their foundations within Christian or humanist values, the current Dutch government has attempted to concretize being Dutch through the mandatory testing for prospective immigrants and long-term visitors to the Netherlands from non-Western countries. Previous policy was primarily confined to language skills and aimed at helping the newly arrived with finding employment, housing, and the basics of daily social interaction. Mandatory testing now includes wider historical and cultural knowledge, as well as taken-for-granted norms of acceptable behavior, such as riding public transport and visiting a public beach. The test, called an "integration examination," consists of two parts: knowledge of Dutch society and competence in the use of the Dutch language (Naar Nederland). Knowledge of Dutch society is examined through answering a series of 100 questions. These questions are provided in written and picture format and the proper answers can be gleaned from the accompanying hour-long video. The video comes in two versions, censored and uncensored, which the purchaser may choose. When I bought mine in an Amsterdam bookshop, the clerk was very clear about explaining the different options to me. The objects of censorship are images of bare-breasted women and men kissing, both of which are part of the section on the liberalization of Dutch sexual mores following the 1960s cultural revolution.

The instructional video is made in the style of a travelogue, the kind often shown on airplanes and buses upon one's arrival in a foreign country. The main difference is that despite the chatty presentation what is shown can be interpreted as an obvious attempt to lower rather than raise expectations about the country and its climate. The moderator, an attractively dressed young woman with a pleasant voice and friendly demeanor, guides us through the landing at Schiphol Airport and onto the public transportation that will take us to Amsterdam. Along the way we are given instructions on what to expect, the cold, damp weather, the individualism of the population, and the punctuality of the public transport. Buses and trains wait for no one in the Netherlands! The history lesson consists of a fifteen-minute sweep through Dutch history, starting with the Eighty Years War to free Protestant Netherlands from tyrannical Catholic rule. The rebellion, we are told, was led by William of Orange, who was later assassinated on the orders of the Spanish king. Images of William are followed by those of the current queen, portraying continuity in the monarchy. The Treaty of Utrecht of 1648 is mentioned as the founding document of the new country, in which religious tolerance, between Catholics and Protestants, is a central feature. The question is raised how such a small country could become so powerful and command so many colonies. The answer given concerns shipping and commerce, with the Dutch East and West India Companies highlighted. Trade is foremost in the presentation, but slavery is also mentioned and pictured, with special reference given to the transport of slaves from Africa to the Dutch colony of Suriname in South America. It is also noted that in the 1700s, half of the Dutch population consisted of foreigners. The French Revolution is mentioned, to suggest that the Netherlands are part of Europe, but also that this event spurred the reigning Dutch king to reform the constitution, to separate church and state, and to found a parliament. The struggle of Dutch Catholics for their own schools is highlighted as having led to the establishment of the first political parties, and the workers' movement is credited with pushing through universal education and other social reforms. The struggle for woman's suffrage is also pictured.

The Second World War and the German occupation form an important segment of the film. The neutrality of the Netherlands at the beginning of the war is mentioned, as is the bombing of Rotterdam. The treatment of Dutch Jews is discussed with reference to Anne Frank, her diary, and the house in which she hid. The fact that Anne Frank was betrayed and died in a concentration camp is mentioned, but nothing about who might have done this or why. Coverage of the postwar period begins with the image of Willem Drees, presented as a politician active in the Dutch resistance who was entrusted by Queen Wilhelmina to form a new government. "Papa" Drees (prime minister from 1948 to 1958), is represented as the father of the Dutch welfare state. The flow of immigrants from former colonies in the 1950s–60s is represented through newsreel images of Moluccans who supported the Dutch in Indonesia arriving in Rotterdam, with small children in their arms. No mention is made of why this occurred. Reconstruction after the war and the building of the welfare state culminates in images of collective labor and smiling faces on the eve of the 1960s. Then the youth revolt is pictured, and the sexual revolution is highlighted. The Dutch economy is also mentioned as having altered during this time, with new technologies and service industries replacing the older forms of manufacture. Workers from Turkey are portrayed as representative of the new "guest workers" in this new economy. This is followed by mention of their choice to remain in the country and to have their families join them. Immigrants from Morocco and Suriname and Aruba are also mentioned. After the rise of terrorism and the attacks on the World Trade Center in New York, increasing protests against immigration and societal tensions are mentioned. Other sections of the video provide information about the political system, health care, education, and employment and income. A picture book is also provided to help in remembering the contents of the video and in preparing for the examination, which consists of thirty questions selected from the video.

Dutchness is here framed as Western and European, a distinctive mode of life, if not a civilization. What is distinctive about this way of life is its cosmopolitanism, its liberalism, and its cultural as well as political and social history. The Dutch people, it is suggested, emerged out of a struggle for religious and personal freedom and have created institutions and norms to protect as well as to extend that freedom. Tolerance toward others, especially with regard to religion is a founding notion of this way of life. The political system, the parliament, and the political parties, all are shown to be formed out of the struggle to construct and maintain religious freedom and to ensure that others, in this case the Catholics, were afforded that right. What now for Muslims?

While notions like tolerance and responses like pillarization can be traced far back into Dutch history, the Second World War with its devastating experience of occupation and the horrendous fate of Jews, along with the humiliating loss of the colonial empire immediately following, mark a watershed in narratives of Dutch collective identity. The war and its aftermath form the background against which current ideas of Dutchness were reframed. Describing the decade between 1940 and 1950, the eminent historian H. L. Wesseling (1980:126) writes, "War, occupation, war again and finally the loss of an Empire were together more dramatic events within ten years than Dutch history had provided in the course of several centuries. In the Netherlands the years following 1945 were characterized by hope and fear: the hope of a new society which would arise out of destruction, the fear of total ruin if the colonies were lost."

In the experience of defeat and occupation, narratives vacillated between hero and victim, or, as F. Abbink (2005) puts it, "from caretakers of England to the winter war" (Van Engelandvaarders tot Oorlogswinter).[16] Since at least the early nineteenth century, the Netherlands had been a bystander to many of the great conflicts that changed the face of Europe, insulating itself behind a policy of neutrality through the First World War. Germany and the Netherlands were closely bound economically as well as culturally at the beginning of the twentieth century, and the Dutch suffered deeply from Germany's defeat and forced reparations. Neutrality was also the official position as the Second World War began. However, in an attempt to avoid the main line of the French defense, the German army swept into the Low Countries in May 1940, opening another pathway to France. This caught the Dutch by surprise, and their army was quickly overrun. In an attempt to capture the royal family, German paratroopers landed in The Hague. However, Queen Wilhelmina and about 5,000 officials managed to escape to England, establishing a government-in-exile in London. One week later, the German command threatened to bomb the port city of Rotterdam, demanding its surrender. Even as the Dutch authorities complied, German bombers attacked the city, killing nearly 800 people and leaving 78,000 homeless. Following this the Dutch army surrendered. Led by the queen, the government in exile focused its armed resistance on the East Indies, especially Indonesia, where the Dutch navy and merchant marine allied with British forces against the advancing Japanese.

In her radio broadcasts from London, Queen Wilhelmina referred to the Dutch people as a "nation of heroes" for their resistance against the occupiers. The situation was a bit more complicated. At first, the occupiers considered the Dutch to be part of the Aryan nation and ordered their policies accordingly, vacillating between indoctrination and repression (Moore 1997). This began to change as the general situation of the war worsened and the need of labor power in German factories increased. The small Dutch fascist party, Nationaal-Socialistische Beweging (NSB), worked together with the occupation authorities and was the only political party legally operating in the Netherlands. In addition, about 25,000 Dutchmen voluntarily served in the German military. Yet, in 1943, when asked to sign a loyalty oath to the German administration, a large majority of Dutch university students refused to sign and many went into hiding (Woolf 1999). Dutch resistance became more active and aggressive after laws requiring Dutch men between eighteen and forty-five to work in Germany. Another factor that spurred active resistance was the treatment of Dutch Jews. In an expression of solidarity that is unique in European history, Amsterdam's sanitary and transportation workers led a strike in February 1941 to protest a round-up of 400 men from the city's large Jewish population just days before (Mooij 2006). Though quickly suppressed, this event became a symbol of national resistance and a stimulus to future actions that began in earnest as the victory of the Allies seemed more likely. Still a matter of controversy as to who actually organized it, the *Februaristaking* (February Strike) is commemorated each year in an Amsterdam square and is a central feature at the city's Resistance Museum.[17] Another act of national resistance came in the closing stages of the war. In 1944 a rail strike was organized as the southern part of the Netherlands was being liberated by Allied forces. In response, the German authorities cut off food supplies to those parts of the country still under their control. This helped ensure the famine of 1945, or Hunger Winter, during which approximately 30,000 people died of starvation. In all, out of a population of about 9 million, 250,000 Dutch citizens lost their lives during the war, including 100,000 Jews (Barnouw 1986).[18]

In an attempt to rouse the spirit of the nation during the first months of occupation, an organization called Nederlandse Unie (Netherlands Unity) formed. In one its first flyers, the organization offered the following "Reasons for national pride: We have a large colonial empire, we struggle heroically against the sea, we cherish our glorious history and a beloved royal family" (*Nederlandse Unie* 1940, on file at the Amsterdam Resistance Museum). Founded in July 1940, the organization was formally banned by the Germans one year later. In the first few months of its existence, Nederlandse Unie attracted nearly 800,000 members, the largest party the Netherlands has ever had. In this appeal for unity, one finds some of the nation's grounding myths and aspects of its collective imagination, the struggle against the sea that required all hands working together, the pride of being a member of a dominant nation (though now being dominated), and, finally, the heritage of the House of Orange, with valiant Queen Wilhelmina now personifying the collective will.

Documented acts of collective resistance were relatively few, and the actual behavior of Dutch citizens during the occupation, especially in relation to their Jewish neighbors, is still a very sensitive and controversial matter (Moore 1997, Haan 2003, Wolf 2007). Two citations from Geert Mak's history of Amsterdam will suffice: "On 20 January 1941, the German authorities requested the Civil Registry to make a colour-coded map showing the distribution of Jews throughout the city. By 29 January it was complete: a map with one stripe for every ten Jews. Not one civil servant so much as hesitated. . . . The Germans never posted more than 60 officers in Amsterdam, even at the height of the persecution of the Jews. The rest was done by the Dutch" (Mak 1999:265). As recently as April 2006 a newly published book (Vuijsje 2006) challenged established interpretations, causing a media sensation. Only 30,000 Dutch Jews survived the war, and many who did were given a cold reception on their return (Wolf 2007). However, the image of the Dutch as active resisters and protectors of Jews became an important element of postwar narratives. An image of the "good" Dutchman was added to the tolerant one. The good Dutchman was one who knew the right side during the occupation, not necessarily one who followed this up with action. The opposite was thus not someone "bad" or evil, but someone who was "wrong," or better, "mistaken." These stories and images were complemented and complicated by the ambiguous shifting between hero and victim, but they solidified a collective narrative about the wartime experience around which the nation could unite.

As a form of agency, resistance to violent repression, whether active or passive, has a heroic component, while being its victim carries other connotations. Victims are passive and often portrayed as weak, while the hero, even when flawed and not successful, reveals a degree of strength, moral as well as physical. The weakness of the victim, however, opens the possibility of redemption through the collective effort of recovery. This became one of the meanings of postwar recovery: lifting the nation out of victimhood. Achieving this would depend, however, on solidifying a story line whereby at least passive resistance to occupation was the main theme. Thus the predominant narrative coming out of the Second World War was that of a nation engaged in resisting occupation and caring about, if not actually rescuing, its Jewish residents and refugees. This image was solidified in official reports and in popular projects, such the restoration of the Anne Frank house in Amsterdam (Gerstenfeld 2002, Wolf 2007). Novels and films also contributed. It would take the dramatic capture and televised trial of Adolf Eichmann in 1960 to open some cracks in this narrative. As Hannah Arendt would report in the *New Yorker* and later in her famous book *Eichmann in Jerusalem*, the trial revealed the "banality of evil" at work in the destruction of European Jews. Spurred by this trial and then by a new generation's curiosity about their parent's behavior during the occupation, the publication of sensitive documents and memoirs of the Dutch war experience led to the shattering of settled images.

The hope and fear that the postwar era would bring about a fundamentally different Dutch society turned out to be unfounded. Even with the loss of its largest colony, the country stabilized itself politically on its traditional pillars, aided of course by the Marshal Plan and, later, the new European Common Market (Wesseling 1980:132–33). The major political change that did occur was membership in NATO, thus ending a long history of neutrality. On a lesser scale, the "pillars" on which the nation stood were expanded to include socialists and liberals, along with Protestants and Catholics, each with their own media, social and sport clubs, and, to a large extent, segregated domiciles. When these segregated and segmented groups met, it was primarily in some form of competition or contest. What united everyone was the imagined community of good Dutchmen being renarrated in the postwar reconstruction. While reinforcing segregation, these pillars actually gave Dutch society an inherent structure, a form of stability under a surface fragmentation. Each pillar was internally ordered, but linked from top to bottom, thus offering individuals within a sense of belonging, as well as relegated position and appropriate status. Identity was thus linked to pillar and to nation at one and the same time.

One of the most dramatic changes in Dutch society was the unexpected, and unprecedented, economic growth and changes in the nature of work and occupation. Between 1950 and 1970, "the Dutch economy grew by 3.5% each year . . . *seven* times the average annual growth rate for the preceding forty years" (Judt 2005: 325). This meant that unemployment rates were very low, another significant change from the recent past. At the same time, a dramatic shift occurred in the ways people made their living, as the focus of the economy shifted from agriculture to industry and the agriculture that still remained an important part of Dutch life was itself industrialized. Finally, a population explosion was in progress, with a 35 percent increase occurring in the population in the Netherlands between 1950 and 1970, with 30 percent of the population under the age of fifteen in 1960 (Judt 2005:331). If this was not enough to demand some fundamental adjustment in national identity, the shift in economic focus from the East Indies to Western Europe demanded by the establishment of an independent Indonesia, clearly did. Added to this was the return home of ex-colonials and their allies. According to Judt (2005:280–81), major consequences followed from these changes: the destruction of a national myth concerning a "Golden Age and a symbol of Dutch commercial and seafaring glory," which necessitated a shift in economic and cultural focus to a Europe more widely defined than previously. The Netherlands helped form the Benelux trading union and was central to the formation of the European Economic Community when it was founded in 1957. The future, in other words, lay in a reconstructed Europe and not in the colonial past.

REMEMBERING TO FORGET

Following the wartime trauma and the dynamics of remembering and forgetting in its aftermath, the fact that sensitive issues, like the treatment of Jews and other ethnic minorities during the occupation and anxieties relating to the arrival of refugees from former colonies, were never fully discussed might help explain some of the explosion of emotion after the murder of van Gogh. After an initial bloodletting, the mood in the Netherlands, and in Europe generally, was to look forward and rebuild and not open up old sores. The new Cold War helped redefine the meaning of "Europe" by dividing West and East by the Iron Curtain, and an emerging consumer society quickly replaced postcolonial fears and any remaining doubts about the moral standing of the nation.[19]

In his comparative account of the postwar narrations in Belgium, France, and the Netherlands, Lagrou (1997:196) writes that "the liberated societies of Europe were traumatized and their now fragile national consciousness badly needed the kind of patriotic epic that only the Resistance could deliver. Persecution, as a more fundamental experience, was unspeakable and unacceptable in this context. Mourning without triumphalism would have undermined post-war national recovery. The threatening memory of impotence, humiliation and loss of meaning at best, and of complicity at worst, could only be commemorated through the prism of resistance and patriotism." The situation for the Dutch was complicated by the nation's neutrality during the First World War. There were no veterans who could be transformed into soldier-heroes, and resistance had a left-wing, even communist taint, so the problem of who could become the national heroes was a difficult one. The queen and the House of Orange remained untainted by any stigma of collaboration, making it possible for the monarchy to reestablish itself as a symbol of national unity. This was different than elsewhere in Europe, where the organized Resistance could put forward such claims.

In the face of postwar efforts to rebuild the nation, there was relatively little public talk about collaboration and resistance; and in the absence of veterans groups and other interest organizations, there were few who could pressure the queen and her government on this point. In addition, among the main organizing forces of the Resistance were communists who, aside from their heavy losses during the Second World War, were much weakened by the Cold War. This and the fact that the Netherlands had joined NATO and participated in the Korean War in 1950 brought the country much closer to the United States and its policies than ever before, a situation that continues to this day. Any discussion of the treatment of Jews was also laid aside in favor of a Dutch-focused rebuilding. The need for national unity took precedence over the aims of any interest group. "The government declared 'veteranism' to be a very un-Dutch and unpatriotic activity . . . it ignored and boycotted all pressure-groups, including those of Resistance veterans. Any group claiming special merit or special suffering not only threatened to be a burden on the national budget, but also endangered the national consensus that heroism and martyrdom had been the collective experience of the Dutch people, symbolized by the emblematic figure of national affection, Queen Wilhelmina." (Lagrou 1997:207–8).

That this laying-aside was successful requires some further reflection on the social mechanisms of remembering and forgetting. What is remembered and forgotten is a contest about what and who will be seen and heard, a contest that occurs in the present, but one that also concerns the future as well as the past. In this meaning conflict, various voices make themselves heard, some more loudly and powerfully than others. This power is related to but not reducible to access to mass media and other institutions that amplify and solidify voice, making it heard over time and space. Only powerful forces, persons and groups, with symbolic and material resources in hand can compete in this meaning struggle. In part because of her actions during the occupation, the Dutch queen commanded such resources and was thus a powerful player who could influence what was said and made visible and thus remembered about the years of the occupation.[20] Other individuals and groups, such as the communists and others active in the Resistance were weakened by the war and the events that followed and were thus less able to command the recognition, or the remembrance, that they did in other countries.

After the exaltation following liberation by Canadian forces in 1945, there were many well-publicized trials of collaborators and war criminals, as well as ritual public humiliations of *moffenmeiden*, those Dutch women accused of having been romantically involved with the occupiers. Over 50,000 people were put on trial for their actions during the occupation, and out of the 132 Dutch citizens sentenced to death (long outlawed, the death penalty was reinstated for this occasion, but has since been rescinded), 32 were executed, as were 5 of the 18 Germans convicted (Barnouw 1986:20). For comparison, 242 people were executed in Belgium, but Dutch retributions were fairly comparable to those in other European countries.

The queen reestablished parliament in 1947, after giving up an attempt to consolidate more power around the monarchy, and the work of rebuilding the country took priority with a fairly strong consensus prevailing. Reconstruction (given the motto "Hands to the Plough") was a spiritual as well as a material project, with, as we have seen, little room for controversy and even less for a nuanced account of the war experience. There would be much more government intervention than before the war and not only in economic matters. The media were singled out for an important role in this process; as the *De Stem van Nederland* (Voice of the Netherlands) pointed out in its April 13, 1946, issue, "The demands which the government makes and must make in reconstruction must be made clear. Film can and must play a significant role in this . . . this task cannot be left only to merchants" (translated and quoted by Barnouw 1986:20). There was only limited artistic resistance to these conformist demands. One of the most prominent was led by COBRA, a loose network of artists from Copenhagen, Brussels, and Amsterdam, who through their paintings hoped to represent a vision of a new society. They became quickly disillusioned, however, and soon disbanded, and their paintings are probably better known today than they were at the time.

The first professional historical accounts of the war appeared already in the late 1940s (Abbink 2005:12) and mainly concerned the treatment of Jews and their place in Dutch society. On the one side were those claiming Jews had already been marginalized prior to the war and on the other those who denied this. Both sides largely agreed however, that the Dutch should not be held responsible for the fate of the Jewish population. At least since the 1950s it has been common to portray the Dutch as bravely resisting their occupiers, while claiming the treatment of Jews belonged to Jewish history, not to the history of the Netherlands (Abbink 2005:16). L. de Jong repeated this view in what became the official version of the war experience, one that would be publicly performed as a television documentary in the mid-1960s. It was this "reassuring" interpretation of the war experience that the youth revolts later in the decade would challenge.[21]

The loss of empire, most particularly Indonesia, also affected Dutch identity and shaped the re-framing of Dutchness. Without empire, it was feared the Netherlands would be reduced to the status of Denmark, a small and quaint European country with a glorious past and little future. An impetus to renarrate the meaning of Dutchness came not only from economic loss and the ensuing political crisis as from the influx of people from the colonies, most importantly those from the Moluccan Islands and from Suriname, those with a darker skin tone. Added to this were those of "mixed-race," the so-called *Indische*, from Indonesia. Dutch society was now visibly multiracial, and the notion of Dutchness was once again made an object of reflection and discussion. It was not only a formal question of who was Dutch, that is, who had the right to Dutch citizenship, though this was an important issue, but also what it meant to be Dutch. "In contrast to the stream of literature about the second world war, there exist only a few unread novels and some forgotten memoirs . . . In short there existed no historical view of colonization and decolonization; no-one needed it; it was the past, but it was not history: 'it was simply pushed aside, obliterated, wiped out' " (Wesseling 1980: 139).

Another impulse to discussion came also from outside, the highly publicized trial of Adolf Eichmann.[22] Two related "inside" events further stimulated debate. The first was the revelations about the atrocities committed by Dutch soldiers in Indonesia. These included an eventual government report that compared them to the Nazi ss. Second, there was the publication of the memoirs of a Dutch Jew who had been convicted after the Second World War of treason for alleged collaboration with the German occupation authorities. The man in question, F. Weinreb (see Weinreb 1971), claimed that he had in fact carried out single-handedly "guerilla actions" against the German and Dutch administration during the war. What was more disturbing and more relevant to the present case was Weinreb's portrayal of the behavior of the majority of the Dutch population, which he described as "passively collaborationist" (Wesseling 1980: 140). The book aroused such a public debate that the government began an investigation, resulting in the publication of the two-volume "Weinreb Report" in 1976. The evidence presented here was even more damning than that presented at the original trial. This mattered little, however, for Weinreb became an antiestablishment hero for a new generation ready to challenge established interpretations of the past.

The result was a new sense of uneasiness regarding the past. "The severe crisis that hit the Dutch consensus model in the late 1960s also led to a crisis in the Dutch politics of memory" (Lagrou 1997:210). Resistance organizations began pressing for recognition and what Lagrou calls a "Jewish memory" was emerging (1997:216). The impact of the memoirs of Weinreb should be understood in this context. The previously mentioned television series produced under the direction of L. de Jong helped reopen the issue of the actions of the Dutch during the war, including the treatment of Jews. Then the first comprehensive account of the latter by

J. Presser was published in 1965; its 10,000-copy print run sold out in two days (Wolf 2007). The postwar desire for national consensus was now being challenged, in part because of representation in the mass media.

The film industry also made a contribution. Founded in the 1930s on the German model, Dutch film production was confiscated during the occupation and used to turn out propaganda films with German casts. One of Amsterdam's most famous movie houses, the art deco Tuschinski, named for its founder Abram Tuschinski, was forced to change its name to the Tivoli because of its Jewish ownership (Beerekamp 1986a:9). The first films made about the occupation were not well received and drew little interest from a population more concerned with getting by and rebuilding for the future. In terms of style, they were greatly influenced by Italian neorealism and several used actual resistance members to play themselves in the style of Roberto Rossellini's *Rome, Open City*. These films "were the first to seek an artistic form to cope with the traumas of the war" (ibid.:10). Things changed in the late 1960s in part because of the founding of the Netherlands Film Academy and the emergence of a group of young film-makers keen on reproducing the French New Wave. One of the prime targets of this group was the official view of the war and the occupation, in part as a criticism of de Jong's televised version, broadcast throughout 1963.[23] In films such as *Pastorale 1943* (Wim Verstappen, dir., 1978) and *Soldier of Orange* (Paul Verhoeven, dir., 1977) the image of the heroic Dutchman was forcefully deconstructed. Verhoeven, whose film was based on published memoirs and was given the approval of the royal family, revealed the flowing line between resistance and collaboration in everyday life during the occupation. There were few heroes and much ambiguity in the character portraits he presents.[24] Television also played its part. Verhoeven's *Voorbij voorbij* (Lest we forget) offered a non-heroic view of the resistance for a television audience. While still banned in France, Marcel Ophuls and Andre Harris's powerful documentary about resistance and collaboration in occupied France, *Le chagrin et la pitié* (*The Sorrow and the Pity*, 1970), was shown on Dutch television in the 1970s. It made such an impression that Dutch journalists demanded their own version be made, and in October 1974 Dutch television broadcast the three-hour documentary *Vastberaden maar soepel en met mate, 1938–1948: Herinneringen aan Nederland* (Determined yet flexible and measured, 1938–1948: Memories of the Netherlands), modeled on French film (Barnouw 1986:24).

The social movements of the 1960s and 1970s provided a major part of the context in which all these issues, and their mediated representations, were brought to public discussion. These movements, especially the student protests and the formation of the European new left and the counterculture as represented in the Provos, Kabouters, and Krakers (squatters) are significant not only for a discussion of the changing meaning of Dutchness but also for an understanding of Theo van Gogh and his murder. As they followed and developed from each other, these social movements stimulated public discussion through their actions and by creating their own media. The movement media became alternative sources of information and representation and included music, theater, and other art forms, along with the more traditional means of communication, such as newspapers, flyers, and pamphlets. These alternative media were augmented by the interest the movements provoked in the established media and art worlds. Suddenly, seemingly settled issues like the behavior of the Dutch population during the Second World War and in the colonies were gaining new attention and interpretation. Activists demanded not only a reopening debate but also new content in the established curriculum of public education that would facilitate the discussion of such issues.

The story of the youth and student revolts in the 1960s is well known and need not be repeated here except for mentioning the significant Dutch variations that affected and were influenced by Dutch identity. In the United States and Western Europe, a new "youth culture" based on free time and age-specific consumer goods was emerging, part and parcel of which was a rebellious attitude toward the status quo. Like other European countries, both population and purchasing power greatly expanded in the Netherlands after the war; as previously noted, by 1960 "30 percent of the population was under fifteen years old" (Judt 2005:331), and youth had money to spend on things other than necessities like food and clothing. Judt points to two seemingly paradoxical forces at work here: the increased role of the state in the economy, the general social welfare of the citizenry, and the relaxing of its "authority over their morals and opinions" (2005:373). The combination of a relaxation of the moral authority of the state and church and an expanding "consumer" economy helped produce a context in which a distinctive generational consciousness could develop. The engine for that development lay in new cultural and social movements.[25]

Pim Fortuyn (2001) gives the social movements of the 1960s a special place in his recounting of Dutch identity, as having helped revitalize as well as transform it. Even more than Fortuyn, Theo van Gogh was a product of those movements; he carried their antiestablishment message into the new century in a much more apparent way. Most important in the early years of youth protest were the Provos and the Kabouters, two interrelated youth movements. Characteristic of both and perhaps of the Dutch protest in the sixties generally was their playful nature and colorful symbolism. The main thrust of their attack was the Dutch "establishment," most particularly the royal House of Orange and new middle-class consumer society, the cornerstones of the postwar consensus. Harry Mulisch (1966) described one of the early Provo "happenings" in this way:

> While their parents, sitting on their refrigerators and dishwashers, were watching TV with their left eye and their car in the front of the house with their right eye, with one hand on the food mixer and the other in De Telegraaf [a conservative newspaper], their kids spent Saturday night on Spui Square [in front of the Athenaeum bookstore near the University of Amsterdam]. . . . And at the stroke of midnight, the high priest appeared from some alley, all dressed up to walk Magic Circles around the nicotine demon [a statue in the square sponsored by a tobacco company], while his disciples cheered, applauded and sang the Ugge Ugge song [an antismoking jingle]. (Quoted in Voeten 1990:4)

Tobacco (and advertisements for cigars and cigarettes), was here taken as symbolic of the Dutch establishment, which the Provos labeled the "Nico-Mafia," and their enjoyment and commercial promotion of products from the colonies, like cigars and cigarettes. If they smoked at all, like their Hippie counterparts in the United States the Provos favored marijuana and were an early source of the liberal drug policies that have since made the Netherlands unique. Influenced by surrealism and the French situationists, as well as the American counterculture, the Provos preferred street theater to violent confrontations. In one of their most famous acts, they sabotaged the royal wedding in 1966, exploding a smoke bomb in the midst of the procession, an image that was televised around the world. One of the reasons for this provocation was that the Dutch princess (now queen) Beatrix was marrying Klas von Amsberg, a former member of the Hitlerjugend. In addition to referencing the Second World War and the Dutch-German ties, the Provos managed also to link Klas von Amsberg with Sinterklaas (Klas/Sinterklaas), a hallowed Dutch Christmas figure and one that continues to arouse controversy because of the presence of his black helper "zwarte-piet" or black peter. The war and the colonial past were thus once again symbolically articulated.[26] The Provos evolved into the Kabouters (gnomes), an anarchist political party that retains an influence in Amsterdam, largely through the "squatters" movement.

Harry Mulisch and other writers, such as Gerard Reve, influenced and were themselves influenced by what the Provos saw as the complacency of the Dutch middle class. Mulisch remains a central figure in Dutch literature, an art form that more generally has played an important part in the articulation of Dutchness and the solidification of Dutch identity. Maintaining and developing the national language is central here. Along with Reve and W. F. Hermans, Mulisch has been called one of the "three most important writers in Dutch literature in the 20th century" (*Volkskrant*, April 10, 2006).[27] Their books form a central part of the educational curriculum, and nearly all school children are exposed to them. Mulisch's novel *The Assault* (1982) and the later filmed version of it won worldwide recognition for the portrayal of ambiguity during the German occupation, and Reve's *De Avonden* (The evenings; 1947) was one of the first novels to give voice to the postwar experience in portraying the days of 1946 through the eyes of a young boy. When Reve died in April 2006, the Dutch media (including Hirsi Ali's Web page) offered a full representation of his life and work, with front-page coverage in the major newspapers and a two-hour discussion on television, in which Mulisch, an outspoken critic, was a featured guest. Not unlike Theo van Gogh, Reve was a writer with a mass appeal and a public figure who thrived on provocation. During the 1970s, Reve was accused of racism for his outspoken attacks on Surinamese immigrants, and his public performances at the time were precursors to the actions of both van Gogh and Pim Fortuyn in their portrayal of immigrants as threats to Dutch culture and way of life. Reve did not stop there, however; as the Provos and van Gogh would later do, Reve attacked many of the sacred cows of postwar Dutch identity.

Like the Provos and the wider countercultural youth subcultures, the student movement in the Netherlands was less aggressive and violent than in other countries. Generally speaking, the aim was to open a dialogue and to reform the society rather than to radically transform it (Zwaan 1981, Moerings 1983). While the Provos eventually were forced to escalate their provocations, due largely to the violently aggressive police response, the student movement staged only a few major confrontations, such as the occupation of the administrative buildings at the University of Amsterdam for several days in 1969. The one occasion around which the Provos and the radical students did unite was the royal wedding mentioned above (Mak 1999:294). Dutch protests did not stem from poverty or exclusion, which might have led to more prolonged and aggressive conflicts over social justice, and the Dutch were not involved in unpopular foreign wars, so student life itself and the behavior of the Dutch elite generally provided a major focus of mobilization. Added to this was the lack of any interest in reflecting on the colonial past and the behavior of the Dutch during the Second World War, which received little attention in the academic curriculum. As in other countries, the humanities and social sciences were a major target of this critique and students in those disciplines were at the forefront of the student revolt.

The Krakers or squatters movement is still ongoing and is in some senses an exception to the rule cited above. This youth movement did spring from relative poverty and social exclusion, in that the housing market in Amsterdam has undergone great changes that have affected low-income people. In the optimistic early 1960s, city planners built whole new areas of high-rise apartments designed to make Amsterdam "a city of the future" (Mak 1999:298). The idea was to provide low- to medium-income families with functional, light, and airy living spaces surrounded by areas of green. As the opening of the largest of these projects, the Bijlmer, coincided with the massive influx of immigrants from the former colony in Suriname, it gained the reputation as a crime-ridden immigrant ghetto, and flats stood empty for years. In other parts of the city, a housing shortage prevailed, while the city went ahead with plans for building an underground metro, which would require tearing down even more houses. Already in the late 1960s, a squatters wing of the counterculture had emerged, and this served as a basis for future confrontations and housing occupations in the 1970s and 80s. In contemporary Amsterdam the movement is still very active and provides both resources and a focal point for protest activity in the city. Squatters are among the most vocal and fiercest opponents of the current government's immigration policies, and many squatted houses in the city bear banners calling for the removal of the controversial Rita Verdonk.

CONCLUSION: WHY THE FRAME WORKS

Already before the murder of Theo van Gogh, debate on the "immigrant question" in the Netherlands had polarized into a clash between Western and Islamic civilizations, a drama of world-historical proportions. Following the meteoric rise of Pim Fortuyn and his eventual assassination, van Gogh's murder helped solidify the contours of this discursive field. While well-positioned actors such as Fortuyn, Hirsi Ali, and van Gogh all made use of metaphors drawn from an imported discourse, their particular formulations and the responses they evoked had specific resonance in the Netherlands. The emotive power of this rhetoric and response can be understood in relation to some of the myths that had given coherence to Dutch identity at least since the Second World War. Theo van Gogh commonly referred to radical Islam as a contemporary form of fascism, and references to fascism are commonly made by other commentators seeking to raise fears about the migration of Muslims to Europe. Hirsi Ali continues to mine this vein. The presence of Muslims has also spurred the rise of neo-Nazi groups among a new generation of Europeans. On the one side, Muslims are portrayed as a new fifth column, which even when nonviolent will soon take advantage of the gift of democracy to use their ever-increasing numbers to form a voting bloc against Christian Dutch to take over the country from within. For this side, they have replaced the Jews as the cancer within. One could well ask why these representations were not reversed, why those who speak in the name of heroic resistance do not see Muslims as today's victims in need of support. In the parliamentary debates in the weeks after the murder, Minister Verdonk proposed that those who perpetrate "crimes against the state" have their passports rescinded, something that had not been discussed since the trials of the collaborators after the war (Hajer and Maussen 2004:2). The use of such dramatic imagery is a central part of the clash of civilizations, which has replaced the multicultural drama outlined by Paul Scheffer in 2000.

Religion is a common denominator on both sides of this clash of civilizations and in the war on terror. This is the case even if Hirsi Ali and

Theo van Gogh identify themselves as nonbelievers. Notions of Dutchness (and Western civilization more generally) are rooted in Christianity, in Calvinism, and a religion-based humanism, where religious beliefs live side by side with a tolerance for believing and nonbelieving others. The meaning of tolerance along with other facets of previously stabilized narratives of Dutch identity has now opened up and is being tested. In the framework of a clash of civilizations, the multivoiced tolerant West is contrasted with an Islam conceived as intolerant and fundamentalist. Islam is represented as based on one word, the Koran, and one voice, the Prophet Muhammad. Whereas the West is multivoiced and democratic, the East is authoritarian; whereas the West is urban and modern, the East is rural and traditional. Against this backdrop, Dutchness is nonviolent and civilized, while Islam is violent and uncivilized, or as van Gogh and Hirsi Ali put it "backward" and "primitive," with allusions to the group mentality and the emotional politics of fascism. This is the master frame through which Muslim immigrants are thus represented and made visible.

Such pronouncements would not have had their enormous effect were it not for the media access commanded by van Gogh and Hirsi Ali—were it not for who they are and what they represent: van Gogh, the consummate sixties bohemian with a famous name, and Hirsi Ali, the Muslim convert who has suffered and therefore knows of what she speaks. However, even as these coded messages were carried forth by such representative figures, they would not have had their impact if they did not draw on specific images that resonated with their chosen audience. These messages were powerful not merely because of who said them, and in what media, but also because they resonated with a specific audience, one that can be identified as those with a however vaguely understood and articulated sense of being Dutch. This resonance was based within frameworks of interpretation rooted in a shared pool of memory, imagery, and imagination. Like classic Greek theater, the mediated performances of van Gogh and Hirsi Ali were successful when these actors and their audience fused with each other, performing together a drama with commonly shared imagery, scripts, and props (Alexander 2006).

There are certainly generational and other aspects at work in this fusion, but the Second World War remains significant in the construction and maintenance of Dutch collective memory and national identity for a large segment of its current population. To all the previous examples, one can add the furor created when a current prince chose to marry the daughter of a former Argentinean general linked to fascism; the wedding was allowed to go on but the father of the bride was not permitted to attend. To say that the war weighs heavily on the Dutch imagination is not necessarily to say anything about the factual content of that memory. A survey-sample of citizens over the age of thirteen carried out in April 2006, for example, found that more that 80 percent thought the war started because of the Holocaust (Volkskrant, April 26, 2006). However remembered, the war weighs heavily on the Dutch collective imagination, providing not only a mechanism of inclusion/exclusion, but also a moral framework for making judgments about what can and cannot be said.[28] In the postwar era, this collective memory helped forge a common will to rebuild the nation, just as in the 1960s a new generation formed in rebellion against it, helping at once to revise as well as revitalize this collective memory. In the contemporary context, the Second World War again makes its appearance as part of the rhetoric to mobilize emotions in a new confrontation between natives and newcomers. Images of the war are used to define who "we" are: a Western nation that is united against tyranny and has rebuilt itself on common values that newcomers must learn to respect. This was one of the taken-for-granted assumptions that provided grounding for earlier notions of pillarization, the idea of tolerance and the vague multiculturalism of the 1990s.

The fact that Hirsi Ali, an outsider, currently most forcefully puts this argument forward must appear ironic to some. Hirsi Ali is very cognizant of her role as outsider with regard to the memory of the Second World War. Asked to give a speech at the annual Memorial commemoration, she began by stating "What can an immigrant add to May 4 [Memorial Day] or May 5 [Liberation Day]? Do I share the collective memory of the Dutch or, for that matter, the European War generation?" (Hirsi Ali 2006a:96). In this sense, being an "immigrant" is defined through being an outsider, or a late-comer, to an established collective memory.

There are layers and fractures in this performative fusion between speaker and audience related to age, gender, and class, but there are also aspects of a common sense of belonging to some imagined, yet deeply felt, community. There is a clear generational appeal here, although younger people might not get the symbolic referents and Moroccans and Turks of whatever age, those Islamic newcomers, are by definition outside this appeal. A sense of collective belonging is especially sensitive in relation to the past, since identities are reconstructed and secured "not only by facing the present and future but also by reconstructing the collectivity's earlier life" (Alexander 2004:26). Such identities are almost necessarily constructed against an Other. During the Second World War, this Other was represented very concretely by the German occupiers. In the context of occupation, Jews and other minorities were once again placed in a precarious position vis-à-vis the "Dutch." However diminished by the war, the Jewish population was rather uneasily reincorporated into the community in the postwar consensus building and in the face of a new Other in "godless" Communism. This consensus concerning who should be included was strong and flexible enough to permit refugees from former colonies. A series of events, beginning with the murder of Pim Fortuyn and concluding with that of Theo van Gogh has led to the collapse of that consensus and to a reopening of the question of who and what should be included in the national community. The issue of the meaning of Dutchness has now also reopened, and a new Other, the Islamic East, has been constituted. We can understand the social drama of the murder of Theo van Gogh as part of a cultural trauma in which the collective identity is being re-narrated as lines of inclusion and exclusion are redrawn.

CHAPTER 5

A DUTCH DILEMMA: FREE

SPEECH, RELIGIOUS FREEDOM,

AND MULTICULTURAL

TOLERANCE

In 1944 Gunnar Myrdal published what would become a classic study of race relations in the United States under the title *An American Dilemma*. The dilemma Myrdal referred to was the discrepancy he and his fellow researchers uncovered between the social ethos, the core values around which American self-identity revolved, and the reality of American life. The central components of that ethos, which Myrdal called the "American Creed," related to the presumed dignity and equality of all American citizens, their "inalienable rights to freedom, justice and fair opportunity." These ideals, he noted, were not matched in the actual treatment and living conditions of American blacks. In this "creed" Myrdal might well have included ideals concerning religious freedom and multicultural tolerance.[1] The murder of Theo van Gogh places the Netherlands and its multicultural drama at the center of a similar predicament: how to maintain a commitment to ideals of individual freedom, religious tolerance and social equality, in a globalizing, postcolonial world. Through the murder of van Gogh the discourse on Muslim immigration and the articulation of the core values of Dutchness finally and forcefully converged.

The murder of van Gogh greatly affected the intellectual and artistic discourse in the Netherlands, as well as the general political climate. Since the murder, commentators have pointed to a relaxation of norms concerning the expression of what are generally considered racist viewpoints. People who might otherwise consider themselves tolerant and liberal feel somehow justified in making negative statements about Muslims. More directly apparent, the murder helped articulate and solidify distinctive positions in the mediated public discussion. In the aftermath of the murder, in the public debate and in demonstrations of solidarity and protest, groups have taken form around various issues, such as the meaning of the film *Submission* and the persons of Hirsi Ali and Theo van Gogh, as well as the murder itself. A group calling itself the "friends of van Gogh" emerged and became very visible spokespersons defending the film and its makers in the cause of artistic freedom through various mass media (Hajer and Uitermark forthcoming). The murder was identified as yet another attack on the right of artists and intellectuals to freely express themselves. On the Internet, bloggers discussed a new awareness of the dangers and responsibilities of being an artist, something that has only intensified with what came to be called the Danish cartoon affair, which will be discussed below.

This chapter will discuss the role of the artist, the arts, and intellectuals more generally around issues of freedom of expression and religious tolerance, with reference to the murder of van Gogh in particular and the broader question of multiculturalism in contemporary Europe. A comparison between what has come to be known as the Rushdie affair and the murder of van Gogh will help us in this. The intellectual is here conceived as public debater, a role taken on by individuals who have already acquired a reputation in some field of endeavor and thus speak from a position of authority, though not necessarily expertise, on the particular issue at hand. In this broad understanding of the term, Ali and van Gogh are intellectuals. For our purposes, a comparison between Rushdie and Hirsi Ali as well is significant on at least two levels. The first has to do with what can be called authority and politics, which requires that the issue of who is speaking and from what position be analyzed in reference to the specific context. The second concerns how the events surrounding the Rushdie affair, Hirsi Ali's challenges to Islamic tradition, and the murder of van Gogh compare as acts of global and mediated performity, including how the news traveled, was framed, and drew reactions.

Threats against Hirsi Ali and van Gogh were directed against them as representative individuals. As targeted individuals, the actions against them were of a different sort than attacks against an indiscriminate, though specified and representative, public, as in the case of "suicide" bombings. Suicide bombers choose a more general category of victim, such as Americans, Jews, business people (not as identifiable individuals, however); people who attack representative figures are more discriminate: they choose particular individuals who represent something more than themselves—an opinion or a value—even if, as in the case of van

Gogh, what exactly the targeted victim represents (and the persona of the actual target) may be fluid. Even though the British author Salman Rushdie was targeted for death but not killed, his case offers an important precedent in regard to the murder of van Gogh. We begin with a comparison with the Rushdie affair, because of the general issues it raises and also because Hirsi Ali and Rushdie are often compared. This will be followed by a discussion of the Danish cartoon affair. The thread linking these highly public and publicized events is not only the issue of the responsibility of artists and intellectuals but also the wider issue of multiculturalism and the new European dilemma.

HIRSI ALI, VAN GOGH, AND RUSHDIE

Before and after the murder of van Gogh, comparisons between Ayaan Hirsi Ali and Salman Rushdie were made by many, including the protagonists themselves. In interviews Hirsi Ali and Rushdie drew inferences from each other's circumstances, especially regarding death threats by Islamic militants. More generally, Koenraad Elst (2002) links the two together with a long list of other artists and intellectuals, Muslim or not, as victims of what he calls the "Rushdie Rules." Following the American writer Daniel Pipes (1990), Elst proposes that the *fatwa* (religious decree) directed by Ayatollah Ruhollah Khomeini in 1989 against the British author altered the rules by which Islam could be publicly criticized.[2] While artists and writers have historically been censured and persecuted under the strictures of Islamic law in Muslim countries, following the death sentence pronounced in the religious decree, along with the promise of a $3 million bounty to be paid to any successful assassin, a new era was opened. The fatwa, an edict based on an interpretation of religious law by a recognized religious authority, "opened the door for Islamist terror against Muslim freethinkers and non-Muslim critics of Islam" (Elst 2002; also Pipes 1990). Under the Rushdie Rules, the murder of van Gogh could then be understood as part of a growing chain of confrontation and intimidation.

Writing before the making of *Submission* Elst included Hirsi Ali in his list of intellectuals and public figures threatened because of their public criticism of Islam. At that point in time, Hirsi Ali, identified as a researcher for the Dutch Labor Party (PvdA), was forced into hiding for remarks she made on a television program concerning the oppression of

Muslim women. Hirsi Ali was threatened with assassination because she, like Rushdie, was a Muslim and could thus be charged with apostasy, a most serious religious transgression involving the attempt to abandon the Muslim faith and punishable by death. Van Gogh was not mentioned of course. Elst ends his recapitulation of the Rushdie affair by asking why more Western intellectuals were not speaking out against this religious-based censorship. Fear, he wrote, should not be a factor, because nonbelievers did not come under the same category of threat as believers, like Rushdie and Hirsi Ali. If Elst can be taken as more or less correctly representing the situation at the time, the van Gogh murder added a new dimension, even if the filmmaker was not the real or first target, in that his murder represented a widening of potential individual targets to include nonbelieving Westerners.

Salman Rushdie's book *The Satanic Verses* (1988) created a sensation even before its official publication and Khomeini's decree. News of its impending appearance spread to India through magazine articles there. The book was banned almost immediately after its British publication (see Pipes 1990 for a full account of the entire affair). The ban in India was followed by similar measures taken in other countries, including South Africa, which has only a small Muslim population. Copies of the book were ceremonially burned in Bolton and Bradford, England, and five persons were killed in Islamabad, Pakistan, during a demonstration protesting the book's publication (Kepel 1997).[3] Then on February 14, 1989, Ayatollah Khomeini, the spiritual and political leader of Iran, broadcast his fatwa over Radio Tehran, saying, "I inform the proud Muslim people of the world that the author of the *Satanic Verses* book which is against Islam, the Prophet and the Koran, and all involved in its publication who were aware of its content are sentenced to death."[4] Khomeini called upon "all zealous Muslims to execute" those involved, and decreed that anyone himself killed in the attempt would be regarded as a martyr and duly rewarded. The strategy behind a Shia cleric claiming to speak for all Muslims has already been discussed. What is of interest here is the meaning of this event in relation to the murder of van Gogh.

In his radio address, Khomeini called Rushdie's book blasphemous and charged its author with apostasy, thus legitimating his death sentence. Evidence for these charges were to be found in the novel itself and in Rushdie's televised defense, in which he proclaimed himself to be a practicing Muslim, something he would later retract. The seriousness of Khomeini's charge was underlined when, ten days later, the $3 million bounty was added, which would later be doubled by the Iranian leadership after Khomeini's death a few months later in 1989. This public performance (in its double meaning of audience-related action and the attempt to do something with words) and media-orchestrated representation only increased Khomeini's standing in the Muslim world, and the consequences were immediately apparent. Rushdie was forced into hiding and bookstores as far removed as Berkeley, California, were firebombed. The Japanese translator of the book was murdered; the Italian translator stabbed and beaten; and the Norwegian publisher was shot outside his home in Oslo. In Sivas, Turkey, thirty-seven people died in a hotel set on fire by people protesting the appearance of the Turkish translator. Those who spoke out against the ban and the intimidation were themselves subject to threats and persecution. According to Elst however, the even more significant consequences of this edict was the fact that it legitimated attacks and censorship on a wide range of intellectual and artistic practices, especially as the newly codified Rushdie Rules became useful to radical Islamic groups as a source of recognition and a resource for mobilization.

In the Netherlands, the Rushdie affair dominated for a time media debate about Islam (see Goossen 2004, for example). One commentator wrote, "Tensions around the Rushdie Affair and Gulf War had been solved in the Dutch way: the Minister of Home Affairs calling all leaders of Islamic organizations to the ministry and giving them a double message: 1) we have rules for disputes that Muslims should respect, so no fatwas and book burnings, and 2) if you are threatened because you are a Muslim, we will protect you!" (Penninx 2005:7 n. 4). To avoid polarization and promote moderation, Dutch authorities contacted Muslim organizations in order to help mediate the opposing sides (Rath et al. 2001:93). These interactions would prove important for further relations between the government and these organizations, something that would be important in the management of tensions after the murders of Fortuyn and van Gogh.

It is here that one direct link to the van Gogh murder can be further articulated. The Rushdie fatwa and the succeeding flow of incidents can be said to have legitimated the early threats against Ayaan Hirsi Ali. After this fatwa was issued, an individual or group could presumably seek and possibly attain the blessing of a sympathetic cleric for such an act against a prominent fallen Muslim living in the West without specifically naming the target. Such requests are traditionally made in a general way: "If a Muslim has blasphemed the faith, is he or she condemned to death and am I justified in carrying this out?" Neither name nor date need be specified, only an anonymous category of person: a fallen believer. In this sense, the targeting of an individual victim is indiscriminate, at least from the point of view of the legitimating religious authority. As previously discussed, killing a non-Muslim like Theo van Gogh would require further legitimation, as the intended victim was not only a non-Muslim but a distinctively identified individual. The question of how legitimation was attained, if indeed it was attained, needs be asked and answered. If it were not attained, then Mohammed B. was acting outside the prescribed script. To claim martyr status, such a request must have been made and granted. It remains questionable however, if such legitimation could be attained for a nonbeliever; it is at least as likely that Mohammed B. (with or without co-conspirators) acted without religious legitimation. Was van Gogh named as a possible target in the appeal for legitimation? Most likely not, if the cleric who was being petitioned was not an active proponent of radical Islam and thus a political activist as much as a religious authority. It seems as likely that the choice of van Gogh was locally arrived at, and as the note on his body made clear that he was a proxy for Hirsi Ali, a more suitable target. If any legitimation by religious authority was sought, it was most likely for Hirsi Ali, which of course explains the letter and even the official suspicion that it was written by someone other than Mohammed B. In this case, van Gogh might not have been mentioned at all or even hinted at in any conversation with a religious authority and that Mohammed B. was acting entirely on his own accord.

Whether or not the fatwa was granted, the murder of Theo van Gogh may have been carried out in order to make it possible for nonbelievers to become legitimate targets for assassination. The assassination of van Gogh in other words, may have created conditions for the possibility of the death threats to those responsible for the creation and publication of the satiric cartoons depicting Muhammad.

Interviewed in the London *Times* (August 11, 2005) Salman Rushdie called for a reformation of Islam, similar to that implemented in the

Christian world by the Protestant movement. More than that, Rushdie offered that the Koran should be treated as an historical document, rather than taken literally as the word of God, something that the anticlerical Enlightenment helped bring about with regard to the Bible. Similar positions have been taken by Hirsi Ali, who, as noted earlier, has been called a "daughter of the Enlightenment" and has herself called for an "Islamic Voltaire." Both Rushdie and Hirsi Ali can be seen as central figures in an ongoing dialogue and confrontation. Like the discursive process that helped legitimate the reemergence of Islamic radicalism, the voicing of untraditional views by intellectuals like Rushdie and Hirsi Ali has been important to the process of Islamic reform. In fact, the two, radicalism and reform, may be seen as competing sides of the same process of reformation or revitalization of religious doctrine in a new context. The same might be said of Hirsi Ali and Mohammed B. In standing for two clear alternatives to the question of integration, they can also be seen as representing alternatives to the meaning of Islam in Western Europe.

While books by individual authors such as Qutb and Mawdudi, as well as networks and organizations such as the (still active and important) Muslim Brotherhood, were significant in grounding radical Islamic movements, mass media has become much more central in the various facets in the current struggle, including the clash between radicals and reformists. For example, in 1997, the year after it was founded, Al Jazeera, the Qatar-based Arab-language television network, transmitted a debate between the secularist Syrian philosopher Sadiq Jalal al-Azm and the conservative Qatari Shaikh Yusif al-Quaradawi, which reached a very wide audience.[5] This was part of their ongoing series titled "The Opposite Direction," in which live debates are a prominent feature. Just as mass media, from cassette tapes to television broadcasts were important in Khomeini's rise to power in Iran, mass communication and mass education and the progressive development of the public sphere have been important in challenging the role of clerics in the interpretation of religious texts and in determining their application to modern life. The Islamic radicalism that attracted Mohammed B. can be seen as a reaction to the reformist process, as much as it is a reaction against Western modernization. It can be interpreted as part of a wider social movement that would, among other things, restore sacred texts and clerical authority to a more central position in social life.

Because it involves direct discursive engagement with Western intellectual and political traditions, the confrontation between reformist and radical Islam is not merely an internal Islamic dialogue. It is also a political struggle played out in public in front of a multilayered global audience. Reformist or liberal movements have been present in Islamic thought at least since the nineteenth century. One prime focus of such movements has been the claim that sacred texts are matters of individual interpretation and that religion is a matter of personal commitment, something very similar to that which has occurred in other world religions. This applies especially to contested areas such as gender roles and the relation to modern cultural practices, including the following of secular law and customs. Seen with generous eyes, Hirsi Ali can be viewed as part of this movement. In this case, differences between Hirsi Ali and others might appear to be more tactical than substantial. The Muslim feminist scholar Leila Ahmed, for example, would most likely agree with Hirsi Ali in problematizing the view of women contained in radical Islam, but she might disagree about how to combat this. One of the most comprehensive alternatives to the confrontational tactics of Hirsi Ali can be found in the writings of Tariq Ramadan, especially his *Western Muslims and the Future of Islam* (2004).[6] A philosophy professor born in Switzerland, Ramadan offers a comprehensive account of what it means to be a Muslim living in Europe and some practical advice about maintaining one's faith while at the same time engaging modern Western society. Just as radical Islam has spread itself through dense networks, the liberal Islamic tradition currently exemplified by Ramadan has developed a following throughout Europe. It is just a matter of time before a new reformist social movement breaks out into the public sphere of European politics. The Dutch imam Abdullah Haselhoef, mentioned in the previous chapter, might well be placed in the same reformist camp.

The murder of van Gogh has proven to be a catalyst in this interpretative, dialogic process, an example being the funding of new initiatives to promote more contact between native Dutch and Muslims and a more positive image of Islam in general and of Moroccans in particular. There are also those who would follow the example of ethnic groups in the United States in attempting to promote the possibility of hybrid identities, as in Dutch-Moroccan and Dutch-Islam.

For reformists, a presumed long-term aim is the development of a reflexive and self-reflective Muslim culture, in which both religious traditions and leaders, on the one hand, and intellectual freedom and intellectuals, on the other, would be respected. A more short-term aim appears to be to counter the forcefulness of Islamic fundamentalism. How best to carry out this confrontation is an issue that also affects how one approaches Hirsi Ali, *Submission*, and the murder of van Gogh. While Hirsi Ali readily stands in the same company as Rushdie, two fallen Muslims in search of reformation, there is a great deal of difference between *Submission* and *The Satanic Verses*. First of all, there is the historical context. Europe in 2004, when *Submission* was broadcast on Dutch television, is not the same as it was in 1988–89. The flow of immigrants from Islamic countries and the problems of assimilating second and third generations raised the temperature, the sensitivities, and the balance of power. Tolerance is being tested on all sides, with more chances to be heard and seen. Rushdie probably could not have predicted the violent response to his book, though some think otherwise (see Pipes 1990, for example). In the last pages of the first edition of *The Satanic Verses*, Rushdie carefully acknowledges the sources of his adaptations from the Koran, revealing a scholarly author concerned with his presumed audience. Yet, Pipes is quite convincing in his argument that Rushdie must have known something of what he was doing when he revitalized the claim that "the entire Qur'an [Koran] derived not from God through Gabriel, but from Muhammad himself, who put the words in Gabriel's mouth" (Pipes 1990:61). This is blasphemy, for "if this is true," writes Pipes, "then the Qur'an is a human artifact and the Islamic faith is built on a deceit." This is so because the faith grounds itself on the Koran being the literal word of God, to which one is compelled to submit, as Hirsi Ali would have it. And it is in part because Rushdie was so scholarly in his approach, carefully checking and recounting the sacred sources of his magical realistic fantasy, that Islamic scholars were forced to address his claims: they were as real to this audience as they were magical and fanciful to another.

Like censorship, blasphemy is a contested concept: a cultural marker that is difficult to define because it is a category of meaning whose borders are fluid and ever changing. For S. Brent Plate, blasphemy in the arts is about transgressing the boundaries between the sacred and profane, exposing some taboo that evokes the foundational values of a society. Plate (2006:27) quotes Leonard Levy as saying that "blasphemy is a litmus test of the standards a society feels it must enforce to preserve its unity, its peace, its morality, and above all its salvation." Blasphemy requires an object; an expression, act, or work of art; and an accuser, someone claiming to be offended by it. The act of blasphemy is performative in at least two senses: in its making and in the claim of being offended. The latter makes the created object into something more than a work of art. In other words, blasphemy must be performed, as it requires a doing and a distinctive reception.

Considered as cultural objects and works of art, there may be significant differences in accessibility and the intensity or speed of impact between a novel of nearly 600 pages, written in the ribald style of magical realism and a visually graphic, eleven-minute television movie. This is partly the difference between the literary and the visual and the relative power of the image. The first is available only to a limited few, while the latter is available to literally everyone. This difference is partly a matter of genre, images have the capacity to make a more immediate impression while written texts must be absorbed in order to be understood and thus to provoke a reaction. However, as Pipes (1990) reveals, the Rushdie texts were made available by various interest groups in excerpted form, with only the most relevant passages translated and made available. They were, in other words, "taken out of context," but still they were read by a great many, most of whom would not have read the entire novel. So the differences in genre and access between a graphic film and a highlighted written text might not be as meaningful as one thinks.

There is then the matter of audience and its capacity to decode meaning. Rushdie could perhaps justifiably claim to have knowingly limited his audience through his choice of literary form, and thus to have controlled for its response. He probably could not have known that his book would be useful to an Islamic leader making a claim for power in a widening political and cultural struggle. However, given the care Rushdie took to acknowledge his sources, he must have known that there would be those reading his novel through what David Morgan (2005) calls "the sacred gaze": viewing an object filtered through a religion.[7] Hirsi Ali and van Gogh could make no such claim. They knew exactly what they were doing, and, if one is to believe Hirsi Ali, she is intent on doing it again. One important difference between the artist and an intellectual should be mentioned: in general artists are more concerned with form than with conveying a distinct message, while for intellectuals the message takes precedence. In this regard, too, Hirsi Ali and not van Gogh was the proper target of wrath. However, since it is so clearly its message that was the driving force behind *Submission*, assumed effects, as well as intentions, must be considered in understanding and judging this film, even if audiences will not always interpret what they see in the way intended by the artist/performer. From the point of view of its creators, *Submission* is not simply an artistic work that can be judged on aesthetic criteria alone, as one might claim in Rushdie's case. Aesthetic criteria might apply, but they are secondary to the political effects. One can justly ask whether the film has helped Hirsi Ali's campaign for Islamic reform and the bettering of rights for Islamic women, or whether the opposite has been the case. To judge from the critical response, the answer appears to be the latter.

REPRESENTATION IN A CHANGING WORLD

One further general issue at stake here needs discussion: how should Muslims be represented in cultural forms and who should decide on that? This is something all minorities face, especially when they are in a position to have some say in the matter. It was the case for blacks in the United States, for example, when black writers, artists, and intellectuals were sufficient in number to assert some control over their own cultural production (Eyerman 2001). What *The Satanic Verses* and *Submission* have in common is that they offer representations of Islam that many who identify themselves with that religion find reprehensible because of the way Muslims are portrayed to those outside the faith. Representation in this sense is an especially sensitive issue in times of cultural clash, both internally, as in the struggle between reformists and traditionalists, and externally. Like Hirsi Ali, who was accused of betraying the immigrant community for making a film that slandered its religion, and therefore was no longer considered "one of us," Rushdie was open to charges of bad faith and betrayal. Even for those who had not read the book, the author's name identified him as a Muslim (Pipes 1990). The fact that a Muslim would write something that opened other Muslims to ridicule was sufficient to condemn him, regardless of the genre involved and the author's claims to artistic license and freedom of speech. As some African American critics argued in the 1920s, these were freedoms that minority artists were not entitled to; or if they were, then they had to take into account the potential harm their works, if made generally available, might have on how their community was viewed by the dominant group in society (Eyerman 2001).

As was the case with the making of *Submission* and perhaps also Salman Rushdie, the Danish cartoonists and the newspaper publishers who printed caricatures of the Prophet Muhammad knew exactly what they were doing and could anticipate some of the response to their actions. The cartoons, twelve in all, depicted the Prophet in various satirical images, the most controversial and most reproduced being a drawing of the Prophet wearing a turban with a fuse, thus representing him as a weapon of destruction. These had been published in Denmark at the end of September 2005, but the real conflict over their appearance began in January and February 2006, after news of their existence had spread throughout the world. Danish Muslim organizations were an important source in this dispersal (especially after having tried and failed to get legal satisfaction in Denmark), as were new telecommunications media and television news networks like CNN and Al Jazeera. What started out as a controversy concerning religious tolerance and freedom of speech in Denmark became a global political conflict that included the boycotting of Danish goods in many places in the world and several violent confrontations in which many died. On the issue of freedom of the press, at least one newspaper editor (of *Le Soir*) was fired for reprinting the most provocative cartoon, and newspaper editors and publishers on all continents were forced to take a stand on whether or not to reprint it. Along with the offices of *Jyllands-Posten*, the newspaper in which the cartoons first appeared, the Amsterdam office of *de Volkskrant* was emptied because of bomb threats as a direct result of the editors' decision to print the cartoons. In the name of freedom of the press and as an expression of solidarity with their Danish colleagues, Sweden's largest afternoon newspaper *Aftonbladet* (February 1, 2006) carried a full-page article by Bjorn Ulvaeus, formerly of ABBA and now a composer of popular musicals, arguing for the right of artists to subject religion to satirical interpretation (no Swedish paper has reprinted the drawings, though many have carried editorials supporting the right to do so).[8] Identifying himself as a skeptic, Ulvaeus proposed that he and others like him have the right to characterize, in whatever fashion they see fit, Jesus or Muhammad or any other deity. Similar words were used by Theo van Gogh in his defense of *Submission*, and more recently an outspoken critic, the Dutch author Leon de Winter, has argued that freedom of speech without the freedom to poke fun at the sacred is no freedom at all (Ellian and Winter 2006). In Ulvaeus's article, a picture of Rushdie, an image from the satiric film *The Life of Brian*, and *Jylland-Posten*'s cartoons are all discussed together. In an interview published in *de Volkskrant* (February 4, 2006) Klaus Bruhn Jensen, professor of media studies at the University of Copenhagen, drew a parallel between the cartoons and the film *Submission*. According to Jensen, *Jyllands-Posten* helped make visible the normally hidden line between what can and what ought not be publicly articulated. As in the case of *Submission*, the motives and the effects of any such articulation are influenced by the surrounding context. Timing may not be everything, but it means a lot in terms of the expected response. One must be careful then to distinguish between the defense of principle and the desire or need to mobilize public opinion, or in the case of leaders in the Islamic world, the need or usefulness in mobilizing opposition.

The Danish editors of this right-of-center newspaper were actively intervening in an ongoing, and very heated, political debate, as were Hirsi Ali and van Gogh. Their decision to print the cartoons at that particular time was taken, one can assume, on more than the principled grounds of freedom of the press.[9] Their newspaper had already taken positions on matters related to Islam and the immigration policies of the Danish government. Their decision to publish must thus also be judged according to effects and not merely values and intentions. Did the editors contribute to developing respect for principles of free speech, to opening dialogue and debate on this issue? The answer is not clear and unambiguous. The publication of the cartoons certainly widened a debate rekindled by *Submission*, moving it from the Netherlands onto the global public stage.[10]

How is this issue to be resolved? Can it be? Understanding the matter as one of free speech and intellectual freedom, a basic right in Western democracies, is a matter of framing that carries with it a source of resolution: the law and the courts in the country where the alleged offense occurred.[11] This means that a religious minority cannot expect that its own laws, such as the sharia in the case of Muslims, necessarily be respected by the majority, at least not in the legal sense. Such minorities may resort to other forms of pressure, such as that exercised through "representatives" in the Dutch multicultural model, or economic and political pressure as in the Danish case. Such pressure can be both local and global, and many protests have emerged around such issues. If we accept that the murder of Theo van Gogh received clerical approval, then his assassination was at the extreme end of a politically motivated response to a violation of Islamic law.

There is reason to doubt, however, that there might be much support among European Muslims for such an imposition. A recent data compilation (Tausch et al. 2006:2) suggests that even as the poverty rates of European Muslims grow, due to a combination of factors including national patterns of discrimination and European Union expansion to include lower-wage workers from Eastern Europe, the "passive support for Islamist radicalism in Europe and the complete distrust of democracy does not exceed 400,000 persons." In addition, as mentioned in the first chapter, the data they provide reveal that "Muslim communities in Europe are not different from other religious communities in their tendency towards secularism." To the extent that this is true, it suggests that the fear of Islamization in Europe is not well grounded in fact and that framing the matter in this way serves political interests as much as it reflects core values.

There exists a long history of judgments on issues of artistic freedom and freedom of expression that can be drawn on, and there are already laws on national and international levels. A general consideration here concerns who the creator of the offensive text or image is and in whose name he or she is acting. In his discussion of Submission, Geert Mak (2005c) drew a comparison to caricatures made by Nazi cartoonists of Jews in Germany in the late 1930s, and similar references were made during the cartoon controversy. There is, however, a difference when such an image is made by a member of a governing party and representing the interests of a powerful group and when one is made by an individual artist, who is then subject to a test in court. This point has been made by those defending the right to artistic expression, and there seems to be an important principle here: the position of the person making the transgression and the social and political context in which this occurs must be a consideration in any well-grounded judgments (Julius 2002).

There remains the issue of who decides how the issue is to be framed, the extent to which freedom of speech or religious freedom has to be given priority and the degree to which recognition and respect for something like a sacred gaze has to be taken into account. If Muslims attain a collective identity as "Muslims" and are viewed as a distinctive group by themselves as well as others, then there are at least two sides in the process of deciding. Part of the struggle in the current case is "who speaks for Muslims": on the one hand, there are elected representatives, like Hirsi Ali, and, on the other, there are neighborhood leaders or political activists, like Mohammed B. There are many claimants to "representative voice." In addition to the elected officials at the local and national level of the political system, there are established groups and organizations designed and designated to represent various religious and ethnic minorities. These are part of what many have called Dutch corporatism and are included within the specifics of multiculturalism. Some of these organizations attempted by formal means to prevent the showing of Submission on Dutch television. Whom did Ayaan Hirsi Ali represent when she and van Gogh made their film? Whom was she elected to represent when she was made a member of parliament? Hirsi Ali was chosen by her political party at least in part because she embodied something they desired and needed in their own representation: a young woman with a Muslim background who had quickly "assimilated" and who had become visible on the basis of statements she made concerning immigration policy and Muslim immigrants. Her attributes also attracted and then alienated her from the Labor Party. Though she claimed to represent Muslim women, election results reveal that such "immigrants" voted for the Labor Party in much greater numbers than Hirsi Ali's vvD. As a public intellectual, Ali claimed that Submission was a part of this representative project, yet, regardless of their political affiliation and social standing, Muslims in the Netherlands were united in their distaste for the film (Buruma 2006b).

A central issue here is what multicultural tolerance means today and in the future. In the highly charged current context, tolerance might include a great sensitivity to the beliefs and customs of others, especially when they are in a relatively powerless position. This might include forms of self-censorship on the part of artists and intellectuals, something that could be seen as temporary until that power disparity has been lessened. The empowerment of European Muslims would have to be stimulated, and any reconciliation would have to be a process of mutual accommodation. Artists and intellectuals have a central a role here as political actors, as they carry the burden of representation, giving voice to the so highly valued and hard-won right to freedom of expression in a way that others find just. Especially in a multicultural context, freedom of expression is a relative, not an absolute value, because it involves tolerance on both sides.

Ayaan Hirsi Ali can be viewed as a representative figure, someone whose status is dependent on social characteristics, that is, what she represents to various others. Like the Moroccan-born Amsterdam alderman Ahmed Aboutaleb, her rise to prominence must be contextualized. Hirsi Ali was chosen to stand for parliament as a representative figure; for party leaders, her being an articulate, young black Muslim woman was at least as important as her ideology. Such representative characteristics made access to the mass media relatively easy for the ambitious and articulate Hirsi Ali, but the content of what she said was no less significant. The same can be said about her role in making Submission. On the other hand, Aboutaleb was a representative figure in a different sense. A self-made man who had climbed the ropes of local politics, he had shaped his career in the context of Dutch multiculturalism, where representative figures were chosen to stand for and to manage a particular constituency. This type of representation requires skill in mediating between the group one 'is selected to represent and the political elites to whom one must deliver a constituency. This is precisely what Aboutaleb did, and he was an important agent in defusing tensions in Amsterdam on the day of the murder. This may well have been the career path Mohammed B. sought through his neighborhood activities and his early membership in the Labor Party. Initially, he sought recognition as a representative figure in local affairs, and in success for himself as well as "his" community. When these hopes were frustrated, due to personal limitations and a changing social context, he turned to the radical Islam that had become available as an alternative.

From the wider perspective of European Muslims, this can be seen as part of a struggle to define who and what will represent Islam and Muslims in the contemporary world. Within this context, radical Islam can be viewed as a social movement in the "war for Muslim minds," as Gilles Kepel (2004:254) describes it; one central issue of this struggle concerns whether Europe itself can be defined as part of the "land of Islam." This is an aspect of what Roy (2004) identifies as the "de-territorialization" of Islam, a product of the migration flows and population shifts in the contemporary phase of economic and cultural globalization. Of consequence here is another question besides that of territory: who is to define what being a Muslim in Europe means? Competing with those who advocate acceptance of the distinction between church and state (deemed central to Dutchness by Pim Fortuyn), including converts to European secularism like Hirsi Ali, are those associated with two predominant strands of salafism (Kepel 2004:255; see also Ramadan 2004:65). Though they insist on defining Europe as part of the "land of unbelief," that is, not part of the land of Islam, salafist leaders have mapped out alternative strategies for those believers who find themselves there. "In traditional Islamic political theory, the 'land of unbelief' is subdivided into Dar al-Harb, the land of war, where jihad is allowed, and Dar al-Sulh [sometimes written dar al-ahd], the land of truce, where Muslims do not instigate violence against unbelievers and infidels. In the pietistic . . . view, Europe is Dar al-Sulh. In the jihadists' view, it is Dar al-Harb" (Kepel 2004:255).[12] A leading figure in the jihadist camp is Osama bin Laden, who in early 2004 offered Europe the opportunity to distance itself from the foreign policy of the United States and become part of the "land of truce" (Kepel 2004:255). Through this rhetorical act, bin Laden was claiming to represent one strand in the struggle to define the situation of European Muslims, at the same time that he was claiming the authority and the power to make such a definition. With regard to the van Gogh affair, Mohammed B., a secularized Sunni Muslim announced his conversion to the jihadist camp when he threatened the lives of Hirsi Ali and Ahmed Aboutaleb and murdered van Gogh.

Like many sociologists studying social movements, Kepel (1997) applies the term *entrepreneur* to individuals seeking to play a leading role in an interpretative struggle. From this perspective, bin Laden functions as an entrepreneur, one who mobilizes resources toward some end when he speaks in the name of Islam, just as when he finances and organizes attacks on the West. Hirsi Ali can as well be characterized as an entrepreneur when she writes books and makes public statements about Islam and its need for reformation. Like bin Laden, she can be described as attempting to mobilize support for her views on the relationship between Islam and Muslim residents of Europe. One could add a generational aspect to this, as Kepel (1997:126) does. Many current activists on the Muslim side in this struggle are part of a younger generation confronted and confused by the changing conditions of Muslims in Europe and the rest of the world. The motivations and the actions of both Hirsi Ali and Mohammed B. can be so seen. While an older generation can be portrayed as accommodating itself to imposed demands for assimilation, a more militant generation of leaders has recently emerged in this period of change and uncertainty. Hirsi Ali has been successful as an entrepreneur; Mohammed B. seems less so. He may well be the "loser" that Anneke van Gogh described after his trial. Appearing at the trial in Moroccan clothes and Palestinian scarf, he failed, at least in her eyes, to represent anything but marginalization. However, to those neighborhood youth who knew him as Mo B., and the Taliban, he clearly represented something else. Which of these representations will prevail is of vital importance to the future of the Netherlands and the European Union of which it is a part.

Kepel (1997) draws a comparison between the black Muslim movement in the United States and radical Islam in Europe. This is a fruitful comparison. Applying this to the current situation of Muslims in Europe, I would propose a wider comparison between African Americans generally and Muslims in Europe. Black Muslims are a religious sect, containing various factions within it that range in their militancy. While it has evolved over the years, its central strategy is closest to what Kepel calls communalism: the attempt to maintain your own distinctive way of life while living as a minority in a larger society. This is a version of what some Dutch leaders call pillarization and is one possible outcome in the redefinition of Dutch-Muslim relations in the aftermath of the murder of van Gogh. However, black Muslims represent only a small fraction of African Americans, a minority within a minority, even though they make a continuous effort at increasing their number through conversion. The European Muslim comparison can be drawn with those in the pietist camp who make similar attempts at converting others and at seeking moderate accommodations to the secular or Christian world surrounding them. The jihadists are more comparable to the Black Panthers, a militant group with some connection (but not an essential one) to black Muslims, who turned to a more confrontational stance against the dominant society. Just as European Muslims are today, black Americans were once viewed as a "problem," as W. E. B. Du Bois famously pointed out at the turn of the twentieth century. The concept of "race" as applied in the United States has functioned in much the same way as "civilization" in the current debate in Europe, as a trope for a fundamental difference that is claimed to be real and objective. However, in their dealings with Muslim immigrants, Europeans probably do not experience any of the collective guilt and the need for reconciliation and repair of a troubled past that at least some citizens of the United States felt regarding slavery. There is no sense of having done wrong; in fact, the opposite seems to be the case. Many Europeans feel resentment against those who are not sufficiently grateful for the benefits of living in a "civilized" society, which is not only tolerant but also generous.

THE RESPONSIBILITY OF INTELLECTUALS

This chapter opened with reference to a dilemma for the Dutch: the disparity between a commitment to religious tolerance and their relations with the Muslims living in their midst. Through its social performance, the murder of van Gogh clearly brought into relief the horns of this dilemma, as the key actors embodied and acted out the clash of civilizations narrative that had come to define the debate. Although they have become obscured due to the funneling effect of this polarization, there remain still-dormant alternatives, including the development of a modernized Islam and an integrated, though not necessarily culturally assimilated Muslim community. Other representative voices than those expressing the clash of civilizations are now being rediscovered and given equal opportunity to be seen and heard. Salman Rushdie and Ayaan Hirsi Ali appeared also to have softened their message by more specifically naming their target, in a widely distributed "Manifesto" (February 2006) which they and ten other prominent intellectuals signed. In their text one can find "Islamism" rather than Islam identified as the source of evil; rather than calling for the reformation of Islam, they take a more positive approach by saying that those who live within Muslim culture "should not be deprived of the right to equality, freedom and secular values."[13]

Writing in Paris in 1924, in the midst of what was widely perceived as a crisis in European culture, Julien Benda called for intellectuals to abstain from political polemic in favor of more dispassionate scholarship. His *Trahison des clercs* is not only well named but also well worth rereading. While Benda's clercs are not the religious leaders so prominent in today's culture wars, his plea for a more "responsible" intellectual debate, and more responsible intellectuals, is fitting in the current climate. What is the role of the intellectual in a polarized discourse like the current clash of civilizations? Is it to be a provocateur, a cultural "terrorist" as van Gogh would have it, or should one withdraw into scholarship or art of its own sake, as Benda proposed? That is certainly one possibility: to stand up and defend the tradition of intellectual criticism and artistic freedom one claims as exclusively "Western" values against an "Eastern" tradition that, so it is claimed, denies them. Susan Buck-Morss (2003:vii) provides another possibility when she invites intellectuals "to suspend existing political identities and reconfigure the parameters of their discourse to recognize overlapping concerns." Of course, Buck-Morss limits Western intellectuals to "critical theory on the left" but I think one could make a wider, more inclusive plea that would include liberals as well. By "overlapping concerns," Buck-Morss means the critical stance toward modernization and the Enlightenment, which one finds in the writings of theorists associated with the early Frankfurt School. This perspective would be as critical of Hirsi Ali's "radical enlightenment" positioning as it would be of its polar opposite, "radical Islam," but could possibly find common ground with a reformist Islam in search of an alternative to the intrusion of "the morally indifferent world of global markets" (ibid.:ix). A first step would be to recognize the existence of a critical discourse within Islam and the rejection of easy stereotyping. This might include, on the basis of civic responsibility, refusing to publish the Muhammad cartoons because they so graphically reinforce stereotypes, making the issue a moral as well as a political one, and not simply a claim to the principle of free speech. Such a position would also criticize those who made Submission. It would recognize that reformist and critical traditions have long existed in the Islamic world and that many more Muslim artists and intellectuals have suffered at the hands of radicals than have Westerners. Hirsi Ali and Salman Rushdie appear now to have recognized that intellectuals have a moral and political responsibility, as well as an artistic one.

The central argument of this book is that the murder of Theo van Gogh was not yet another incident of senseless individual violence that can be suitably explained through reference to the individuals involved; it was not simply attributable to the frustrations or psychological state of the perpetrator or to provocations on the part of the victim. Nor do I suggest that the murder was an expression of collective violence, the work of a terrorist network, with or without links to an international organization. While that may well turn out to be the case, no substantial evidence has yet come forth. Rather, I have analyzed the murder through the prism of social drama, as an act of symbolic violence, where actions are scripted within highly stylized frameworks of meaning and targets selected for what they are thought to represent. As Robben and Suárez-Orozco (2000:1) write, such "violence cannot be reduced to a single level of analysis because it targets the body, the psyche, as well as the socio-cultural order." Such actions make reference to and help constitute collective representations, as much as they reflect individual motives. In this book I have extended the theory of social drama to include the central actors themselves, who are interesting not so much for their biographies or their intentions as for what they symbolize. The actors in this drama are interesting for the tropes they carry and the potentialities they mobilize in audiences and other actors, including the mass media.

The theory of social drama provided an interpretive frame for uncovering layers of meaning in the occurrence itself. Within that frame, I applied analysis geared to three levels of approach. First, I applied performance theory to highlight the actors, the acts, and the setting. The issues here concerned who was killed, why, and where, as well as how the murder was carried out and what this meant to actors and audience. Second, use was made of discourse theory to analyze how the murder was represented and reconstructed in mass media and, in the process, transformed into a public event. The question of who was killed and why was raised again, but with a focus on framing and media representation. Third, by means of a macrohistorical approach, the interpretation was turned to the past and to collective memory in understanding the emotions unleashed by the murder. Issues of concern here were the meaning of "Dutchness," of multiculturalism and the very nature of collective identity. In this final chapter, I will add yet another dimension through invoking the theory of cultural trauma, which was outlined at the start of the book.

CULTURAL TRAUMA

The murder of Theo van Gogh opened festering sores in Dutch society, including some that were very deeply hidden. As it occurred in real time and unfolded in the mass media, the event had effects that could be called "traumatizing," making it possible to speak of its "traumatizing potential" (Sztompka 2004, Smelser 2004). This is to walk a line between realist and constructivist approaches, whereby actual occurrences can be graded according to their (potential) effects and whereby all effect is not merely "constructed" or added on after the fact. I take this position in the foregoing analysis, and I will seek to further clarify it in my concluding discussion.

In the wake of the murder of Pim Fortuyn, the murder of van Gogh registered a major impact; how powerful can be gauged by the public reactions, from those more predictable from elected officials to those less so from the general public and the royal family.[1] Subtler anecdotal evidence of "traumatizing effects" can also be uncovered, such as those recounted to me by residents of the Amsterdam neighborhood in which the murder occurred. One person recalled how she had been at work in another part of the city when the first accounts were broadcast over the radio. At this point the identity of the victim was not announced, but the place was. Assuming that such a bulletin would not have been broadcast for just any victim and also curious about her neighbors' reactions, this woman cycled to the crime scene and, along with many others, remained there the entire day. The murder not only broke her daily routine; she could recall the precise details almost two years later. A second account comes from a person who heard only the barest details over the radio while awaiting a taxi to drive her to the airport for an overseas trip. On returning home a month later, she found her neighborhood a different place. None of the "Dutch" were speaking to their "Muslim" neighbors, as they had done previously. While things would eventually return to normal, as she described it, the event had significantly affected the routine behaviors that make up daily life.

Why an incident like the murder of van Gogh may have "traumatizing" effects needs to be explained, and this explanation can be situational, limiting itself to the immediate conditions. Here one would focus on the brutality of the killing, the chilling behavior of the murderer, the well-known victim, the "senselessness" of the attack on an open street, and so on. All of this could in itself be shocking and numbing and possibly cause a short- or even longer-term change in the routines of social interaction, as the examples above suggest. One could also link this reaction to other recent incidents as a further example of "senseless violence" (Stengs n.d.), which would give it broader meaning but not necessarily imply cultural trauma. The argument that I have been building, especially since chapter 4, is meant to show that, while plausible, framing the event in terms of senseless violence would not sufficiently get to the root of explaining the emotional impact and deep cleavages exposed through the murder of Theo van Gogh.

The theory of cultural trauma allows us to focus on more than a single event, no matter how powerful it may by itself be. From this perspective one should speak of an accumulating "traumatizing potential" in relation to a series of events, such that a number of incidents experienced as a series and connected through a narrative adding to their cumulative effect might result in cultural trauma. In this case, framing and the content of the narration would be determinant. As developed previously (Eyerman 2001; Alexander, et al. 2004), cultural trauma refers to a tear in the fabric of a social order precipitated by a shocking occurrence that sets up a meaning struggle and that demands reparation. What I am suggesting is that there may be a series of such events, which call forth this demand.

Once interpretations have been stabilized and a relatively robust consensus about the meaning of the event is achieved, that consensus becomes more than a "preferred" reading or interpretation because it has real effects in the sense of supporting new ways of acting, including changes in policies and protocol. To be more concrete, once it is established who was killed by whom and why, changes in the boundaries demarcating the collective may follow, along with new policies of inclusion and exclusion, which would affect changes in the collective itself. In other words, Dutchness, the foundation theme of the collective, might be redefined and re-performed.

Cultural trauma is a theoretical construct, a heuristic that permits us to set borders around an occurrence that reaches back into the past and forward into the future. The aim is to make deeply buried culture structures available to the analyst. Framing the murder of Theo van Gogh as cultural trauma means placing the event within a distinctive conceptual frame, with a longer time line than indicated in the anecdotal examples given above. Like the frame around a painting, the theory of cultural trauma allows us to mark off a historical process, to distinguish foreground and background, and to highlight specific features. Unlike the construction of a theoretical model, the aim is not to construct hypotheses or to predict outcomes; rather it is to uncover layers of meaning that help us gain a deeper understanding of significance and consequence.

First of all, the theory of cultural trauma permits us to further analyze the process from occurrence to event, as discussed in the opening chapters. As argued there, occurrences, even relatively rare ones like murders, become events through mediated representations, whereby they are reconstituted as broadly significant and meaningful. This process of event making necessarily involves conflicting interpretations and the attempt by various agents and agencies to define the situation in a particular way and from a particular perspective. Not all occurrences, of course, become events. Turning an occurrence into an event involves a struggle to affix meaning. As a meta-framework of interpretation, cultural trauma allows one to highlight these meaning struggles, while at the same time making possible a multilayered analysis of the entire process, including the "meaning" of the event-making process itself. In this analysis, individual responses to and mediated representations of powerful, event-generating occurrences are interpreted in the light of scripted frameworks and internalized collective representations, sediments of individual and collective memory. This permits not only the identification of key agents in the struggle to affix and stabilize meaning but also allows the identification of significant collective processes. Analyzing the process of event making helps make visible deeply rooted collective representations, which in turn may aid in explaining why the occurrence is powerful or contains the traumatizing potential that it does. The aim of such analysis is at one and the same time to identify the agents and the scripted representations and to articulate the deep structure of collective representation.

At one level, one can identify "the mediating role of intellectuals, social movements, the media, journalists, educational institutions and various other moral entrepreneurs," as important actors in transforming an occurrence into an event (Demertzis n.d.:7). Such agents are positioned on a discursive field, which they themselves help constitute through their own practices in the struggle to define the situation. In what has been called a spiral of signification (Sahlins 1985), the representations these agents provide are a vital factor in realizing the trauma potential in any occurrence. For example, Smelser (2004:40) notes how the attribution of negative affect as implied in such phrasing as "national tragedy, national shame, national catastrophe" is essential in the realization of trauma potential. It is through mass media that such attribution is made with maximum effect. In this case, agents are, at the same time and through the same process, claiming to speak for a collective, the nation, while calling it into being. They are, in other words, performing the collective.

That such phrasing may have a powerful effect and be effective in mobilizing emotions in collective will-formation points to another level of meaning and interpretation. Calling upon the nation or any other collective is to call forth identities and identifications that exist as discourses of a shared history and a shared future. Such representations are performative in the sense that through signification and denotation one hopes to create that collectivity of which one speaks. Whether or not such attempts are successful, whether or the not a "collective" responds and how large or consequential it will be, cannot be known at the outset, as the audience in a modern society is multiple and varied. One point to be emphasized is that speaking of the nation and of national trauma is itself positional, being always related to some individual or collective actor. In speaking of cultural trauma, one must always ask, "Whose trauma? Trauma for whom?" as Bernhard Giesen (2004) does when he distinguishes between the trauma of the perpetrators and the trauma of the victims.

In the process of affixing meaning, agents (including the central actors themselves) search for antecedents and predict consequences in order to motivate, strengthen, and dramatize their positions. Here preexisting narrative genres and tropes enter the scene, as the current incident is discursively linked to scripts culled from a shared past or projected future. This means that part of the process of affixing meaning contains the potential for initiating collective movements and practices such as grounding new laws and policies, which may affect the future of the collective. It is here that past and future connect in and through an occurrence, adding significance.

There are other levels beyond the situational that the theory of cultural trauma helps elucidate. Speaking of cultural trauma requires both deeper and more permanent changes in thinking and behavior and a longer time line or horizon of explanation. In cultural trauma, the traumatizing incident is given deeper significance, triggering a spiral of interpretation and emotionally charged response that eventually arrive at the foundations of collective identity. Both the struggle to fix meaning on the event, to name the perpetrators and the victims, and the attempts to repair or to redefine the collective involve more deeply rooted emotions and foundational narratives. In other words, an occurrence gains significance both through exposing the "roots" of the collective and being "signified and socially accepted as trauma" (Demertzis n.d.:5, Sztompka 2004). What is essential is the breaking of a social bond, of the collective frames of reference and the apparatuses for the reproduction of the social subsystems and or of the social system in its totality. Even if there are various and competing accounts, a cultural trauma exists and has permanent effects; the deepness and the indelibility of the effects are key. Understanding this requires a longer-term perspective than one that limits itself to the situation or immediate context within which the shocking incident occurred.

ACCUMULATED TRAUMA

In *Trauma Culture* (2005), E. Ann Kaplan links the conceptualization of trauma to modernity, suggesting that the "shocks" caused by rapid social change created conditions necessitating new concepts and theories to understand them. A key figure in this process was, of course, Sigmund Freud, whose development of psychoanalysis was a response to individual trauma. Jürgen Habermas (1989) makes a similar argument, though with no direct reference to trauma, when he links the emergence of psychology to modern subjectivity and the differentiation of public and private spheres as a characteristic of modernity. In addition to developments in scientific understanding, the experience of modernity created conditions for developments in artistic expression, creating new genres, like the novel and the melodrama in theater and then film, in which the shocks of modern life could be represented as fiction and fantasy. Like Kaplan, I have suggested that such media serve as mechanisms not only for the psychological reworking of collective trauma, but also for its maintenance and transmission over time and space (Eyerman 2001).

My aim in the present book has been to propose that to gain a deep understanding of the reactions to the murder of van Gogh one has to grasp the emotional effects of some significant events in Dutch history at least since the Second World War; their significance lies in the fact that they have left a mark on the collective memory and are part of the narration of national identity, of Dutchness. Important here are the lingering emotions attached to the German occupation, the tragedy of Dutch Jews, the myth of resistance, and the painful recounting of the humiliations of daily life during and immediately after the war. Here the myth of resistance and the celebration of heroism, the Anne Frank house as shrine, for example, are mixed with the history of collaboration and indifference. As was discussed in an earlier chapter, the memory of the Second World War still weighs heavily in the Dutch collective memory and shapes the meaning of Dutchness, helping determine who is included in the collective and who is not. More closely connected in terms of time and topic are the painful effects of defeat as a colonial power, most especially the loss of the East Indian colonies and the forced recognition of an independent Indonesia. The memory of the colonial past and its continuing relevance is evidenced by its reevaluation, in academic texts as well as in film and literature. The Second World War and the closely connected loss of colonies provide a moral framework through which contemporary events are filtered. This has long been the case, but following the murders of Fortuyn and van Gogh, the interpretative framework has become politicized in new directions. Van Gogh heard the stomping of Nazi boots when he saw Muslim beards and head scarves, and Hirsi Ali equated Islamic radicals with fascism, while Amsterdam mayor Job Cohen is more prone to see Dutch Muslims as an oppressed minority, in need of protection as were Dutch Jews during the war. In one autobiographical account, Hirsi Ali similarly draws on both the Second World War and the colonial experience to explain why the Dutch were so open to the demands of some Muslim immigrants for their "own pillar in Dutch society": "The Dutch adopted these policies because they wanted to be good people. Their country had behaved unspeakably in Indonesia, and didn't (much) resist Hitler; in Holland, a greater percentage of Jews were deported during the Second World War than in any other country in Western Europe. Dutch people felt guilty about this recent past" (Hirsi Ali 2007:245–46).

ACCUMULATED TRAUMA: REDEFINING COLLECTIVITY

A potent reminder of the past came in December 1971, when a group calling itself the Free South Moluccan Youths seized a train and attempted to pressure the Dutch government to support independence for the islands from which their parents had been forced to flee. Two people were killed, and some fifty hostages held for twelve days. During the hijacking, another group attacked the Indonesian consulate in Amsterdam and also seized hostages. Both groups eventually surrendered to the police and were imprisoned. In May 1977, Moluccans seized a train near Groningen and a school in Bovensmilde, demanding that those who had earlier been imprisoned be released. After nearly three weeks of negotiations, the Dutch army stormed the train, killing six of the nine Moluccans; two hostages also died in the assault. Media coverage of these events and the trials that followed them was extensive. Perhaps even more painful than these events was the memory of the last years of Dutch rule in Indonesia and the forced repatriation of Dutch civilians and their Indonesian families in the 1950s. As the approximately 270,000 people arrived in the decade between 1950 and 1960, a new ethnic group, the Indie, was created. A 1990 report estimated the number of people born in Indonesia or having at least one parent born there living in the Netherlands at 472,000 (Dieleman 1993:120). If still neglected in the official memory, there is ample evidence of a distinct popular memory maintained within this group concerning the behavior of the Dutch authorities.

The concept of trauma was applied by Dutch authorities and then the mass media in discussing the experience of Dutch troops in Srebrenica in 1995 (Zarkov 2002). In July of that year, Dutch troops failed to defend Bosnian Muslims from Serbian troops, and an estimated 7,500 Muslims died. When an official report on this event was published in 2002, the Dutch government, led by Wim Kok, resigned. The actions of the Dutch military at the time were broadcast by the mass media, which invoked the concept of trauma. The concept was first applied to the Dutch forces, to the guilt and helplessness they were said to have felt as a result of their failure. This was called the "Srebrenica-trauma" in the Dutch press (see, for example, de Volkskrant, October 30, 1995). The term was later applied in the Dutch mass media as a "national trauma" to explain the reluctance of later governments to use Dutch troops in similar international conflicts, just as the term Vietnam syndrome has been used in the United States. One might also speak of the trauma of Muslims in the Netherlands and around the globe, as they viewed once again the failure of Western institutions in the face of aggression against Muslim civilians. The wars in Bosnia, Afghanistan, and Chechnya had a cumulative affect on young Muslims, confirming their perception that the "West" could not be trusted and was indeed their enemy. As mentioned earlier, members of the so-called Hofstad group had volunteered for service in Chechnya and had viewed videos of atrocities in those countries, which conditioned their feelings of alienation and anger while living in the Netherlands.

Closest in time and meaning was the trauma associated with the murder of Pim Fortuyn, just a year and half before the murder of van Gogh. While some have pointed to his rise to prominence as the greatest shock in modern Dutch political history, the murder of Fortuyn left an indelible mark on the national conscience. If murder is a relatively rare occurrence in the Netherlands, the murder of a public figure is extremely rare. At the time of his murder, Fortuyn was a national celebrity, as much as a representative figure of Dutchness as a leader of a political party. A television poll in November 2004, weeks after the murder of van Gogh, designated Fortuyn the "greatest figure in Dutch history" (Buruma 2006b:45). His murder left not only scars but also great anger and frustration. These emotions were rekindled through the murder of van Gogh. The murder of Fortuyn most directly contributed to that necessary set of conditions for trauma that Marshall Sahlins (1985) called a "structure of conjuncture."

With the help of such concepts, one can identify two distinct processes at work in creating a cultural trauma: (1) the accumulated traumas that help shape collective memory and the identity of a collective and (2) the "spiral of signification" creating a "culture structure" (Alexander 2004: 203) that turns particular occurrences with traumatic potential into traumatic events.

Cultural trauma always poses the question trauma for whom? As Sztompka (2004:166–67) puts it, not everyone suffers from trauma in the same way, nor does everyone adopt the same strategies for dealing with it. Smelser (2004:37) suggests that events may be traumatic at one moment in a nation's history, but not at another; he states that "cultural traumas are for the most part historically made, not born." Individual and collective memory may be selective and various; much depends on the location of the individual doing the remembering and on the interpretive frame of those who seek to represent the memory of the collective. Memory is subject to recall, as well as interest and intention, and what is recalled may well be filtered through mass-mediated representations. Significant events such as the Holocaust have been forged into memory through films and documentaries, novels and textbooks, all of which necessarily involve selection and the constitutive effects of narration.

Alongside the accumulated traumas resulting from war, occupation, and the loss of colonies that helped articulate and reconstitute a sense of Dutchness at various historical moments are those accumulated traumas that contributed to the shaping of Mohammed B.'s life. His traumatic experiences are just as essential to understanding his conversion to radical Islam and the decision to murder Theo van Gogh as the accumulated traumas are to understanding the murder's effect on the Dutch nation. The prime trauma here was being brought up as the son of marginalized and stigmatized immigrant parents, occupants of the lower rungs of the social hierarchy in contemporary Dutch society. As bad as it was from the beginning, the status of Berbers from rural Morocco in the Netherlands only worsened with time, as they moved from being relatively welcomed "guest workers" to problematic "immigrants" in the context of a changing national and global economy. Neither Dutch nor Moroccan, but a little of both, many in the second generation felt that they fit nowhere and had nowhere to go in search of a better life. Here personal biography mixed with history, as some succeeded and some did not. Then there were the more personal, emotionally charged events, like Mohammed B.'s viewing his father's declining health and failing ability to rise above both marginalization and work-related injury to play the designated role of patriarch in the household. As the eldest son in tradition-bound Berber culture, which places a special burden on that position, Mohammed B.

must have been extremely frustrated, as well as angered, by this failing. It was now up to him to uphold the honor of the family. To this one can add his own frustrations in the neighborhood, the closing of the youth center and his loss of status there and the failure to settle on a career path. Mohammed B. was caught in both a personal and a national failure; it was a matter of failed social policy as much as insufficient individual will. Added to this was the changing status of Islam itself, especially after September 11, 2001, and the declaration of the war on terror within the framework of the clash of civilizations.

In his account of what might motivate relatively well-integrated Muslim youth living in Europe to join radical Islamic movements, Quintan Wiktorowicz (2005:5) proposes that the crucial first step is conditioned by a "cognitive opening" that "shakes the certitude in previously accepted beliefs." While Wiktorowicz sees this as a more or less sudden occurrence, similar to the breach in Victor Turner's general theory of social drama, I would suggest that this can also be a longer-term cumulative process.

It is possible to dismiss Mohammed B. as a "loser," as Theo van Gogh's mother Anneke did (Buruma 2006b:191). After all, other immigrants from the Rif Mountains successfully assimilated into the Netherlands, such as Amsterdam alderman Ahmed Aboutaleb, one of Mohammed B.'s hate objects. One could also focus on his apparently problematic personality, his paranoia and megalomania, as Buruma (2006b:194) does. All of this might be true from some perspective, but it has the effect of individualizing the murderer and the murder. As such, it represents an attempt, conscious or not, to defuse cultural trauma and move toward reconciliation.

There are generational aspects to these accumulated traumas, affecting the meaning of events and the formation of a specific generational consciousness. Second-generation immigrant youth experience marginalization and discrimination differently than their parents, in part because they can view their parents' lives as one of humiliation and often experience a doubly felt sense of shame. They can feel shame about and for their parents and for their own inability to do anything to help. Mohammed B.'s anger at his father's inability to discipline his sister and at his own inability as the eldest son to effectively replace him, an anger that drove him from the family home, was an expression of generational anger as much as it was individual and personal. Such anger can also be explained as accumulated shame and humiliation at the community level and as the result of a breakdown of a traditional family structure in a liberal setting. Mohammed B. was just a child during the Rushdie affair, but the sense of humiliation and anger it aroused in the already marginalized Muslim neighborhoods in the Netherlands must have been felt and recorded in his experience. The film *Submission* was his Rushdie affair, but not only his, as this film was part of the longer process of misunderstanding and marginalization affecting Muslims in the Netherlands and in Europe more generally.

The presence of the colonial past is something that unifies European Muslims, even where there are national differences, both between colonized and colonizer. The Netherlands never colonized Morocco, so Mohammed B. would not have felt the humiliation of subordination directly. However, he likely felt this by proxy as Khosrokhavar (2005) uses the term, especially after Islam became the dominant identification of his life, making the notion of *umma* or Islamic community a fundamental category of his experience. This notion implies that what happens to other Muslims happens to oneself, and one not only experiences empathy but also shares the responsibility to act. In the postcolonial era, one of the most traumatic events for Muslims was the defeat suffered at the hands of the Israeli army in 1967. For Fatima Mernissi (1987), this marked a decisive cultural as well as political turning point where looking back to the past replaced looking ahead to the future for hope and glory. It also marked a shift in power in the production of ideas, and in politics, from secular to religious leaders. More recently, the slaughter of Muslims in Srebrenica, where the United Nations and Dutch troops failed to protect innocent civilians in a murderous civil war, was strongly experienced as betrayal by Muslims worldwide. This event drove at least one member of the so-called Hofstad group to radical Islam. The trauma experienced then was not the "national trauma" of the Dutch, but the trauma of the vulnerable and exposed Muslim community at the lower end of the society. As Mohammed B. would later discover, radical Islam offered a new definition of this situation, which permitted the transformation of frustration and negative social ascription into something seemingly positive. Radical Islam provided a heroic narrative that could turn tragedy into triumph, as least symbolically. As part of the process, the mundane routines of everyday life became charged with symbolism, even when things remained much as they had been. The murder of Theo van Gogh was

Mohammed B.'s act of redemption. Through this act he sought to redeem not only himself but also, more importantly, the community he sought to represent. Although it did not end the way he planned, the social drama he helped promote could end happily for Mohammed B. if his murderous act contributed to a widening breach and toward a cultural trauma in Dutch society. Whether he is a winner or loser remains to be seen. It all depends on how individual and collective actors attempt to resolve the Dutch dilemma and repair the collective.

The example of Mohammed B.'s identification with an imagined Muslim community can be used to illustrate the process through which various levels are incorporated into the idea of cultural trauma. The slaughter of Muslims in the Bosnian civil war affected the experience of Muslims in the Netherlands, making it into a national issue and for some a national trauma. This was the case not only because of the direct involvement of the Dutch army and the national debate this sparked, but also because it was experienced and discussed by Muslims living in the Netherlands. For some of these Muslims—Mohammed B., for example—this was strongly felt as a sense of betrayal and a further indication that one could not trust Western ideals of democracy and citizenship or multiculturalism.

Since the murder of van Gogh, the Netherlands has become a "normal" European nation, with an anti-immigrant/immigration right wing gathering a significant proportion of the vote in both local and national elections. In the November 2006 election, which itself was brought about due to the fall of the ruling coalition in the wake of the threatened removal of Hirsi Ali's citizenship, a new right-wing party led by Geert Wilders, the former VVD-member of parliament who once coauthored a manifesto with Hirsi Ali, gained nine seats in parliament. Given the necessity of coalition in Dutch politics, the issue is now how much influence this anti-immigration right wing will have and how long lasting that influence will be. It is clear that one of the central issues for any new government will be redefining the meaning of Dutch multiculturalism. One of the more positive outcomes of the van Gogh murder has been to transform Dutch politics from management to public debate, thus returning the political sphere to its tradition function.

1. ASSASSINATION AS PUBLIC PERFORMANCE

1 I use the term "Muslim" to refer to an ethnic group as officially categorized by Dutch authorities. This group is composed of those "having an Islamic cultural background" (Shadid and Koningsveld 1995:3).

2 Dutch criminal law was amended in August 2004 to make the life sentence applicable to "terrorist acts." Mohammed Bouyeri was the first to be sentenced under the new law and the twenty-eighth person since 1945 (excluding war criminals) to receive the life sentence. The trial led to the following pronouncement: "The defendant rejects our democracy. He even wants to bring down our democracy. With violence. He is insistent. To this day. He sticks to his views with perseverance. This calls for a strong response. By literally placing him outside our democracy. This means that he will not be allowed to vote. This means deprivation of active and passive suffrage. Taking everything into consideration, the severity of the facts, the underlying circumstances, and the personality of the defendant, I find only one punishment suitable and this is life imprisonment" (www.wikipedia.org/wiki/moham med—Bouyeri).

3 In the reportage, when the 60 Minutes host asked Hirsi Ali how it felt to rise from being an immigrant to a member of parliament, Ali replied, "The American Dream." The program also included interviews with Nabil Marmouch, identified as a "Muslim community leader" and as someone starting a Muslim political party and also with Paul Scheffer, of the University of Amsterdam, who will figure in our story. Hirsi Ali attended a gala dinner sponsored by Time magazine, where she was an honored guest. Introduced as a freedom fighter, she toasted van Gogh as a hero who made a film for Muslim women he would never know, and who, she said, bravely insisted on having his name appear as director in the face of great danger. Dutch television in its film coverage of this event called it "Hollywood in New York" and carried footage of the exquisitely dressed Hirsi Ali signing autographs for fans, as photographers in the background yelled out, "Ali, you look gorgeous."

4 What Bouyeri actually said was, "I don't feel your pain, I can't. I don't know what it is to lose a child that was brought into this world with pain and tears. It is in part because I am not a woman. But it is also in part because I can't feel with you. That's because I believe that you are an infidel" (trial transcript posted on http://dutchreport.blogspot.com).

5 The concept of "moral panic" emerged in accounting for public alarm over the consumption of drugs among youth in the early 1970s (Thompson 1998). It was made famous by Stanley Cohen (1972) in his study of British youth cultures in the 1960s. Cohen (1972:9) wrote, "Societies appear to be subject, every now and then, to periods of moral panic. A condition, episode, person or group of persons emerges to become defined as a threat to societal values and interests; its nature is presented in a stylized and stereotypical fashion by the mass media; the moral barricades are manned by editors, bishops, politicians and other right-thinking people, socially accredited experts pronounce their diagnoses and solutions; ways of coping are evolved or (more often) resorted to; the condition then disappears, submerges or deteriorates and becomes more visible."

6 This need not be as dramatic as it might appear; they also reported that those claiming "no religion" were the largest group (nearly 40 percent), Roman Catholics were next with just over 31 percent, Protestants about 14 percent, then members of the Dutch Calvinist church 7 percent, followed by Muslims at about 5 percent (http:www.cbs.nl).

7 I use ritual here to mean highly determined, stylized actions, where behavior follows rigidly set traditions (one acts out, rather than acts); performances are scripted in a difference sense, where the possibility of reflective distance, and thus action, is possible. The dagger was the weapon of choice for the original "assassins," the members of the Ismaili order in eleventh-century Iran. Their crusade was directed against rival Sunni religious leaders, as well as the political elite. After carrying out an assassination, "the assassin either took his own life or was put to death" (Khosrokhavar 2005:24). In discussing the continuity as well as the differences between the ancient and modern martyr, Khosrokhavar points out that "members of premodern sects were usually willing to die and to kill their enemies because of their millenarian convictions . . . the Ismaili disciple who put a Seljuk dignitary to death believed that he was helping to construct a new *polis* in a new world. Modern martyrs . . . act out of hatred for a world in which, as they see it, they are being denied access to a life of 'dignity.' . . . Whereas the sectarian martyrs of the Islam of the premodern age were convinced that their actions would bring about the advent of a new world and the destruction of the old, the actions of the modern Muslim martyrs are intended to destroy a world in which there is no place for them as citizens of a nation or an Islamic community. In most cases, they do not cherish any chiliastic ideal as a central theme in their motivations" (24–25). What Mohammed B.'s thoughts were in this regard would be something of interest.

8 Mohammed Bouyeri lived in an Amsterdam neighborhood that not only was highly populated with immigrants but also had produced its share of radicals. A neighborhood-centered analysis might be useful to counter the focus on

individuals. Mohammed Bouyeri had also spent several months in prison (summer 2001) for his part in a neighborhood fight. His neighborhood was also the target of intensive investigation by the social authorities, and his building was subject to regular visits by social workers, something that he viewed as an intrusion and reacted strongly against, advising his family not to speak with them (Kranenberg 2005). Kranenberg describes the transformation of Bouyeri from a second-generation immigrant youth with aspirations toward integration to a holy warrior.

9   The terms "autochthonous" and "allochthonous" are constructions that in and of themselves are revealing in reference to the Dutch debate. The terms are opposites and meant to refer to native and nonnative Dutch citizens. The terms were chosen over more commonplace alternatives presumably because "allochthonous" appeared more neutral and thus less offensive than, for example, "immigrant" or "ethnic minority." Yet, from their Greek origins and geological usage, the concept connotes a sense of fundamental difference, of a different sort, and thus of being present yet "not one of us."

10 It could well be, however, that van Gogh's, if not Hirsi Ali's, intentions were just that of blasphemy. As Benschop (2005:84) points out, "Atheists find these sections of the law hard to digest . . . atheists are accused of insulting a god, who they deny exists"; citing George Bernard Shaw's statement "All great truths start as blasphemies," Benschop writes that van Gogh would have reacted to lawsuits by awarding them his "Audacity Prize," for attempting to prevent something from being said before it was actually uttered— which could imply that a group of believers were unwilling to live among nonbelievers. The free speech issue is one that emerges continually and from all sides. When Rotterdam artist Chris Ripke painted "Thou shalt not kill" in the form of a mural on the wall next to his studio, the act led to protest from the mosque next door and to the mural's being forcibly removed on orders of the city mayor as a "racist utterance directed at the neighbors." Buruma (2006b) adds a class dimension to this when he suggests that van Gogh belonged to a section of the Dutch elite that believed they could say whatever they felt like.

11 A recent data compilation (Tausch et al. 2006:2) suggests that even as the poverty rates of European Muslims grow, due to a combination of factors including national patterns of discrimination and European Union expansion to include lower-wage workers from Eastern Europe, the "passive support for Islamist radicalism in Europe and the complete distrust of democracy does not exceed 400,000 persons." In addition the data they provide reveal that "Muslim communities in Europe are not different from other religious communities in their tendency towards secularism."

12 According to Kennedy (1995:311), free speech rights were loosened in the 1960s, after being restrictive throughout Dutch history. This occurred in the

midst of student demonstrations. As Kennedy recounts, "By 1967, fining demonstrators for slandering [American president] LBJ became much less frequent, with the fines milder, and in 1969 prosecutions for this offense stopped altogether." However, also in 1969, "a student received a three-month sentence from an angry Amsterdam judge for shouting, 'Away with the Orange whores!'" (ibid.). Defaming a foreign politician, in other words, was less of an issue than speaking ill of the royal house. Article 137d of the Dutch penal code states: "He who in public, orally or in writing or image, incites hatred, discrimination, or violent action against person or property on account of race, religion or philosophy of life, gender or hetero- or homosexual inclination is punishable with imprisonment for a maximum of one year or a fine."

In 1998 the Landelijk Expertiscentrum van het Openbaar Ministerie (National Center on Discrimination or LECD) was charged with enforcing laws against discrimination under the offices of the public prosecutor. One of its concerns has been the balance between free speech and "scornful blasphemy" as defined by Dutch law. For example, Article 147 of the Penal Code states, "He who publicly expresses scornful blasphemies that are offensive to religious feelings will be punished with imprisonment for a maximum of three months," and Article 147a says, "He who distributes a document or image that contains utterances which are offensive to religious feeling as scornful blasphemies, will be punished with imprisonment of a maximum of two months" (Benschop 2005: 83–84). On this basis, van Gogh and Hirsi Ali were subject to criminal charges that would hinge on the meaning of "scornful" and on the intentions of the filmmakers. At least one group of Dutch Muslims has sought legal help in prohibiting the release of the sequel *Submission II*, promised by Hirsi Ali.

13 Smelser's (1962:15–18) determinants are: structural conduciveness, structural strain, the growth and spread of a generalized belief, precipitating factors, the mobilization of participants for action, and the operation of social control.

14 Khosrokhavar (2005:20–25) offers an extensive analysis of the meaning of martyrdom in Islam, including differences between Sunni and Shiite versions. He distinguishes between "defensive" and "offensive" martyrdom in his discussion of Islamic militancy. A defensive martyr (the word itself stems from the Greek word for "witness," a meaning which is preserved in the Koran), according to this distinction, is one who offers one's death as a witness to the sincerity of one's beliefs in the face of a denying authority. Examples come from the early Christians who chose to die rather than submit to "inauthentic" Roman authority. It is a testimony to God, as much as to earthly beings, about the strength of one's faith. Rather than sadness or grief, these martyrs faced death with "radiant joy," something that provoked later

Christian authorities to denounce "the conscious wish to die and thirsting after a holy death . . . to be blasphemous" (Khosrokhavar 2005:9). Offensive martyrdom on the other hand, "is inspired by a desire to destroy the enemy by resorting to a legitimate violence that is sanctioned by religion" (9). "Self-sacrifice for the sake of religion is part of the struggle against irreligious oppressors" (10). "The underlying sense of 'bearing witness' makes the martyr both the protagonist of a holy death and a witness to the truth of his faith" (11). Here one can see how the religiously inspired assassin and that of the martyr can coincide in Islamic thought. Sageman (2004) makes a similar point when he concludes that radical Islam provides a framework for an individualistic form of ascetic suicide. Reviewing some of the studies of suicide terrorism, Bergesen (2006) notes a tension between those like Pape (2005) who stress collective pressures and those like Sageman who put emphasis on the individual.

One can see how it is possible to interpret the killing of Theo van Gogh as a sideshow in an internal Islamic struggle, Hirsi Ali's interpretation of Islam as condoning the oppression of women and Mohammed B.'s fundamentally different reading of the sacred texts. It can also be interpreted as a struggle between two interpretations of the meaning of integration or engagement with Dutch society in particular and Western society more generally. According to Khosrokhavar (2005:18), at least three strategies have been adopted by the new wave of Islamic immigrants to Western Europe since the 1960s: integration, with various degrees of acculturation, non-acculturation with proselytism (da'wa) as a goal, and outright confrontation or jihad. There is of course a fourth option (hijra), the return to an Islamic country.

15 Fortuyn was shot in the parking lot of a radio station where he had just given an interview. This in itself is significant, as the mass media is of course a central player in contemporary politics. The mass media and Dutch politicians, as well, were accused by critics of having created an environment in which the murder could take place, some arguing that they turned his political emergence into a social drama through their imagery and rhetoric. This was an atmosphere in which the image-conscious and photogenic Fortuyn thrived; he was as much a creation of the media as its victim. Even before he was murdered, it was often said that he transformed "dull" Dutch politics into something exciting. On a more somber note, Storm and Naastepad (2003) link Fortuyn's rise to changes in the Dutch economy. They point out that "the replacement of the consensus-oriented corporatist relations of the post-war period by the anonymous, globalized and highly competitive structures of the neo-liberal order has left large numbers of Dutch citizens feeling insecure, atomized and powerless" (2003:139–40). Looking for an explanation as to why this would push voters to the right instead of the left, they turn to social psychology and to Erich Fromm (Escape from Freedom).

16 Also: "*Breach* of regular, norm-governed social relations occurs between persons or groups within the same system of social relations. . . . Breach is signalized by the public, overt breach or deliberate non-fulfillment of some crucial norm regulating the intercourse of the parties . . . ('a symbolic trigger of confrontation or encounter')" (Turner 1974:38).

17 If one reverses the story, it is reminiscent of the assassination of Malcolm X, a hugely popular symbolic figure who had to be eliminated because he seemed to be offering a middle path between an inward-turning Islam and a more open engagement with the "West."

2. MEDIATING SOCIAL DRAMA

1 This attempt to control and fix meaning has some resonance with the analysis of framing in social movement research, something that will be further developed in a later chapter.

2 According to Peter Mair (2006), who calls him a "thriller writer," Ross and van Gogh were planning to write a satirical novel together. The topic was to be Mabel Wisse Smit, a colorful personality with a shady past who was romantically involved with Prince Johan-Friso, a son of the current queen.

3 In a personal conversation with the author, Marc de Leeuw and Sonja van Wichelen, authors of a perceptive article on *Submission* (2005), pointed out that before this and because of his anti-Semitic remarks, van Gogh was considered indecent by many in the Dutch middle class, insofar as being "decent" or *fatsoenlijk* is considered a public virtue. They suggested that one could perhaps compare these sentiments with a popular saying concerning Jews during the Second World War: "We houden niet van Joden maar het zijn wel onze Joden" (We didn't care much for Jews, but they were *our* Jews). In regard to van Gogh, one could say, "We didn't like him or his style, but he was still *our* van Gogh."

4 That Hirsi Ali's move from one political party to another can be painted as opportunism is something that could be analyzed. All politics is to some degree opportunism and that she would make such a move is not necessarily negative opportunism, but merely logical political behavior. Her explanation, then, is not odd or morally suspect. She defined herself in terms of one specific issue, the rights of Muslim women, and, after deciding that organized party politics was the way to go, she could then be expected to move to the party that offered her the best chance of representing this issue and of achieving practical ends in its regard. The same can be said of the VVD. Smaller parties in what is relatively speaking the political center often have problems with a fixed identity, since they do not have a firm constituency and must shift issues to find more support. They are by definition "opportunistic," so it would be neither unusual nor morally suspect from a political point

of view for the vvd to seize this issue and this person for its own ends. The pvda, on the other hand, had a more worked-out ideology and constituency and thus had less room to maneuver, in addition to being encumbered by the other issues and problems that Hirsi Ali herself mentions.

5 Pels offers an insightful analysis of the new right as a wider European phenomenon and of Fortuyn's place in it. He develops the idea of a right-wing "third way," a form of liberal fascism, to characterize this development, as opposed to the classical models of fascism that emerged in the middle of the last century out of a combination of nationalism and socialism. For Pels, the new forms combine liberalism with populism, articulated through the same sort of strong, charismatic leader. Most significantly, these new movements choose to work within the parliamentary system, which means they do not seek to overthrow democratic institutions as their historical predecessors did.

6 Hajer and Uitermark (Forthcoming) offer a brilliant analysis of Aboutaleb's "performance of authority," which also draws on Turner's notion of social drama. They argue that such authority can be media derived, noting how much press coverage Aboutaleb's speech received the day following its actual performance.

7 There exists strict regulation of the Dutch mass media, organized through the Commissariaat voor de media (cvdm). The Media Authority is a commission appointed by the sovereign and placed under the Ministry of Education, Culture, and Science, yet formally independent. The role of the commission is to see to it that the strictures of the Media Act are followed. According to its mandate, it "allocates national broadcasting time to educational broadcasting organizations, religious and spiritual organizations, political parties, and for government information." Each year, the minister establishes how much national broadcasting time is available. The Media Authority authorizes commercial broadcasting as well. "Commercial broadcasting includes: general interest channels, thematic channels, subscription channels, so-called 'electronic newspapers' broadcasted via the cable-networks." (See the website for the Commissariat voor de Media website, http://www.cvdm.nl/pages/English .asp?m=f&ID=6.) There is room for regional variation in this system as two regional television stations, rtv Noord Holland and rtv Utrecht, refused to broadcast Submission.

In response to the wave of ethnic tension and violence that erupted in the Netherlands after the murder of Theo van Gogh, Dutch leaders debated invoking a rarely used law banning blasphemy. Justice Minister Piet Hein Donner told the parliament that he wanted to revive a 1932 law to isolate radicals and curb hate speech. On November 26, 2004, the Dutch Journalists' Union (nvj) sent a letter to Prime Minister Balkenende, requesting a meeting to discuss the role of the media in the coverage of the murder of van Gogh and its aftermath, as several ministers had criticized the media coverage, claiming that the media had contributed to the social tension.

Reportedly, the Minster of Justice said that journalists should not give a stage to "idiots," such as those individuals who expressed their joy at van Gogh's death. The NVJ agreed that the media have a social responsibility. However, the union believes that the media must also fill "an independent, multiform role" in "the reporting concerning the attack (on Van Gogh) and the consequences of this for society." (International Press Institute, 2004 World Press Freedom Review, http://www.freemedia.at.) On their website, the murder of van Gogh is listed under the heading of journalists killed in the line of professional duty.

8 The Dutch cabinet is composed of fourteen ministers and fourteen state secretaries.

9 The title refers to van Gogh's last words to his workmates before cycling home on the weekend before the murder. The implication of this version of an alleged conspiracy behind the murder of van Gogh is that the AIVD had sufficient information to have prevented it. As to why the police authorities did not act, the film suggests that Mohammed B. was an AIVD informer who then turned on the police for reasons unknown and beat them at their own game. The alleged involvement of the AIVD is also the plot of van Gogh's own film about the murder of Fortuyn. The narrator of the *Prettig Weekend* DVD is Katja Schuurman, a well-known Dutch celebrity and one of van Gogh's favorite actresses. She appeared in van Gogh's film *Cool* along with then minister of finance Gerrit Zalm. Like van Gogh, Schuurman has tested the borders between art and life, in part by provoking audiences with her expressive sensuality. Voted the sexiest woman in the Netherlands, her nude photos in the Dutch *Playboy* attracted at least as much attention as van Gogh's interview in the same magazine. In *Prettig Weekend* Schuurman plays the role of an investigative reporter trying to make sense of the actions of police authorities in reference to van Gogh's murder. The film itself is done in the documentary style of Michael Moore's *Roger and Me*, where Moore traces his attempts to speak with the chief executive of General Motors.

10 In an interview with the author in April 2006, Minister Zalm regretted making this statement, saying that it was in the heat of the moment and that he was, in any case, referring more to the global war on terror than to the van Gogh murder in itself. After the fall of his government in the controversy surrounding the threatened revocation of Hirsi Ali's Dutch citizenship, Zalm retired from active political life.

11 Conspiracy theories form a genre, and there exists a rather large sociological literature on the topic. Brian Keeley (1999:116) defines a conspiracy theory as a "proposed explanation of some historical event (or events) in terms of the significant causal agency of a relatively small group of persons—the con-

spirators—acting in secret." A defining characteristic is that these narrative accounts of an event seek to locate an ultimate cause "as a secret, and often deceptive, plot by a covert alliance of powerful or influential people or organizations" (Wikipedia, s.v. "Conspiracy Theory," August 22, 2007). Conspiracy theory is a social version of paranoia; there is an already existing, ready-made, genre about what happens; it is a free-floating detective story. In the case of the murder of van Gogh there were conspiracy theories on all sides.

12 How direct the linkage between Al Qaeda and the Hofstad group is has been the subject of discussion on blogs. Writing at the Windsofchange.net site in December 2005, Dan Darling summarizes a report by "Norwegian researchers" to the effect that "the killing of Theo Van Gogh was not the work of a lone fanatic but rather the deliberate work of an ad-hoc group of al-Qaeda supporters that viewed the world within the context of the network's global jihad" (Darling 2005).

13 An article from the *New York Times* Internet service dated May 25, 2005, and signed by Marlise Simons, reports that "two Chechens have been arrested in connection with the killing of the filmmaker Theo van Gogh . . . , Dutch prosecutors said. Bislan Ismaliov, 25, was detained in Tours, France, on an international arrest warrant on May 18 and French authorities said he would be extradited to the Netherlands. The second man, identified only as Marad, 22, was arrested in the Dutch city of Schiedam last month. . . . They said the men were wanted because their fingerprints had been found on items that belonged to Mohammed Bouyeri, the Dutch-Moroccan who has confessed to the killing. The three men, who knew each other in Amsterdam, are believed to belong to the same group of Islamic radicals." Another twelve were arrested directly after the murder and remain in custody. Claims such as these make the killing political, but they push responsibility outside the Dutch domain and thus do not of themselves point toward breach. Neither the existence of al-Issar nor the involvement of any conspiratorial group has even been legally proven. A summary of the murder offered by a Swedish news account in July 2006, following the fall of the Dutch government after a series of crises surrounding Hirsi Ali, stated simply, "[Ali] helped make the film which led to the death of film director Theo van Gogh; he was murdered on an open street by a fundamentalist who believed the film scandalized Islam" (*Sydsvenskan*, July 1, 2006, A19).

3. PERPETRATORS AND VICTIMS

1 According to Buruma (2006b:196), Hamid Bouyeri funded the building of a mosque in his native Moroccan village in the Rif mountains, in addition to a house for his family. He also owns a summer home in another part of the country.

2　That they did nothing further was later to be a cause of great embarrassment, and the Algemene Inlichtingen- en Veiligheidsdienst (AIVD) has since apologized for underestimating the role of Mohammed B. in this organization. Not only had the head of the Amsterdam region police authority denied having previous knowledge of van Gogh's killer in early reports, the AIVD claimed that Mohammed B. was not a member of any terrorist group. Benschop (2005:91) offers two explanations for this. The first is that at this time the AIVD was focused on the threat of large-scale terrorist attack and thus was more interested in other members of the group, because Mohammed B.'s role was viewed as secondary. The other explanation is that the AIVD underestimated the importance of Internet communication in the activities of the group; and even while it was aware of Mohammed B.'s inflammatory messages, it did not take real notice. This is because the AIVD was looking for more visible forms of organization and missed the shift to new, networked forms of collective action. In its 2004 annual report, which was compiled after the murder, the agency now acknowledges this mistake: "Many discourses that can be found in the letters of Mohammed B. had been circulating for a considerable time in news groups and chat rooms or originating on international web sites, where one can find treatises on the 'true' Islam. The Hofstad group was not only nourished ideologically via the Internet, but in the same way also made contact with young people who were open to the mental world of the group" (Benschop 2005:92). Investigations continue to expose new "terrorist networks" in the Netherlands and recent reports suggest that these are "homegrown" and largely autonomous ("De geweld-dadige jihad in Nederland" [Global jihad in the Netherlands] AIVD Report, as reported in the *Volkskrant*, March 31, 2006, 3). Another explanation for the "failure" of the AIVD is offered in *Prettig Weekend* (Jong 2005) where it is proposed that Mohammed B. was an AIVD informer and thus the agency's failure to account for him had more sinister reasons.

3　The distinction between "thick" and "thin" identifications seems applicable here. While Mohammed B. had been raised a Muslim and had apparently followed the rituals associated with this religion, his identification could be called "thin" in that it was multilayered. At this time, in 2003, he appears to be moving toward a much "thicker" identification with Islam and with a particular "radical" and politicized version. Following Armstrong (2006) one can say that "Islam" refers both to the official name of those who follow the religion of the Koran and the Prophet Muhammad and also to those who have made the act of surrender or submission (islam).

4　The number of conversions to Islam by members of non-Muslim minority groups in the Netherlands should be taken into account in accessing the perceptions of Islam by the Dutch.

5　A Swedish study carried out in the southern port city of Malmö found to the contrary that segregation could also lead to finding social networks that provide jobs in a highly stratified labor market (IMER Malmö Högskolan, as reported in the Swedish media in July 2006).

6 The term *fundamentalism* is problematic. Shadid (1991:368) discusses different ways the term has been used in reference to Islam: most generally, if it can refer to "the wish to apply Islamic norms and values in daily life and in the state constitution, then most Muslims, especially those from rural areas, are to be described as fundamentalists." In this case fundamentalism collapses into a form of traditionalism. On the other hand, the term can be applied to "resistance movements aimed at promoting the application of Islam both as a religion and as a political ideology." Here fundamentalism is a source of resistance to secularization and, as Islamic fundamentalism, to societies founded on Judaic and Christian values. Buck-Morss (2003:2) would position radical Islam at one extreme in what she calls "Islamism," a wide postcolonial Muslim "discourse of opposition and debate, dealing with issues of social justice, legitimate power, and ethical life in a way that challenges the hegemony of Western political and cultural norms." In her account, Islamism is not as much a religious discourse as a political one. "It is a debate about modernity, expressed in multiple voices, encompassing varied and conflicting theoretical positions that are meant to have practical, political effects" (43). I use radical Islam in a similar way.

7 In the early stages of its development in the United States, the black Muslims were more an urban sect than a cultural movement (Eyerman 2001). They were at first most successful in recruiting unskilled laborers who had recently migrated from rural areas. This changed in the 1960s, when their appeal widened greatly. Similarities with radical Islam should not be overstated, especially since the latter is more aggressive in its confrontation with the surrounding society and also is a sworn enemy of nationalism, cultural or otherwise. The main similarity I would like to draw concerns the level of individual identity and how "conversion" might offer a positive sense of self to those who find themselves on the social margins of a society. The attainment of this new sense of self is linked to a range of symbolic practices, as well as to a new social network. Black Muslims changed their names to remove the stigma of slavery; radical Islamists alter their appearance, growing beards and adorning themselves with "traditional" styles of dress. Both have invented much of this "tradition" as part of a search for authenticity to distinguish themselves from the perceived shallowness of the surrounding culture that has marginalized them.

8 Following the work of the psychologist Geert Hofstede, Pels (2005) discusses the differences between Moroccan and Dutch culture in terms of individualism versus collectivism and the masculine versus the feminine. According to this scale, Moroccan youth are bound by more collective and masculine

norms in a Dutch culture that is more individualistic and feminine. Hirsi Ali (2004a) uses a similar form of argument.

9 Sayyid Qutb was a member of the Cario intellectual elite, part of a circle that included many liberal and Westernized writers and poets (Ruthven 2004:37–38). He was educated in the United States, and a spark to his conversion to radical Islam was his long exposure to American culture. The following passage taken from his prison writings might well have been written by Theodor Adorno (with the possible exception of the passages concerning sexuality) after similar exposure to Hollywood at around the same time: "Humanity today is living in a large brothel! One has only to glance at its press, films, fashion shows, beauty contests, ballrooms, wine bars, and broadcasting stations! Or observe its lust for naked flesh, provocative postures, and sick, suggestive statements in literature, the arts, and the mass media! And add to all this the system of usury which fuels man's voracity for money and engenders vile methods for its accumulation and investment, in addition to fraud, trickery, and blackmail dressed up in the garb of law" (cited in Ruthven 2004:37).

10 For Qutb and Mawdudi, the greatest enemy of Islam was nationalism. They opposed religion and nationalism in a way that has not often been repeated in practice. More on the theoretical or rhetorical level, Islamist movements have challenged the nationalism of their opponents, who often share the same religion. Thus, the Palestinian Hamas challenges the nationalism of the Palestine Liberation Organization.

11 For a discussion of Islamic protest through the eyes of social movement theory, see Wiktorowicz 2004. Especially relevant to our discussion is the chapter in that volume by Diane Singerman, "The Networked World of Islamic Social Movements." Singerman argues that Islamic movements are characterized by their challenging the borders between the public and private in ways very different from social movements in Western societies. Singerman (2004:150–51) writes, "The Islamic vision of the 'good life' is not simply about 'religion' or 'politics,' but is part of a cultural battle over the very definition of these terms. Islamic movements have framed their agenda around fundamental questions about the meaning of life and how Islamic beliefs and practices should inform daily life, law, morality, the economy, and governance. . . . Battles over dress, morality, marriage, celebrations, entertainment, sexuality, and faith as well as conflicts over governance and law are at the center of Islamist oppositional frames that have attracted sympathetic support." Gwenn Okruhlik's article on Islamism and reformism in Saudi Arabia in the Wiktorowicz 2004 collection also makes use of cultural aspects of social movement theory to show how opposition in a strictly regulated society can form by "tapping into recognizable rhetoric and symbols" (2004:251). In this case, the relevant "rhetoric and symbols" were those of Islam. When the

Saudi universities were closed during the Gulf War (1990–91), "the mosques became centers of political sermons, ideological debate, and opposition. Both mosques and private homes served as safe havens for opposition activists . . . In these sanctuaries, narratives were woven that provided people with a vocabulary to utilize in distilling their discontent. These safe sites of contention allowed people to construct oppositional alternatives to the dominant history, status quo dogma, and prevailing ideology" (2004:256). Similar claims can be made for the development of radical Islamism in cities like Amsterdam.

12 Ruthven (2004:162) reveals similarities in the thinking and ritualized practice of "fundamentalist" martyrs. Interesting in our case are the similarities between the motivations and ritual practices followed by Jewish extremists, such as Baruch Goldstein, who killed close to thirty worshippers at a Muslim prayer meeting in Hebron, Israel, in 1994, and Yigael Amir, who assassinated Israeli prime minister Yitzhak Rabin in 1995. Goldstein, an American-educated doctor was proclaimed a "holy martyr" who "heard the cry of Israel . . . and acted to relieve the cry of that Land" (quoted in Ruthven 2004:162), and Amir, "a serious, deeply religious and thoroughly well-adjusted student" (163), viewed Rabin as a traitor to the idea of Israel and acted in the name of community self-defense. Before the assassination, Amir obtained the permission of a rabbi to legitimate his deed. Khosrokhavar (2005) discusses not only differences between Christian and Islamic martyrdom but also those between Sunni and Shiite martyrdom. In his interviews with imprisoned suicide bombers, he found that while both groups shared in a "subculture of death," the meaning of martyrdom was different. Shia martyrs more closely resembled their Christian counterparts in that they could be compared with saints once they "embraced a holy death" (2005:4). Sunnis on the other hand do not recognize sainthood, and any heroism associated with martyrdom is of this world and not the next: "The Sunni martyr is one who dies 'in the path of God' by taking part in a jihad." In personal conversation with the author, Khosrokhavar noted that this difference also affected the way these imprisoned and thus failed martyrs experienced their forced life after death. For Shia Muslims, feelings of guilt and humiliation were only intensified in prison; they had failed in their quest for sainthood. But Sunnis felt that prison was only another god-given test of their will to struggle for the greater good of Islam.

13 Recent Sunni commentators focus on Afghanistan and the expulsion of Russian troops as the high point of collective Islamic militancy (see Kepel 2000:361). In her autobiography, Hirsi Ali (2007:133) suggests that widespread corruption in government was a major contributing factor to the mass appeal of radical Islam. This was based on her own activism in Somalia, where she took part in the revivalist Muslim Brotherhood movement in the

early 1990s. Interesting also in her account of this movement was its appeal to youth and the way the divide between East (Islamic revival) and West (modernism) was expressed in modes of dress, skirts and high heels for girls and fitted shirts for boys, versus the jilbab and cloth wrap for girls and white robes for boys (128).

14 Abdulhadi Khalaf (2006) points out how moving their place of worship was common to all the "Islamic volunteers" he interviewed. In personal correspondence, Khalaf mentioned that this process has an even deeper symbolic meaning, in that the original Muhammad, the Prophet, was forced to migrate from one place to another and that this hegira came to signal a new beginning. "From being a harassed outcast on the margins of Mecca, Mohammed became a respected and powerful leader with the help of newly found allies in Medina."

15 Shadid and Koningsveld (1995:4) were one of the first to notice this. They list several factors that might explain this shift in visibility: the Iranian revolution of 1979, civil war in Lebanon, the Rushdie affair, the Gulf War, and the collapse of the Soviet empire. They also mention the rise of Islamic fundamentalism as a possible contributing factor.

16 Rath et al. (2001:89) note that these organizations were first viewed as "fascist" and "right-wing extremist" by the Dutch. This is something that might have influenced van Gogh.

17 Buruma (2006b:141–42) cites the lyrics of the rap song that prompted the arrest and conviction of its singers, the group from The Hague called DHC, made up of three men of Moroccan origin: "Fuck Hirsi Ali Somali, Just two months in Holland, and already all-knowing. Cancer whore, shit stain, I'll smash your face . . ."

18 Rath et al. examine this process on the national and local level. Political participation is important to study at the local level, as Dutch law prohibits noncitizen permanent residents from voting in national elections, but allows them to vote in local elections. In the same way, there are no national Muslim political parties, yet there are local parties, such as Muslim parties in Rotterdam and Utrecht.

19 The last barrier was cleared when it was shown that ritual slaughter was no more painful to animals than the "normal" practice at Dutch slaughterhouses. This study was carried out after environmental groups held protests about the matter (Shadid 1991:363).

20 According to Khosrokhavar (2005:45), "In its modernized and radical versions, martyrdom is an expression of an extreme situation characterized by the difficult advent of a process of individuation and by the failure of secular forms of modernization, which have raised expectations of autonomy without actually satisfying them. Violent death is the result of a choice made because self-realization is impossible, and it also results in the death of those

the martyr identifies as the cause of his suffering." Choice and self-realization are also modern conceptions, and in its contemporary version martyrdom is a curious blending of tradition and modernity.

21 According to police accounts and as referred to above, the murder of Theo van Gogh was the work of a locally based network they labeled the Hofstad group, which was at least virtually connected to a wider network. However, after two trials both the workings of the group and Mohammed B.'s position in it remain matters of controversy. Still, the issue is crucial to any analysis of the latter's intentions. Drawing on the trial transcripts, Benschop (2005:99) writes, "The group was built around Mohammed B. and was inspired by his texts. More than friends, the other twelve 'students,' followers and confidents . . . formed and concentrated around him." Just how central Mohammed B. was in this group can be discussed. According to official allegations, the Hofstad group emerged in 2002 and was eventually composed of thirteen persons. The more stable members have been identified as Samir Azzouz (born 1986), who grew up around the corner from Mohammed B.; Ismail Akhnikh (1983); and Jason Walters (1985), a Dutch citizen with an American father. The last two probably had a special status in the group due to their allegedly having fought or received training abroad (in Pakistan). Jason's younger brother Jermaine Walters (1986) was also a member. Samir Azzouz was detained by custom officials in the Ukraine on his way to Chechnya to join the jihad in the struggle against the Russians. In October 2003, Samir Azzouz, Jason Walters, Redouan al-Issar, and one other member of the group were arrested for allegedly plotting acts of terrorism. They were soon thereafter released for lack of evidence. Azzouz was arrested again in June 2004 for attempting to hold up a food store where he worked as a stock boy (Benschop 2005:46). When police searched his home and that of his accomplice, they discovered maps and photos of important government buildings and a list of prospective targets. After being tried, Azzouz was convicted of possession of firearms and not of terrorist conspiracy, in part because he was arrested before a new law on terrorism went into effect (he probably would have been convicted under the new law, which was implemented on August 10, 2004). As Mohammed B. would later do, Samir Azzouz chose to remain silent during the court proceedings. In November 2006, Azzouz was convicted and sentenced to eight years in prison for his role in planning attacks "with a terrorist intent." Singerman (2004:157–58) points out the importance of participation in militant actions in both the recruitment and political socialization of Islamic activists. She writes " . . . many returned to Europe or the Middle East with greater ideological commitments, deeper loyalties to a particular community, and military experience." She goes on to compare this "transforming" experience to that of civil rights activists in the American south in the 1960s.

22 Following Evan, Arquilla and Ronfeldt distinguish three fundamental types of networks: the chain, the star, and the all-channel, where the first two are more leader-integrated (1999:196).

23 Thomas Scheff (1994:3) also points out the importance of shame and pride in explaining the emotions that bind tighter groups, calling them "the emotional facets of a relationship." Pride and shame are central features in the model Scheff offers to explain the forceful nature of nationalist movements, something that is very applicable to understanding the difference between a network and a group.

24 Making use of the same clan-based network that helped Hirsi Ali escape to the Netherlands, her father tracked her down in the refugee camp. While still living there, she was visited by a group of male clan members from all over Europe, including her husband and a high-ranking elder. A formal meeting was organized to reconcile the couple. Hirsi Ali writes, "For this full confrontation, I planned to obey the codes of good behavior. But I didn't dress in my long skirt. I wore jeans and a tunic. And I didn't cover my hair with a headscarf. My clothes were correct—they didn't display any skin—but my message was clear: things had changed" (Hirsi Ali 2007:206). From the traditional point of view, Hirsi Ali's actions made no sense: her father had arranged an advantageous marriage; her husband had done nothing to offend her and had followed all the appropriate norms of behavior. In response to the question from the elder, "So why did you do this?," Hirsi Ali answered: "It is the will of the soul, the soul cannot be coerced" (Hirsi Ali 2007:208). It was, she writes, an answer he had to respect.

25 These arguments are repeated in her published work (for example in Hirsi Ali 2004:61). In her more recent role as public intellectual, Hirsi Ali formulates herself in more polemical fashion, arguing against multiculturalism in the book cited above. She writes that multiculturalism, the idea that integration is possible without a loss of traditional identity, will never function with Muslim immigrants because of the intimate links between religion and cultural practices. What can only be hoped, and thus promoted by the "West," is a reformation on the scale of the Protestant Reformation led by Martin Luther. She understands her own role as public intellectual as that of convincing others of this.

26 This was confirmed in an interview with leading figures in the VVD. In 2003, Cherribi (2003:197) noted that in the Netherlands there were "seven Muslims spread across four political parties." This number included himself, but not Hirsi Ali, who in a way was his replacement representing Muslims for the VVD.

27 Her "normative liberalism" (Chorus and Olgun 2005:24–25) has always created problems, for herself and for others. Buruma (2006b:170) puts it more personally and dramatically: "It was only to be expected . . . that Ayaan would

leave the Social Democrats to join the free enterprise party, the VVD. Delighted to have a beautiful black critic of the welfare state and Muslim radicalism in a party that was, overall, very male and very white, she was welcomed as a walking Statue of Liberty." According to Buruma, Hirsi Ali finally proved "too radical for the VVD too" (ibid.). By her own account, Hirsi Ali uncovered a dilemma in the demand to critically acknowledge what she sees as the shortcomings in ethnic cultures and on the other side the demand for religious and other kinds of freedom, which are at the core of liberal philosophy. After the court ruled that the Hofstad group was a "terrorist organization" and sentenced its leading members to long prison terms, Hirsi Ali pointed out some of the weakness of this judgment. Speaking in parliament, she said that the evidence was weak and that it should not be a crime to hold and express extreme political views, as long as they did not lead to action (Volkskrant, March 13, 2006). In true liberal fashion, she defended the right to free speech, just as she had with regard to the Danish cartoons and to her own film Submission.

There were early signs that this was changing. In a speech given in Berlin in February 2006, Ali stated that "humiliation might be a good way to open up a group to discussion." This comment is at odds with some influential VVD leaders, who question its morality, as well as the apparent lack of understanding that even liberals recognize limits to the freedom of speech (Trouw, February 18, 2006). Members of her party confirmed this; one said that the problems really emerged when Hirsi Ali became "an atheist." The same person noted a lack of nuance in Ali's view of Islam.

28 Mamdani (2004:20) labels this "culture talk" and uncovers two strands, one represented by Bernard Lewis and the other by Samuel Huntington. In this sense, Hirsi Ali has managed to combine the two. There are other precedents for her views on the role of cultural heritage in determining the success or failure of assimilation, for example, Thomas Sowell, author of Ethnic America (1981), Race and Culture: A World View (1995), and Black Rednecks and White Liberals (2005). An economist and a conservative African American, Sowell is also courted by the political right. Orlando Patterson (2006) remarks on the importance of "cultural" factors in explaining the failure of young African American males to achieve social mobility.

29 Pim Fortuyn was also influenced by Norbert Elias, and Pels's biography contains a photograph of the two at a conference that Fortuyn organized to celebrate Elias's contribution to sociology.

30 This is not simply a local issue. The right of artists to free expression is about to be challenged and perhaps curbed by new laws proposed in Great Britain. Part of the antiterrorist legislation being discussed there include provisions like those already put in place in the Netherlands following the murder of van Gogh. These discussions have raised concerns about censorship (New York

Times, December 8, 2005, E3). In Denmark cartoonists were forced into hiding because of death threats after a national newspaper printed their satirical caricature depicting the prophet Muhammad. A local Islamic party has been reported as offering 50,000 Danish Kroner to any successful assassin. Demonstrations against the cartoon have occurred in Copenhagen and as far away as Pakistan (as reported in *Sydsvenskan*, January 2, 2006, A12–13). Previously, Danish Radio Broadcasting (DR) was sued for showing *Submission* on its television stations. The lawyer representing DR argued for free speech, saying that in a case like this, one must side with the victim (van Gogh) and not the "legalists" (as reported on the Militant Islam Monitor.com site, December 6, 2004, *www.militantislammonitor.org/pf.php?id=339*). In January 2006 Saudi Arabia and Kuwait recalled their Danish ambassadors, and Saudi Arabia initiated a boycott of Danish products in protest against the cartoon. This was reported to have enormous economic consequences, especially as other Arab nations joined suit. The following day, the editor of the newspaper in question published an open letter in which he tried to explain the meaning of the cartoon, but he did not apologize for its publication. A poll found that the majority of Danes did not think an apology was in order (*Sydsvenskan*, January 28–29, 2006). The point to be taken from this, at least so far, is that the more moderate Saudi Arabia has found a powerful way to influence the representation of Islam in the West. By resorting to the traditional means of protest and economic pressure, it may have found a new way to counter the influence of radical Islam.

31 Buruma (2006b:177) disputes this. He writes of Hirsi Ali's intentions in making the film: "She meant it to be provocative." He also cites a later interview in which she told him that "a section of the Muslim world would come down on me."

32 There is of course nothing new in this. The history of film is filled with examples of taboo breaking that mixes sexuality and religious belief. Buruma (2006b:180) suggests that Adelheid Roosen's theater piece *Veiled Monologues* provided Hirsi Ali with a model.

33 As in most small European countries, Dutch film production is largely financed through state and private agencies aimed at overcoming the problems connected to limited markets. Van Gogh's personality was a liability in this world of subsidized funding and bureaucratic regulation. He was constantly in need of money for his film production, and this also put constraints on the length and distribution of his films.

34 Leila Ahmed (1992:131) reveals how the veil has been a "potent signifier" of issues relating to the social and political meaning of gender in Islamic culture, since it first came into discussion in Koranic verses about the clothing of the wives of the Prophet (see also Armstrong 2006). It has been an issue at the core of the "postcolonial" debates at least since the Algerian-French war (see

Wichelen 2007). Franz Fanon's much discussed *The Wretched of the Earth* (1965) contains an essay on the significance of the veil in the anticolonial struggles. Fanon argued that for the French colonizers the veiled Muslim woman symbolized most clearly the necessity of their "civilizing" mission, while for the rebels wearing the veil became a highly politicized symbolic act for even the most "liberated" females. Both of these positions can be heard in our contemporary debates, as is especially clear in the French attempt to ban the wearing of religious symbols in public institutions. Similar debates have occurred in the Netherlands and in other parts of the world. In 2006 the Dutch government announced that it was considering a ban on the wearing of certain types of garments worn by Muslim women in public places. *Snow*, a best-selling novel by the Turkish writer Orhan Pamuk centers on this issue as well. Further back in Turkish history one finds that when the great modernist Kemal Atatürk declared himself president of the new republic in 1926, he organized a sailing exhibition to reveal to the major cities of Europe Turkey's new modern face. Here one could see an unveiled Turkish woman dancing in Western dress as an important part of the display (Horst 2006). In October 2006, political leaders in the United Kingdom, including its prime minister Tony Blair, posed the issue of the veiled Muslim as one of chosen "separation," not as a matter of religious conviction or style. As in Pamuk's novel, the effect was to lead many Muslim women to wear the face cloth as a symbol of rebellion, even against the apparent wishes of their parents.

4. A MULTICULTURAL DRAMA

1 Buruma (2006b:126) describes Scheffer thusly: "Scheffer, with his jeans, wild curly hair, and casual shirt, looked every inch the progressive Dutch journalist, the kind who would have been a Provo in the 1960s. Once a romantic Maoist, he has had a serious impact on liberal public opinion."

2 The concept of civilization as commonly used by anthropologists refers to a complex form of society defined by a distinctive way of life, such as rural or urban civilizations. For Huntington (1996, 43), a civilization is "the highest cultural grouping of people and the broadest level of cultural identity people have short of that which distinguishes humans from other species." It is thus "culture" that defines a civilization, and religion is the centerpiece of any culture. So it is the culture and the religion of the immigrants that make them into a different civilization, one that is treatening to the Dutch or to Dutchness. Huntington's ideas were not new, of course, as they built on a long tradition of attempting to capture a collective through naming its other. At least as far back as the struggles against the Ottoman Empire, ideas of Europe and of Western civilization have been a source of collective mobilization, as well as a line of demarcation, however fluid and imprecise. During the

Cold War, it was the Soviet Union, communism, and the "Eastern Bloc" that helped to unify the "West" and "Europe" in the attempt to give cultural substance to NATO and the fledgling European Community. The Dutch were not merely Dutch; they were also European and part of Western civilization.

3 Meuleman (2007), an expert on Southeast Asia, offers three factors explaining why "Western public discourse" has difficulty conceiving this as a religious conflict and not one involving civilizations. First, the largely secular West has difficulty seeing religion as something other than a cultural phenomenon. Second, for legal-historical reasons Western states have difficulty dealing with religious communities. And, third, many Muslims themselves feel that Islam is all-encompassing, and thus much broader than Western religions in affecting daily life. Huntington's ideas were discussed in the Dutch media already in 1995, with a discussion in the *NRC Handelsblad* concerning the journal *Foreign Affairs*. A few months later, the same newspaper printed an article on NATO that discussed Huntington's concept more directly. There is a distinctive rise in the appearance of the concept in the Dutch media since that time.

4 Another of Samuel Huntington's books, *Who Are We?* (2004), was an important influence here.

5 The drama began with a television documentary on Hirsi Ali's life that once again revealed that it was a forced marriage and not politics that spurred her immigration to the Netherlands, something that Hirsi Ali had readily admitted as long ago as 2002. When she again made the same admission in a televised interview following the documentary, Verdonk apparently felt compelled to act. Under pressure from parliament, Verdonk later revoked her own decision and reinstated Hirsi Ali's Dutch citizenship and passport. One international commentator, Miranda Hussain, writing in the Pakistani *Daily Times* (web edition, May 31, 2006:1) called this the "submission of Ayaan Hirsi Ali." For Hussain, Hirsi Ali's case raises the issue of whether or not in the Netherlands "it is more difficult to ignore a false asylum claim than the systematic abuse of the country's Muslim women" and she claims that in denying the forced marriage issue in favor of a more directly political one "Ali is guilty of underplaying the violation of women's fundamental rights—a charge she routinely levels against both Dutch Muslims and their European 'appeasers.'"

6 John Rex (2000) offers an overview of multiculturalism for a sociological perspective in a European context and Seyla Benhabib (2002) a more philosophical and gender-related analysis related most specifically to issues of citizenship. Benhabib includes the Netherlands in her discussion of the incorporation of immigrants, see especially page 77.

7 Penninx's claim (2005:7) that Bolkestein was at this point "apparently inspired by Huntington's Clash of Civilizations" seems unlikely, unless the two had personal contact. This influence is more apparent in Bolkestein 1997.

8 Geddes (2003:104) might disagree. In a chapter comparing immigration policies in Sweden and the Netherlands and citing census figures from 1997, he
writes, "One person in six in the Netherlands belongs to an ethnic minority
group, defined as either being born or having a parent who was born outside
of the Netherlands. . . . This is more or less the same proportion as the USA,
but it wasn't until the late 1990s that a Dutch minister officially recognized
that the Netherlands was indeed a country of immigration." Being a country
with flows of immigration is not the same as being a country that understands itself to be a land of immigrants, and I think this is the difference
between the United States and the Netherlands that a focus on the relative
proportion of immigrants does not catch.

9 Vesta (2006:4) reports slightly different numbers: "By 2003 there were
700,000 foreign residents in the Netherlands. But the foreign-born population stood at 1.7 million, since many immigrants had obtained Dutch citizenship. Taking into account the children of immigrants, the population of
non-Dutch ethnic origin stood at 3.1 million—nearly one in five of the Netherlands' total population of 16.3 million. . . . the population of 'non-western'
origin (including children of immigrants), . . . stood at 1.7 million in 2003,
that is 10.7 per cent of the total population." For unemployment rates of
"indigenous" people versus "foreigners" in the Netherlands and Germany,
see Thranhardt (2000:175).

10 The government report on the success of the assimilation drew its examples
from Israel.

11 Judt (2005) remarks that if not for the Cold War, which in effect cut off cheap
Eastern European labor from Western Europe, the nations of the European
Community would most likely have looked to Poland and other "Christian"
countries for their needs.

12 The beating and the name of the victim as well as the ethnicity of the perpetrator were the subject of a popular rap song in 2004.

13 I use collective representation here in the Durkheimian sense of a reservoir of
meanings that are stored as aspects of a group's self-understanding.

14 Hirsi Ali and Wilders wrote a common manifesto in 2003 in the NRC Handelsblad at a time when they both represented the VVD in parliament. Appearing
under the headline "Het is tijd voor een liberale jihad" (The time has come for
a liberal jihad), they argued for a war against what they saw as the "intolerance of Islam" that would promote the liberal message of tolerance through
the "prime vehicles of socialization (schooling, mass media, clubs and voluntary associations)." This would be a counteroffensive against the Islamic
extremism that was, in their eyes, being expounded in mosques and Muslim
schools.

15 Fortuyn is clearly speaking in a political discourse; most of his pamphlet
reads like a campaign speech by a university professor.

16 Abbink also chronicles the changing picture of the war in Dutch literature more generally. He lists five phases, the last of which (2000–2005) he labels "the naked truth."

17 Every February 25 flowers are laid at the foot of a statue of a dock worker to commemorate the strike. See Mooij (2006) for a definitive account of the strike and the controversy over who actually organized it. Wolf (2007) gives a less sympathetic account.

18 Wolf (2007:55–7) puts this in comparative perspective: "Although Holland's prewar Jewish population was less than half that of France's, more Dutch than French Jews were deported and killed, in both absolute and relative terms. Twenty-five thousand more Dutch Jews were killed than French Jews— fully a third more." In her account, the Netherlands has the worst record vis-à-vis Jews in Western Europe, where "the number of Dutch collaborators with the Nazis exceeded the number of those in the Resistance."

19 Judt (2006) bases his account of postwar Europe on the necessity of forgetting.

20 It would not be until the fiftieth anniversary of the war's end that the current queen Beatrix would say in a speech during the May 4 Memorial Day ceremonies, "For an objective account of what happened we must not conceal the fact that the occupier encountered the heroic resistance of some, as well as the passive acceptance and active support of others" (cited by Hirsi Ali 2006a:97).

21 While suppressed in this call for national unity, some of these "forgotten" voices would make themselves heard later on. There are generational aspects and mechanisms, such as what could be called cultural templates, at work to be discussed in a later chapter. In this process of national identity construction, minorities, such as Jews and later migrants would have to find ways of being included. Jews have managed; Moroccans, for example, are having a more difficult time, though an exhibition at the Museum of the Resistance in Amsterdam has had a special exhibition called "Moroccans during the War" in an attempt to make visible their role in a common fight against fascism, if not against the German occupiers in the Netherlands itself. The Amsterdam branch of the committee in charge of the memorial celebrations for the victims of the Occupation, the May 4 and 5 Committee, has long sought ways to incorporate the local Muslim community. However, their attempt to remove a white cross placed in an Amsterdam neighborhood now heavily populated by Muslim families was met with such uproar from the Dutch population that it was rescinded. Like the Resistance Museum, the committee is now seeking ways to commemorate the Moroccan contribution to the allied war effort. These efforts were spurred by the acts of Moroccan youths who desecrated a memorial to members of the Dutch Resistance killed during the German occupation. A group of Moroccan boys had played football with

wreaths placed on the memorial. There had been a series of such occurrences in an Amsterdam neighborhood with a large Moroccan population.

The controversy over the representation of the relationship between the majority population and the Jewish minority during the Second World War continues to this day. In April 2006, Ies Vuijsje published a book that accuses the authors of the leading accounts—Herzberg, Presser, and de Jong—of misreading evidence regarding the knowledge the Dutch had about the ongoing murder of Jews during the war and thus of misrepresenting the effects of Dutch passivity in the face of the deportations during the German occupation. Mak (1994:252) remarks on the significance of trade-unions and the labor movement as sources of integration of Dutch Jews. The show of solidarity by Amsterdam's workers as they courageously protested the deportation of Jews during the early days of the war can also be viewed as a sign of integration: the Jews are part of us!

22 Recently made part and parcel of the new consumer society, television added another dimension to public debate and to shaping national identity. It was the television series on the occupation produced by L. de Jong (director of the State Institute for War Documentation) and broadcast in 1960–64 that visualized and disseminated the official view to a very broad population. The program was immensely popular and de Jong was proclaimed a national hero.

23 This is challenged by the Flemish filmmaker Harry Kumel in an interview in Mathijs 2004. Using the examples of Fons Rademakers's *De Aanslag* (*The Assault*), the film version of Harry Mulisch's novel, and Paul Verhoeven's *Soldaat van oranje* (*Soldier of Orange*), Kumel says "Both Dutch films support the fable that Holland was one big 'pièce de résistance' during World War Two" (Mathijs 2004:xvii).

24 In his voice-over commentary to the DVD edition of the film, Verhoeven comments on the negative reviews the film received at the time of its release. This was in part due, he claims, to the very ambiguous sequence at the film's end, which depicts the reconciliation of two of the main characters—one a member of the resistance who also joined the RAF and the other his former school mate who spent the war years buried in his law books. The former, Verhoeven suggests, may be a hero to some, but he also is an ambiguous figure who was responsible for the deaths of some innocent people. The latter, based on a real person, will go on to be a judge on the Dutch Supreme Court and play an important role in the post-war reconstruction of Dutch democracy. Who is the real hero? Verhoeven asks. He who acts or he who stands and waits?

25 By cultural movements, I mean those in the arts.

26 Contemporary immigrant organizations continue to protest the use of blackface by white Dutch youths on December 5, the traditional Dutch Christmas.

27 Like many smaller, wealthy countries with a well-developed educational system and a relatively small language base, the Netherlands had sought the means to encourage and preserve its literary output by supporting Dutch writers and subsidizing the translation of foreign works into Dutch. Students are required to read selected works by Dutch writers as part of their basic education, and literary figures appear prominently on radio and television programs, as well as in the print media. As in the case of film production, state and private foundations provide financial support for literary endeavors as a way of compensating for the small commercial market. From a sociological perspective, the most important role of literature in the articulation and maintenance of national identity is the protection of the Dutch language itself. Beyond contributing to the robustness of a language, literary works help articulate and communicate a national experience. On Dutch cinema and national identity, see the perceptive introduction by the editor in Mathijs 2004.

28 For example, when a former government official accused Minister Verdonk of "deporting" Muslim immigrants, he was forced to retract his statement because the word recalled Nazi policies against Jews. That this is not restricted to the Netherlands or to the right wing is attested to by Lebow (Lebow et al. 2006:3) in his introduction to The Politics of Memory in Postwar Europe: "Even the most cursory review of European policies about national identity, ethnic conflict, immigrants, and antidemocratic politicians and parties indicates the extent to which these issues are refracted through the lens of the 1930s and World War II. These points of reference appear independent of the political views and policy preferences of those involved."

5. A DUTCH DILEMMA

1 Samuel Huntington (2004) makes ample use of Myrdal's notion, but with a much different emphasis. Whereas Myrdal devised the American Creed as a standpoint from which to make critical judgments concerning the difference between ideals and reality, Huntington uses it as the foundation in his quest to answer the question "Who Are We?," that is, as a cornerstone in an American national identity. The term "multiculturalism" has many meanings; in the present context it means the mutually respectful acknowledgment of cultural differences between groups.

2 Goossen (2004) corrects this by using the concept hukum, which means that a sentence, rather than a decree, was pronounced.

3 According to De Ley (2007:1) much of this protest was carried out by members of the Barelwi movement, with roots in India and Pakistan. "This neo-sufi movement has a tradition of venerating Muhammed to the point of

almost deifying him (making themselves subject to heavy criticism for heresy from orthodox Sunni theologians)."

4 The title refers to specific verses in the Koran that are thought to represent the voice of the devil rather than those of God.

5 According to the *Economist* (July 5, 2003:27), "Al-Jazeera claims 45 million Arabic-speaking viewers." Looking at the Internet pages of the English-language version of Al Jazeera around the time of the murder, one is struck by the similarity of its reportage with, for example, the BBC. That is not to say that it is similar to the Dutch newspaper reports. The headlines in their "global news section" contain phrases like "Dutch Muslims rally against violence" (November 10, 2004), "Muslim sites attacked in Holland" (November 10, 2004), "Dutch PM stresses communal harmony" (November 17, 2004). Reportage from the day of the murder appears to have been drawn from syndicated news sources and thus was no different from the information broadcast by the BBC.

6 Ramadan's grandfather was Hassan al-Banna, the founder of the Muslim Brotherhood, a movement in which his father was also active. Tariq Ramadan was born in Switzerland because his father was forced to flee his native Egypt on account of his Islamic activism.

7 Morgan (2005:3) defines a sacred gaze as something "that designates the particular configuration of ideas, attitudes, and customs that informs a religious act of seeing as it occurs within a given cultural and historical setting. A sacred gaze is the manner in which a way of seeing invests an image, a viewer, or an act of viewing with spiritual significance." This is to recall a way of seeing in which the distinction between art and religion is at least problematic. It implies that there are at least two ways to view the same object, a secular and a religious, something that emerged again in the so-called Danish cartoon affair, to be discussed shortly. To many Muslims even the attempt to make an image of Muhammad would constitute blasphemy; "what is at stake, then, with a public attack against Muhammad, is not just a simple personal act of blasphemy, offending the private feelings of any believer, but it . . . (now perhaps more than ever) is perceived to be a fundamental challenge as well against the Islamic way of life itself" (De Ley 2007).

8 By March 2, 2006, a total of 143 newspapers in fifty-six countries around the world had printed one of the cartoons (*Volkskrant* March 2, 2006:1). Sevennty of these were European newspapers, fourteen in the United States, three in Canada, two in Australia, three in New Zealand, and one in Japan. The cartoons were also reprinted in eight newspapers in Muslim countries (Algeria, Morocco, Jordan, Saudi Arabia, Malaysia, Indonesia, and Bosnia-Herzegovina). In the United States, no national paper reprinted the cartoons; they appeared only in local papers.

9 De Ley (2007:7) writes that the responsible editor had been in close contact with American neoconservatives and was a proponent of the clash of civilizations thesis.

10 Another event involving a similar issue and Salman Rushdie occurred in 2006, when public protests were incited by the film production of the popular novel *Brick Lane*. Written by Monica Ali, a young British writer of Indian descent, the novel portrayed everyday life in an ethnically mixed London neighborhood. Brick Lane is an actual London thoroughfare; when film production was to begin, some groups in the neighborhood protested what they saw as the stereotyped portrayals contained in the novel. Part of the protests included the burning of copies of the book. Salman Rushdie wrote an open letter in support of Ali and her rights as an artist. This was countered by Germaine Greer, a well-known author, who claimed that the characterizations in the novel warranted the protests, stating that "Ali did not concern herself with the possibility that her plot might seem outlandish to the people who created the particular culture of Brick Lane. . . . As British people know little and care less about the Bangladeshi people in their midst, their first appearance as characters in an English novel had the force of a defining caricature" (*The Guardian*, July 29, 2006, 11.).

11 The general issue of "framing" is important here: how was the debate over the film to be understood—as an issue of free speech or the necessity to respect the religion of others? The notion of "framing" (Snow et al. 1986; Snow and Benford 1988), an important concept in recent social movement theory, is a middle step here. According to theorists, framing has three functions: punctuation, modes of attribution, and modes of articulation. The first emphasizes a perceived injustice and defines corrective action. The second is diagnostic and prognostic, attributing blame and offering alternative futures. The third relates to the mobilization potential of a "frame," its resonance and empirical credibility and narrative fidelity. Framing calls attention to the cognitive processes of making sense and the often contentious struggle to define a situation, but it can also involve dramatization, placing an event—a demonstration, for example—within a narrative that lifts it from being seen as a single occurrence and gives it wider significance through connecting it to others. In a sense, framing links with ideology. This particular framing was in part determined by these representatives and their relative power to "define the situation," and it was also an effect of already established discourses and the norms of those who are authorized to decide the issue. This is not something limited to cases of freedom of expression or religious beliefs; it applies to any social conflict. Environmentalists who have attempted to represent the rights of nature in the courts have been forced to transform their claims into a language acceptable to the legal system and have also encountered a fundamental values conflict between the right to work and the desire to protect nature.

12 These terms are elaborated and explained in Ramadan (2004). Kepel (2004: 285) compares salafists to Hasidic Jews and evangelical Christians. According to Armstrong (2006), the term "jihad" should be translated as "struggle," making reference to the need for Muslims to fight against temptation and to remain faithful, rather than to armed combat or confrontation.

13 Another signatory was Irshad Manji, author of *The Trouble with Islam* (2003). Manji and Hirsi Ali have appeared together in public discussions about the possibility of reforming Islam.

6. CULTURAL TRAUMA AND SOCIAL DRAMA

1 The actions of Queen Beatrix following the murder of van Gogh can be contrasted to those of England's Elizabeth following the accidental death of ex-princess Diana in 1995. At least as reported in the mass media, the British royal family remained aloof from the unfolding drama, creating the potential for a national crisis. It was the actions of political leaders, particularly those of Prime Minister Tony Blair, that helped avert such a crisis by mediating between the royal family and the general public. In the Netherlands, by contrast, there was a concerted effort by political authorities to defuse the event's repercussions.

BIBLIOGRAPHY

Abbink, F. 2005. *Van Engelandvaarders tot Oorlogswinter* [From guardians of England to Winter War]. Utrecht: Walburg Pers.

Abrams, Philip. 1982. *Historical Sociology.* Ithaca, N.Y.: Cornell University Press.

Ahsan, M. M., and A. R. Kidwai, eds. 1991. *Sacrilege versus Civility: Muslim Perspectives on the Satanic Verses Affair.* Leicester, U.K.: Islamic Foundation.

Ahmed, Leila. 1992. *Women and Gender in Islam.* New Haven, Conn.: Yale University Press.

Alexander, Jeffrey. 2004. *The Meanings of Social Life.* New York: Oxford.

——. 2006. "Cultural Pragmatics: Social Performance between Ritual and Strategy." In Alexander et al. 2006, 29–90.

Alexander, Jeffrey, and Jason Mast. 2006. "Symbolic Action Theory and Practice: The Cultural Pragmatics of Symbolic Action." In Alexander et al. 2006, 1–28.

Alexander, Jeffrey, et al., eds. 2004. *Cultural Trauma and Collective Identity.* Berkeley: University of California Press.

Alexander, Jeffrey, et al., eds. 2006. *Social Performance: Symbolic Action, Cultural Pragmatics, and Ritual.* Cambridge: Cambridge University Press.

Armstrong, Karen. 2006. *Muhammad: A Prophet for Our Time.* New York: Harper-Collins.

Arquilla, J., and D. Ronfeldt. 1999. "The Advent of Netwar: Analytic Background." *Studies in Conflict and Terrorism* 22:193–206.

Bagley, Christopher. 1973. *The Dutch Plural Society.* London: Oxford University Press.

Barnouw, David. 1986. "The Image of Occupation." In Beerekamp 1986a.

Beerekamp, Hans, ed. 1986a. *Occupation, Collaboration and Resistance in Dutch Films.* Amsterdam: Kring van Nederlandse Filmjournalisten.

——. 1986b. "Dutch Films and World War II." In Beerekamp 1986a.

Benhabib, Seyla. 2002. *The Claims of Culture: Equality and Diversity in the Global Era.* Princeton, N.J.: Princeton University Press.

Bennett, W. Lance. 2003. "Communicating Global Activism: Strengths and Vulnerabilities of Networked Politics." *Information, Communication and Society* 6, no. 2: 143–68.

Benschop, Albert. 2005. "Chronicle of a Political Murder." http://www.sociosite .org/jihad—nl—en.php.

Bergesen, Albert. 2006. "Suicide Bombers." *Contemporary Sociology* 35, no. 5: 459–62.

Bolkestein, Frits. 1997. *Moslim in de Polder* [Muslims in the country]. Amsterdam: Contact.

Boltanski, Luc, and Laurent Trevenot. 1999. "The Sociology of Critical Capacity." *European Journal of Social Theory* 2, no. 3: 359–77.

Boomgaarden, Hajo, and Claes de Vreese. Forthcoming. "Dramatic Real-World Events and Public Opinion Dynamics." *International Journal of Public Opinion Research*.

Boomkens, René. 2004. "Why the Netherlands Is Not a Progressive Country." *De Gids* 167, nos. 5–6: 21–25.

Boxsel, Matthijs van. 2004. "Birth of the Water Wolf." *De Gids* 167, nos. 5–6: 30–36.

Brieven aan Ayaan Hirsi Ali [Letters to Ayaan Hirsi Ali]. 2005. Amsterdam: Prometheus.

Brinks, Jan Herman. 2005. "Les Pays-Bas, entre Islam et Populisme" [The Netherlands, between Islam and populism]. *Politique étrangère*, no. 3: 587–98.

Brubaker, Rogers. 2001. "The Return of Assimilation? Changing Perspectives on Immigration and Its Sequels in France, Germany, and the United States." *Ethnic and Racial Studies* 24, no. 4: 531–48.

Buck-Morss, Susan. 2003. *Thinking Past Terror*. London: Verso.

Buruma, Ian. 2005. "Final Cut." *New Yorker*, January 3, www.newyorker.com.

———. 2006a. "Hard Luck for a Hard-Liner." *New York Times*, May 19, A25.

———. 2006b. *Murder in Amsterdam*. New York: Penguin Press.

Buruma, Ian, and Avishai Margalit. 2004. *Occidentalism*. New York: Penguin Press.

Caldwell, Christopher. 2005. "Daughter of the Enlightenment." *New York Times Magazine*, April 3, www.nytimes.com.

Caryl, Christian. 2005. "Why They Do It," *New York Review of Books*, September 22, 28–32.

Casanova, José. 2005. "Catholic and Muslim Politics in Comparative Perspective." *Taiwan Journal of Democracy* 1, no. 2: 89–108.

Cherribi, Oussama. 2003. "The Growing Islamization of Europe." In Esposito and Burgat 2003, 193–214.

Chorus, Jutta, and Ahmet Olgun. 2005. *In godsnaam: Het jaar van Theo van Gogh* [In God's name: The year of Theo van Gogh]. Amsterdam: Contact.

Cockburn, Cynthia, and Dubravka Zarkov, eds. 2002. *The Postwar Moment*. London: Lawrence and Wishart.

Cohen, Stanley. 1972. *Folk Devils and Moral Panics: The Creation of the Mods and Rockers*. London: Routledge.

Cohn-Sherbok, Dan. 1990. *The Salman Rushdie Controversy in Interreligious Perspective*. Lewiston, N.Y.: Edwin Mellen Press.

Cottle, Simon. 2004. *The Racist Murder of Stephen Lawrence*. Westport, Conn.: Praeger.

Darling, Dan. 2005. "Al-Qaeda: The Scope of the Threat." *WindsofChange.net*, December 8, windsofchange.net/archives/005992.php.

Davis, Joyce. 2003. *Martyrs: Innocence, Vengeance, and Despair in the Middle East.* New York: Palgrave.

Davis, Nancy, and Robert Robinson. 2006. "The Egalitarian Face of Islamic Orthodoxy: Support for Islamic Law and Economic Justice in Seven Muslim-Majority Nations." *American Sociological Review 71*, no. 2: 167–90.

Dayan, Daniel, and Elihu Katz. 1992. *Media Events.* Cambridge, Mass.: Harvard University Press.

Deben, Leon, Willem Heinemeijer, and Dick van der Vaart, eds. 2000. *Understanding Amsterdam.* Amsterdam: Het Spinhuis.

de Leeuw, Marc, and Sonja van Wichelen. 2005. " 'Please, Go and Wake Up!' Submission, Hirsi Ali and the 'War on Terror' in the Netherlands." *Feminist Media Studies 5*, no. 3: 325–40.

De Ley, Herman. 2007. "The Danish Cartoons." *Centrum voor Islam in Europa* (C.I.E.), March, http://www.flwi.ugent.be/cie/CIE2/deley36.htm.

Demertzis, Nicolas. N.d. "Traumas, Emotions, and the Media." Unpublished manuscript in the author's collection.

Deurloo, Rinus, and Sako Musterd. 2001. "Residential Profiles of Surinamese and Moroccans in Amsterdam." *Urban Studies 38*, no. 3: 467–85.

Dieleman, Frans. 1993. "Multicultural Holland: Myth or Reality?" In *Mass Migration in Europe*, edited by Russell King, 118–35. London: Belhaven Press.

Dudnink, Stefan. 2002. "The Unheroic Men of a Moral Nation: Masculinity and Nation in Modern Dutch History." In Cockburn and Zarkov 2002, 146–61.

Ellian, Afshin, and Leon de Winter. 2006. "Islam rechtvaardigt agressie tengen ongelovigen" [Islam justifies violence against nonbelievers]. *De Volkskrant* 7 February, 14.

Elst, Koenraad. 2002. "Afterword: The Rushdie Affair's Legacy." The Koenraad Elst Site, http://koenraadelst.voiceofdharma.com.

Entzinger, Hans. 2003. "The Rise and Fall of Multiculturalism: The Case of the Netherlands." In *Toward Assimilation and Citizenship: Immigrants in Liberal Nation-States*, edited by Christian Joppke and Eva Morawska, 59–86. New York: Palgrave Macmillan.

Esposito, John, and François Burgat, eds. 2003. *Modernizing Islam.* New Brunswick, N.J.: Rutgers University Press.

Eyerman, Ron. 2001. *Cultural Trauma Slavery and the Making of African American Identity.* Cambridge: Cambridge University Press.

——. 2006. "Performing Opposition: How Social Movements Move." In Alexander et al. 2006, 193–217.

For Rushdie: Essays by Arab and Muslim Writers in Defense of Free Speech. 1994. New York: George Braziller.

Fortuyn, Pim. 2002. *De islamisering van onze cultuur* [The Islamisation of our culture]. Amsterdam: Karakter.

Frenkel, F., ed. 1967. *Provo*. Amsterdam: Polak en Van Gennep.

Geddes, Andrew. 2003. *The Politics of Migration and Immigration in Europe*. London: Sage.

Geertz, Clifford. 2000. *Interpretation of Cultures*. New York: Basic Books.

Gerstenfeld, Manfred. 2002. "The Jews' Unfinished Moral Battle for Dutch Postwar Memory," Yad Vashem Web site, www1.yadvashem.org.

Giesen, Bernhard. 2004. *Triumph and Trauma*. Boulder, Colo.: Paradigm Publishers.

Gijsberts, Merove. 2004. "Ethnic Minorities and Integration." The Hague: Social and Cultural Planning Office.

Gogh, Theo van. 2004. *De Gezonde Roker* [The healthy smoker]. Amsterdam: De Prom.

Gole, Nilufer. 2000. "Snapshots of Islamic Modernities." *Daedalus* 129, no. 1: 91–118.

Goor, J. van. 1987. *Indië/Indoneisië: Van Kolonie tot Natie* [East Indies/Indonesia: From colony to nation]. Utrecht: HES.

Goossen, J. P. 2004. "Moslims en islam in Nederland 1947–1992" [Muslims and Islam in the Netherlands 1947–1992]. Stichting Interreligieuze Dialog site, http://www.interreligieuzedialoog.nl/downloads.html.

Goudsblom, Johan. 1967. *Dutch Society*. New York: Random House.

Graaf, H. de. 1985. *Plaatselijke organisaties van Turken en Marokkanen* [Turkish and Moroccan political organizations]. The Hague: Nederlands Instituut voor Maatschappelijk Werk Onderzoek.

Guazzone, Laura, ed. 1996. *The Islamist Dilemma: The Political Role of Islamist Movements in the Contemporary Arab World*. Reading, U.K.: Ithica Press.

Gurr, Ted. 1970. *Why Men Rebel*. Princeton: Princeton University Press.

Habermas, Jürgen. 1989. *The Structural Transformation of the Public Sphere*. Translated by Thomas Burger. Cambridge, Mass.: MIT Press.

Hajer, Maarten, and Marcel Maussen. 2004. "Links en de Moord." *Socialisme en Democratie*, no. 12: 10–18.

Hajer, Maarten, and Justus Uitermark. Forthcoming. "Performing Authority—Dealing with the Assassination of Theo van Gogh." *Public Administration*.

Haan, Ido de. 1998. "The Construction of a National Trauma: The Memory of the Persecution of the Jews in the Netherlands." *Netherlands Journal of Social Sciences* 34, no. 2: 196–217.

———. 2003. "Paths of Normalization after the Persecution of the Jews." In *Life after Death*, edited by Richard Bessel and Dirk Schumann, 65–92. Cambridge: Cambridge University Press.

Heinich, Nathalie. 2000. "From Rejection of Contemporary Art to Culture War." In *Rethinking Comparative Cultural Sociology*, edited by Michèle Lamont and Laurent Thévenot, 170–212. Cambridge: Cambridge University Press.

Haan, Willem, de. 1997. "Minorities and Crime in the Netherlands." In *Minorities*,

Migrants, and Crime: Diversity and Similarity across Europe and the United States, edited by Ineke Haen Marshall, 198–223. London: Sage.

———. 2007. "Migration and the Changing Culture of Control in the Netherlands: From Multicultural Drama to Cultural Trauma" *Kriminologisches Journal* 38, no. 1: 32–48.

Hermassi, Karen. 1977. *Polity and Theater in Historical Perspective*. Berkeley: University of California Press.

Hirsi Ali, Ayaan. 2002. *De zoontjesfabriek* [The son factory]. Amsterdam: Uitgeverij Augustus.

———. 2004a. *Kräv er rätt!* [Demand your rights!] Stockholm: Bonniers.

———. 2004b. "Open Brief ann burgemeester Job Cohen" [Open Letter to Mayor Cohen]. *Trouw*, March 6, 37.

———. 2004c. *Submission: De tekst, de reacties en de achtergronden* [Submission: Text, reaction, and reality]. Amsterdam: Augustus.

———. 2006a. "Confrontatie, geen verzoening" [Confrontation, not appeasement]. *Volkskrant Forum*, April 8, 19.

———. 2006b. *The Caged Virgin: An Emancipation Proclamation for Women and Islam*. New York: Free Press.

———. 2007. *Infidel*. New York: Free Press.

Holman, Theodor. 2006. *Theo Is dood* [Theo is dead]. Amsterdam: Mets en Schilt.

Horst, Hilje van der. 2007. "Appropriating Modernity and Tradition: The Turkish-Dutch and the Imaginative Geography of East and West." In *Reframing Dutch Culture: Between Otherness and Authenticity*, edited by Peter Margry and Herman Roodenburg, 83–108. Aldenshot: Ashgate.

Huntington, Samuel P. 1996. *The Clash of Civilizations and the Remaking of World Order*. New York: Simon and Schuster.

———. 2004. *Who Are We?* New York: Simon and Schuster.

Hussain, Dilwar. 2003. "The Holy Grail of Muslims in Western Europe: Representation and Relationship with the State." In Esposito and Burgat 2003, 215–50.

Ireland, Patrick. 2004. *Becoming Europe*. Pittsburgh: University of Pittsburgh Press.

Israel, Jonathan. 1998. *The Dutch Republic: Its Rise, Greatness and Fall, 1477–1806*. Oxford: Clarendon Press.

Jacobs, Ronald. 2000. *Race, Media and the Crisis of Civil Society*. Cambridge: Cambridge University Press.

Jansen, Hans. 2004. "How to Kill an Unbeliever" (interview with Jansen). *Radio Netherlands*, November 5, www2.rnw.nl.

Jong, Stan de. 2005. *Prettig weekend* [Pleasant weekend]. Amsterdam: XTRA.

Judt, Tony. 2005. *Postwar: A History of Europe since 1945*. New York: Penguin.

Juergensmeyer, Mark. 2003. *Terror in the Mind of God*. Berkeley: University of California Press.

Julius, Anthony. 2002. *Transgressions: The Offenses of Art*. Chicago: University of Chicago Press.

Junger, Marianne, and Wim Polder. 1992. "Some Explanations of Crime among Four Ethnic Groups in the Netherlands." *Journal of Quantitative Criminology* 8, no. 1: 51–78.

Kamrava, Mehran, ed. 2006. *The New Voices of Islam*. Berkeley: University of California Press.

Kantorowicz, Ernst. 1957. *The King's Two Bodies*. Princeton, N.J.: Princeton University Press.

Kaplan, E. Ann. 2005. *Trauma Culture*. New Brunswick, N.J.: Rutgers University Press.

Keeley, Brian. 1999. "Of Conspiracy Theories." *Journal of Philosophy* 96, no. 3: 109–26.

Kelly, Robert, and Jess Maghan. 1998. *Hate Crime: The Global Politics of Polarization*. Carbondale: Southern Illinois University Press.

Kennedy, James C. 1995. *Building New Babylon: Cultural Change in the Netherlands during the 1960s*. Ann Arbor, Mich.: UMI Dissertation Services.

Kepel, Gilles. 1997. *Allah in the West*. Stanford: Stanford University Press.

———. 2000. *Jihad*. London: Tauris Publishers.

———. 2004. *The War for Muslim Minds*. Cambridge, Mass.: Harvard University Press.

Khalaf, Abdulhadi. 2006. "De Arabiska frivilliga" [The Arabic volunteers]. In *Sociala Rörelser—politik och kultur*, edited by A. Wettergren and A. Jamison, 131–49. Lund, Sweden: Studentlitteratur.

Khosrokhavar, Farhad. 2005. *Suicide Bombers: Allah's New Martyrs*. Translated by David Macey. London: Pluto Press.

King, Russell, ed. 1993. *Mass Migration in Europe*. London: Belhaven Press.

Klomp, Aranka, and John Kroon. 2006. *The Netherlands, 2006*. Amsterdam: Prometheus.

Koopmans, Ruud, and Paul Statham, eds. 2000. *Challenging Immigration and Ethnic Relations Politics*. New York: Oxford University Press.

Kranenberg, Annieke. 2005. "Nachbarsjunge, Gotteskrieger" [Neighborhood youth, holy warrior]. *Die Zeit*, no. 31, http://www.zeit.de/2005/31/Van—Gogh—31.

Lagrou, Pieter. 1997. "Victims of Genocide and National Memory: Belgium, France and the Netherlands, 1945–1965." *Past and Present*, no. 154: 181–222.

Laucella, Linda. 1998. *Assassination: The Politics of Murder*. Los Angeles: Lowell House.

Lebow, Richard, Wulf Kansteiner, and Claudio Focu, eds. 2006. *The Politics of Memory in Postwar Europe*. Durham: Duke University Press.

Le Naour, Jean-Yves. 2006. *The Living Unknown Soldier*. London: Arrow Books.

Lijphart, Arend. 1966. *The Trauma of Decolonization*. New Haven, Conn.: Yale University Press.

Linklater, Alexander. 2005. "Danger Woman." *Manchester Guardian*, 17 May.

Loroux, Nicole. 2006. *The Invention of Athens: The Funeral Oration in the Classical City*. New York: Zone Books.

Lucassen, Jan, and Rinus Penninx. 1997. *Newcomers: Immigrants and Their Descendants in the Netherlands, 1550–1995*. Amsterdam: Het Spinhuis.

Luin, Ton van, ed. 2005. *Hoe nu verder?* [How do we go on?]. Utrecht: Spectrum.

Mahmood, Saba. 2005. *Politics of Piety: The Islamic Revival and the Feminist Subject*. Princeton, N.J.: Princeton University Press.

Mair, Peter. 2006. "What's Going On?" (Review of Ian Buruma's *Murder in Amsterdam*). *London Review of Books*, December 14, 11–13.

Mak, Geert. 1999. *Amsterdam: A Brief Life of the City*. London: Harvill Press.

——. 2005a. *Nagekomen flessenpost* [Breaking news]. Amsterdam: Atlas.

——. 2005b. *Gedoemd tot kwetsbaarheid* [Condemned to vulnerability]. Amsterdam: Atlas.

——. 2005c. *Der Mord an Theo van Gogh: Geschichte einer moralischen Panik* [The murder of Theo van Gogh: History of a moral panic]. Frankfurt: Suhrkamp.

Mamdani, Mahmood. 2004. *Good Muslim, Bad Muslim*. New York: Pantheon.

Manji, Irshad. 2003. *The Trouble with Islam*. N.Y.: St. Martin's Press.

Mast, Jason. 2006. "The Cultural Pragmatics of Event-ness: The Clinton/Lewinsky Affair." In Alexander et al. 2006, 115–45.

Mathijs, Ernest, ed. 2004. *The Cinema of the Low Countries*. London: Wallflower Press.

Mernissi, Fatima. 1987. *The Veil and the Male Elite*. Reading, Mass.: Addison-Wesley.

Meuleman, Johan, ed. 2007. *Islam in the Era of Globalization: Muslim Attitudes towards Modernity and Identity*. London: Routledge.

Moerings, Martin. 1983. "Protest in the Netherlands: Developments in a Pillarized Society." *Crime, Law and Social Change* 7, no. 2:95–112.

Mollenkopf, John. 2000. "Assimilating Immigrants in Amsterdam." In Deben et al. 2000, 197–218.

Molotch, Harvey, and Marilyn Lester. 1974. "News as Purposive Behavior: On the Strategic Use of Routine Events, Accidents, and Scandals." *American Sociological Review* 39, no. 1: 101–12.

Mooij, Annet. 2006. *De strijd om de Februaristaking* [The Struggle around the February Strike]. Amsterdam: Uitgevrij Balans.

Moore, Bob. 1997. *Victims and Survivors*. London: Arnold.

Morgan, David. 2005. *The Sacred Gaze: Religious Visual Culture in Theory and Practice*. Berkeley: University of California Press.

Mulisch, Harry. 1966. *Bericht aan de rattenkonig* [The coming of the rat king]. Amsterdam: De Bezige Bij.

——. 1985. *The Assault*. Translated by Claire Nicolas White. New York: Pantheon.

Nijman, Jan. 2000. "The Global Moment in Urban Evolution." In Deben et al. 2000, 19–58.

Okruhlik, Gwenn. 2004. "Making Conversation Possible: Islamism and Reform in Saudi Arabia." In Wiktorowicz 2004, 250–69.

Pantti, Mervi, and Liesbet van Zoonen. 2006. "Do Crying Citizens Make Good Citizens?" *Social Semiotics* 16, no. 2: 205–22.

Pape, Robert. 2005. *Dying to Win*. New York: Random House.

Patterson, Orlando. 2006. "Culture and the Fate of Black Men." *New York Times*, April 2, www.nytimes.com.

Pels, Dick. 2004. *De geest van Pim: Het gedachtegoed van een politieke dandy* [Pim's spirit: The reflections of a political dandy]. Amsterdam: Anthos.

———. 2005. *Een zwak voor Nederland* [A soft spot for the Netherlands]. Amsterdam: Anthos.

Penninx, Rinus. 2005. "Dutch Integration Policies after the van Gogh Murder." Lecture presented at the Expert Panel on Social Integration of Immigrants, Ottawa, January 24. Transcript in the author's collection.

Pipes, Daniel. 1990. *The Rushdie Affair*. New York: Birch Lane Press.

Plate, S. Brent. 2006. *Blasphemy: Art That Offends*. London: Black Dog Publishing.

Prins, Baukje. 2000. *Voorbij de onschuld* [Beyond innocence]. Amsterdam: van Gennep.

Ramadan, Tariq. 2004. *Western Muslims and the Future of Islam*. New York: Oxford University Press.

Rath, Jan, Rinus Penninx, Kees Groenendijk, and Astrid Meyer. 2001. *Western Europe and Its Islam*. Leiden: Brill.

Rauer, Valentin. 2006. "Willy Brandt's Kneefall at the Warsaw Monument: The Ritual Foundation of Germany's New Democracy." In Alexander et al. 2006, 257–82.

Renier, G. J. 1944. *The Dutch Nation*. London: George Allen and Unwin.

Rex, John. 2000. "Multiculturalism and Political Integration in Europe." In Koopmans and Statham 2000, 57–73.

Richardson, Louise. 2006. *What Terrorists Want: Understanding the Enemy, Containing the Threat*. New York: Random House.

Ricoeur, Paul. 1973. "The Model of the Text: Meaningful Action Considered as a Text." *New Literary History* 5, no. 1: 91–117.

Riding, Alan. 2005. "Navigating Expression and Religious Taboos." *New York Times*, January 22, www.nytimes.com.

Riesebrodt, Martin. 1993. *Pious Passion: The Emergence of Modern Fundamentalism in the United States and Iran*. Berkeley: University of California Press.

Robben, Antonius, and Marcelo Suárez-Orozco. 2000. *Cultures under Siege: Collective Violence and Trauma*. Cambridge: Cambridge University Press.

Rooijendijk, L., Francien van der Meulen-Wieringa, Mohamed Mea, and Sahanim Genc, eds. 1988. *Turken en Marokkanen in Hollands Welzijnsland* [Turks and Moroccans in Holland's welfare state]. Baarn: H. Nelissen.

Ross, Tomas. 2005. *Take Care! Omzien naar van Gogh* [Reflections on van Gogh]. Amsterdam: Aspect.

Roth, Michael, and Charles Salas. 2001. *Disturbing Remains: Memory, History, and Crisis in the Twentieth Century*. Los Angeles: Getty Research Institute.

Roy, Olivier. 2004. *Globalized Islam: The Search for a New Ummah*. New York: Columbia University Press.

Ruthven, Malise. 2004. *Fundamentalism*. Oxford: Oxford University Press.

Sageman, Marc. 2004. *Understanding Terror Networks*. Philadelphia: University of Pennsylvania Press.

Sahlins, Marshall. 1985. *Islands of History*. Chicago: University of Chicago Press.

Said, Edward. 1979. *Orientalism*. New York: Vintage Books.

———. 1981. *Covering Islam*. New York: Vintage Books.

Schama, Simon. 1987. *The Embarrassment of Riches: An Interpretation of Dutch Culture in the Golden Age*. New York: Knopf.

———. 1995. *Landscape and Memory*. New York: Knopf.

Schenk, Hans. 2006. "Ayaan Hirsi Ali is deel van het problem" [Ayaan Hirsi Ali is part of the problem]. *De Volkskrant*, 11 April 2006.

Scheff, Thomas. 1994. *Bloody Revenge: Emotions, Nationalism, and War*. Boulder, Colo.: Westview Press.

Schogt, Henry. 2003. *The Curtain: Witness and Memory in Wartime Holland*. Waterloo, Ont.: Wilfrid Laurier University Press.

Schoondergang, Huub. 1971. *En toen kwamen de kabouters* [And then came the kabouters]. Leiden: Sijthoff.

Sen, Amartya. 2006. *Identity and Violence: The Illusion of Destiny*. New York: W. W. Norton.

Shadid, W. A. 1991. "The Integration of Muslim Minorities in the Netherlands." *International Migration Review* 25, no. 2: 355–74.

Shadid, W. A., and P. S. van Koningsveld. 1995. *Religious Freedom and the Position of Islam in Western Europe*. Kampen, Netherlands: Kok Pharos.

Singerman, Diane. 2004. "The Networked World of Islamic Social Movements." In Wiktorowicz 2004, 143–63.

Slootman, Marieke, and Jean Tillie. 2006. *Processen van radicalisering: Waarom sommige Amsterdamse moslims radicaal worden* [The radicalization process: Why some Amsterdam Muslims become radical]. Amsterdam: Instituut voor Migratie-en Ethnische Studies.

Smelser, Neil. 1962. *Theory of Collective Behavior*. New York: Free Press.

———. 2004. "Psychological Trauma and Cultural Trauma." In Alexander et al. 2004, 31–59.

Snow, David A., and Robert D. Benford. 1988. "Ideology, Frame Resonance, and Participant Mobilization." In *From Structure to Action: Comparing Social Movement Research across Cultures*, edited by Bert Klandermans, Hanspeter Kriesi, and Sidney G. Tarrow, 197–217. Greenwich, Conn.: JAI.

Snow, David A., E. Burke Rochford Jr., Steven K. Worden, and Robert D. Benford. 1986. "Frame Alignment Processes, Micromobilization, and Movement Participation." *American Sociological Review* 51, no. 4: 464–81.

Sowell, Thomas. 1981. *Ethnic America*. New York: Basic Books.

Stengs, Irene. N.d. "The Art of Mourning." Unpublished manuscript in the author's collection.

Stephenson, Peter. 1989. "Going to McDonald's in Leiden: Reflections on the Concept of Self and Society in the Netherlands." *Ethos* 17, no. 2: 226–47.

Sztompka, Piotr. 2004. "The Trauma of Social Change: A Case of Postcommunist Societies." In Alexander et al. 2004, 155–95.

Storm, Servaas, and Ro Naastepad. 2003. "The Dutch Distress." *New Left Review* 20 (March-April): 131–51.

Tausch, Arno, et al. 2006. *Why Europe Has to Offer a Better Deal towards Its Muslim Communities*. Centro Argentino de Estudios Internacionales (CAEI) and Entelequia, e-book available at http://www.eumed.net/entelequia/es.lib.php?a=b001

Thompson, Ken. 1998. *Moral Panics*. London: Routledge.

Thranhardt, Dietrich. 2000. "Conflict, Consensus, and Policy Outcomes." In Koopmans and Statham 2000, 162–86.

Turk, Austin. 2004. "Sociology of Terrorism." *Annual Review of Sociology* 30:271–86.

Turkle, Sherry. 1995. *Life on the Screen: Identity in the Age of the Internet*. New York: Simon and Schuster.

Turner, Victor. 1974. *Dramas, Fields, and Metaphors: Symbolic Action in Human Society*. Ithaca, N.Y.: Cornell University Press.

——. 1980. "Social Dramas and Stories about Them." *Critical Inquiry* 7, no. 1 (Autumn): 141–68.

——. 1982. *From Ritual to Theatre: The Human Seriousness of Play*. New York: PAJ Publications.

Uitermark, Justus. N.d. "Anti-multiculturalism and the Governance of Ethnic Diversity." Unpublished manuscript in the author's collection.

Uitermark, Justus, and Jan Willem Duyvendak. N.d. "Participatory Logic in a Mediated Age: Neighborhood Governance in the Netherlands after the Multicultural Drama." Unpublished manuscript in the author's collection.

Uitermark, Justus, Ugo Rossi, and Henk Van Houtum. 2005. "Reinventing Multiculturalism: Urban Citizenship and the Negotiation of Ethnic Diversity in Amsterdam." *International Journal of Urban and Regional Research* 29, no. 3: 622–40.

Ulvaeus, Bjorn. 2006. "Religionerna maste kunna utmanas" [Religion must be open to provocation]. *Expressen* 1 (February): 4.

Vanderwal Taylor, Jolanda. 1997. *A Family Occupation: Children of the War and the Memory of World War II in Dutch Literature of the 1980s*. Amsterdam: University of Amsterdam Press.

Vasta, Ellie. 2007. "From Ethnic Minorities to Ethnic Majority Policy: Multiculturalism and the Shift to Assimilationism in the Netherlands." *Ethnic and Racial Studies* 30, no. 5: 7–13.

Veer, Peter van der. 2006. "Pim Fortuyn, Theo van Gogh, and the Politics of Tolerance in the Netherlands." *Public Culture* 18, no. 1: 111–24.

Verkuyten, Maykel. 1991. "Self-Definition and Ingroup Formation among Ethnic Minorities in the Netherlands." *Social Psychological Quarterly* 54, no. 3: 280–86.

———. 2002. "Ethnic Relations in Local Contexts: Beyond a Dualist Approach to Identities and Racism." In *Europe's New Racism: Causes, Manifestations, and Solutions*, edited by the Evens Foundation, 131–42. New York: Berghahn Books.

Voeten, Teun. 1990. "Dutch Provos." *High Times*, January, 32–36, 64–66, 73, http://www.marijuanalibrary.org/HT—provos—0190.html.

Von der Dunk, H. W. 1967. "Holland: The Shock of 1940." *Journal of Contemporary History* 2, no. 1: 169–82.

Vuijsje, Herman. 1986. *Vermoorde onschuld: Etnisch verschil als Hollands taboe* [Murdered innocence: Ethnic difference as Holland's taboo]. Amsterdam: Bert Bakker.

Vuijsje, Ies. 2006. *Tegen beter weten in*. Amsterdam: Augustus.

Wagner-Pacifici, Robin. 1986. *The Moro Morality Play: Terrorism as Social Drama*. Chicago: University of Chicago Press.

———. 2000. *Theorizing the Standoff: Contingency in Action*. Cambridge: Cambridge University Press.

Weinreb, F. 1971. *Collaboratie en varzet* [Collaboration and resistance]. Amsterdam: Meulenhoff.

Wesseling, H. L. 1980. "Post-Imperial Holland." *Journal of Contemporary History* 15, no. 1: 125–42.

Wichelen, Sonja van. 2007. "Embodied Contestations." PhD diss., Amsterdam School for Social Science Research.

Wiktorowicz, Quintan, ed. 2004. *Islamic Activism: A Social Movement Theory Approach*. Bloomington: Indiana University Press.

———. 2005. *Radical Islam Rising*. Lanham, Md.: Rowman and Littlefield.

Wilkinson, Doris, ed. 1976. *Social Structure and Assassination Behavior: The Sociology of Political Murder*. Cambridge, Mass.: Schenkman.

Willems, Wim, and Annemarie Cottaar. 1989. *Het Beeld van Nederland* [The Image of the Netherlands]. The Hague: Ambo.

Wolf, Diane. 2007. *Beyond Anne Frank: Hidden Children and Postwar Families in Holland*. Berkeley: University of California Press.

Woolf, Linda. 1999. "Survival and Resistance: The Netherlands under Nazi Occupation." http://www.webster.edu/woolflm/netherlands.html.

Zarkov, Dubravka. 2002. "*Srebrenica Trauma*: Masculinity, Military and National Self-KaboutersImage in Dutch Daily Newspapers." In Cockburn and Zarkov 2002, 183–203.

Zwaan, Ton. 1981. "Coping with the Crisis in Dutch Sociology." *Theory and Society* 10:707–20.

INDEX

iconoclasm, 35
"ideal" plot, 24
immigration: Dutch perspectives on, 11,
40, 44, 60, 177 n. 9, 198 n. 28; Dutch
policy on, 5, 20, 24, 45, 65, 76–77,
105–6, 111, 139, 173, 197 n. 26; identity construction and, 33, 74–76, 110;
integration and, 19, 37, 52, 62, 65–
66, 85
inclusion: in the community, 140
intellectual: role of, 142, 163–65; Western, 144, 148–50
Internet: 10, 59, 71; identity and, 80
interpretive frames, 3, 51–52, 115, 130,
161
Iranian Revolution, 91
Islam: 9/11 and, 72; democracy and, 76;
fundamentalist, 50, 103; identity and,
113; ideology of, 61–62, 64–68, 70–
74, 103–4, 146, 156, 160, 185 n. 6, 187
nn. 12–13; institutionalization of, 46;
modernization and, 21; perceptions
of, 11, 24–25, 55, 92, 148; as political,
74; radical, 67–68, 73, 89; war on
terror and, 19, 72, 81, 111, 171;
women and, 36, 63, 76–77, 98, 112–
13
Islamic studies, 50
Israel, 195 n. 10

Jesus, 152
jihad, 50, 67, 73, 83, 158

Kabouters, 134
Kaplan, E. Ann, 166–67
Kennedy, John F., 13, 32
Kennedy, Robert, 32
Khaled, Abu, 64–65, 82
Khomeini, Ruhollah, 69, 71, 143–45,
147
Khosrokhavar, Farhad, 84
King, Martin Luther, Jr., 32

Koran, 9, 33, 70, 199 n. 4
Korean War, 128
Krakers, 134–36
Kumel, Harry, 197 n. 23

Leefbaar Nederland, 44
Leiden University, 88
Levy, Leonard, 149
liberalism, 120, 190 n. 27
Lijst Pim Fortuyn (LPF), 45
Lincoln, Abraham, 32
Lindh, Anna, 32
Livable Netherlands, 44
Locke, John, 118
Luther, Martin, 118, 190 n. 25

Mak, Geert, 3, 125
Malcolm X, 180 n. 17
martyrdom, 70, 84
mass media: 168, 181 n. 7; film and television, 48, 99, 132, 152, 192 nn. 32–
33; newspapers, 31–33, 151–53, 192
n. 30; representing social drama
through, 21, 25, 34, 41, 43, 132–33,
179 n. 15
meaning: 180 n. 1; conflict and, 115;
frameworks of, 101; immigrant status
and, 28; violence and, 34
Mernissi, Fatima, 172
Metro, 31
moffenmeiden, 129
Mohammed B. See Bouyeri, Mohammed
Moondriaans Doenia, 59
moral authority, 133, 150
Moro affair, 25, 27–28
Moroccans, 4, 48, 57, 108, 112–14, 183
n. 13, 185 n. 8, 196 n. 21; female, 60;
unemployment and, 60–61
Muhammad (the Prophet), 92, 138, 184
n. 3, 188 n. 14; images of, 152–53,
192 n. 30, 199 n. 7
Mulisch, Harry, 134–35, 197 n. 23

social mobility, 66
social movements, 133
social performance, 27, 35, 43; authority and, 53; paradigms and, 28
Spain, revolt against, 117, 121
squatters movement, 135–36
Srebrenica-trauma, 169
Submission, 24–25, 143; audience of, 18, 65, 99–100, 172; interpretation of, 10, 18, 93, 98–100, 151; murder of van Gogh and, 33, 36, 38, 65, 93, 100, 142, 183 n. 13; subject of, 1, 9, 33, 98
suicide bombers, 142
Sweden, 106, 110, 195 n. 8
Switzerland, 148, 199 n. 6
symbolic types, 41
Syrian, the, 51

television, 99, 132, 152
terrorism, 2, 25, 42, 50–51, 72–73, 82–83
tobacco, 134
tolerance, 93, 195 n. 14; religious, 98
trauma, 170; national, 172; wartime, 127. See also cultural trauma
Treanor, Paul, 39, 45
Turks, 77, 102, 108, 112, 145
Turner, Victor, 14 25, 30

United States, 2, 12, 72, 104, 110, 195 n. 8; slavery and, 158
urban culture, 10

van Gogh, Theo: appearance of, 93; Dutch identity and, 22; as event, 55; friends of, 142; funeral of, 16; life of, 8, 30, 53, 94; murder of, 1, 4–6, 9–10, 15, 24, 28, 33, 44, 48, 51, 55, 93, 104, 162–63, 169; Muslims and, 5, 97; symbolification of, 19, 29, 74, 79, 95–97, 138, 141, 183 n. 13
Veiled Monologues, 192 n. 32
Verdonk, Rita, 37, 47, 52, 93, 105, 137, 194 n. 5, 198 n. 28
violence against women, 11, 100
volkswoede, 54

Wallace, George, 32
Walters, Jason, 189 n. 21
Weber, Max, 117
Weinreb Report, 131
Wilders, Geert, 120, 173
Wilhelmina, Queen, 123, 129
Winter, Leon de, 152
World War II, 22, 47, 116, 121, 123
Wretched of the Earth, The, 192 n. 34

youth culture, 133

Zalm, Gerrit, 50

Ron Eyerman is a professor and codirector (with Jeffrey Alexander) of the Center for Cultural Sociology at Yale University. He is the author of *Between Culture and Politics: Intellectuals in Modern Society* (Polity Press, 1994) and *Cultural Trauma: Slavery and the Formation of African American Identity* (Cambridge University Press, 2001). He is the coauthor (with Andrew Jamison) of *Music and Social Movements: Mobilizing Traditions in the Twentieth Century* (Cambridge University Press, 1998), *Seeds of the Sixties* (University of California Press, 1994), and *Social Movements: A Cognitive Approach* (Pennsylvania State University Press, 1991), and (with Andrew Jamison and Jacqueline Cramer) of *The Making of the New Environmental Consciousness: A Comparative Study of the Environmental Movements in Sweden, Denmark, and the Netherlands* (Edinburgh University Press, 1990). He has also edited the following books: (with Lisa McCormick) *Myth, Meaning, and Performance: Toward a New Cultural Sociology of the Arts* (Paradigm, 2006); (with Mario Diani) *Studying Collective Action* (Sage, 1992); and (with Lennart G. Svensson and Thomas Söderqvist) *Intellectuals, Universities, and the State in Western Modern Societies* (University of California Press, 1987).

Library of Congress Cataloging-in-Publication Data
The assassination of Theo van Gogh : from social
drama to cultural trauma / Ron Eyerman.
p. cm. — (Politics, history, and culture)
Includes bibliographical references and index.
ISBN 978-0-8223-4387-5 (cloth : alk. paper)
ISBN 978-0-8223-4406-3 (pbk. : alk. paper)
1. Gogh, Theo van, 1957–2004—Assassination.
2. Murder—Netherlands—Case studies. 3. Muslims
—Netherlands—Case studies. 4. Islamic funda-
mentalism—Netherlands—Case studies.
I. Eyerman, Ron.
HV6541.N4A77 2008
364.152'4092—dc22   2008013489